A SURVIVAL GUIDE FOR
NEW FACULTY MEMBERS

ABOUT THE AUTHORS

Jeffrey P. Bakken, Ph.D., is Professor and Chair, Department of Special Education at Illinois State University. He has a Bachelor's Degree in Elementary Education from the University of Wisconsin–LaCrosse, and graduate degrees in the area of Special Education-Learning Disabilities from Purdue University. Dr. Bakken is a teacher, consultant, and scholar. His specific areas of interest include transition, teacher effectiveness, assessment, learning strategies, and technology. He has written more than 100 academic publications, including books, journal articles, chapters, monographs, reports, and proceedings; and he has made over 200 presentations at local, state, regional, national, and international levels. Dr. Bakken has received the College of Education and the University Research Initiative Award, the College of Education Outstanding College Researcher Award, the College of Education Outstanding College Teacher Award, and the Outstanding University Teacher Award from Illinois State University. Through his work, he has committed himself toward improving teachers' knowledge and techniques as well as services for students with exceptionalities and their families.

Cynthia G. Simpson, Ph.D., is Associate Professor and Coordinator of Special Education Programs at Sam Houston State University. She received her terminal degree from Texas A&M University and did her undergraduate studies at Texas State University–San Marcos. Dr. Simpson has more than 17 years of experience in the public and private sector as a preschool teacher, special education teacher, elementary teacher, educational diagnostician, and administrator. She is currently in the higher education sector. She maintains an active role in the field of special education as an educational consultant in the areas of assessment, family advocacy, and inclusive practices. Her professional responsibilities include serving on the National Council for Accreditation of Teacher Education (NCATE)/National Association of Young Children (NAEYC) Review Panel, as well as holding the position of State Advisor to the Texas Educational Diagnostician Association (TEDA). She also represents college teachers as the Vice President of Legislative Affairs for Texas Association of College Teachers. Dr. Simpson holds many recognitions such as the recipient of the 2008 Susan Phillips Gorin Award, the highest honor that can be bestowed on a professional member of the Council for Exceptional Children by its student membership; the 2007 Texas Trainer of the Year (awarded by the Texas Association for the Education of Young Children); the 2007 Katheryn Varner Award (awarded by Texas Council for Exceptional Children); the 2009 Wilma Jo Bush Award (awarded by the Texas Educational Diagnostician Association); the 2010 Teacher Educator Award (awarded by the Texas Council for Exceptional Children); and the Sam Houston State University College of Education Service Award. Through her work, she has committed herself toward improving the lives of children with exceptionalities and their families.

A SURVIVAL GUIDE FOR NEW FACULTY MEMBERS

Outlining the Keys to Success for Promotion and Tenure

By

JEFFREY P. BAKKEN

Illinois State University

and

CYNTHIA G. SIMPSON

Sam Houston State University

CHARLES C THOMAS • PUBLISHER, LTD.
Springfield • Illinois • U.S.A.

Published and Distributed Throughout the World by

CHARLES C THOMAS • PUBLISHER, LTD.
2600 South First Street
Springfield, Illinois 62794-9265

© 2011 by CHARLES C THOMAS • PUBLISHER, LTD.

ISBN 978-0-398-08629-9 (hard)
ISBN 978-0-398-08630-5 (paper)
ISBN 978-0-398-08631-2 (ebook)

Library of Congress Catalog Card Number: 2010039941

With THOMAS BOOKS *careful attention is given to all details of manufacturing
and design. It is the Publisher's desire to present books that are satisfactory as to their
physical qualities and artistic possibilities and appropriate for their particular use.*
THOMAS BOOKS *will be true to those laws of quality that assure a good name
and good will.*

*Printed in the United States of America
MM-R-3*

Library of Congress Cataloging in Publication Data

Bakken, Jeffrey P.
A survival guide for new faculty members : outlining the keys to success
for promotion and tenure / by Jeffrey P. Bakken and Cynthia G. Simpson.
p. cm.
Includes biographical references and index.
ISBN 978-0-398-08629-9 (hard)–ISBN 978-0-398-08630-5 (pbk.)–ISBN
978-0-398-08631-2 (ebook)
1. First year teachers–Professional relationships. 2. First year teachers–in-
service training. 3. Mentoring in education. 4. Teachers–Training of. I.
Simpson, Cynthia G. II. Title.

LB2844.1.N4B28 2011
378.1'2–dc22   2010039941

We would like to dedicate this book to our families who have offered us unconditional support throughout the writing process and to all the newly appointed faculty members embarking on the challenges and rewards of higher education.

FOREWORD

At last! *A Survival Guide for New Faculty Members: Outlining the Keys to Success for Promotion and Tenure* fills one of those "I wish someone would write . . ." niches for new faculty members. It's the book that we all wish we had available when we first entered the job market. And, it's the book that we all thought about writing at one time or another but never got around to.

In nearly thirty years in higher education, I have worked directly or indirectly with hundreds of faculty members fresh from their graduate school experiences and anxious to begin their careers. All of them knew how to do research in their disciplines, albeit often more or less under the direction of others. Some of them had taught before, but rarely did they have any formal training in teaching or classroom administration. A few had taken on service roles, usually as a sponsor for a student organization or as the token grad student on a committee. Very few had any idea of how to navigate the political and administrative shoals on the way to tenure and promotion. Most naively and idealistically believed those systems were straightforward, logical, and apolitical.

Most have ultimately been successful, after a fashion. Most have acquired the knowledge found in this compact volume, but often only through experience, trial and error, the always-dangerous practice of listening to "hall talk," and a modicum of good luck. Some were fortunate enough to have an experienced and beneficent chair or senior faculty mentor. Most learned some of the complex vocabulary of higher education, but only in context of specific issues. Most navigated the convoluted committee structures without a clue as to the underlying politics or the real import of committee decisions or letters, often written in a code unique and traditional to that institution. It is not easy, but most new faculty do make it.

But too many new and promising faculty members crash and burn. Far too many new faculty members are nonreappointed prior to tenure, or even worse, are denied tenure. Often new faculty fail to appreciate the importance of determining the institution's relative emphases on teaching, research, or service, both within the official guidelines and unofficially. Far too many fail to read carefully the tenure and promotion rules and guidelines of their departments, schools, and colleges and ask questions when they do not understand those (often) turgid and dense rules. A few lucky souls make midcourse corrections, often after early intervention by senior faculty or chairs. But still some very good young faculty fall through the cracks, ultimately to resurface at other institutions, bruised, weary, and (with luck) wiser.

A Survival Guide for New Faculty Members: Outlining the Keys to Success for Promotion and Tenure provides new faculty members with practical, down-to-earth wisdom and suggestions for successfully working through to tenure and promotion. The authors–both successful and experienced administrators and experts in higher education–have provided an extremely well-organized and useful guide for new faculty members.

Of particular utility is Part II, "The Nuts and Bolts of Success." Too often–it is sometimes difficult to believe–new faculty do not truly comprehend the three facets of faculty life of teaching, research, and service. This volume clearly sets out, compares, and separates those three components with clarity and provides very useful advice for putting the three together. Taken together with Chapters 7 and 8, "Documenting Your Progress" and "Promotion and Tenure," new faculty are provided with a solid, practical introduction to building a foundation for success in higher education.

The last chapter, "Creating a Harmony for Being Successful," introduces the critical concept of *balance.* An academic career is not a 100 meter dash–it is a marathon, often lasting several decades and often well past traditional retirement age. It is a calling, not just a career or a job. As such, academic careers often overwhelm every other aspect of "personhood." Our families, our health, our other interests, and sometimes our very beings are subordinated to the wrenching demands of discipline, research, and students.

As the authors contend, "[i]t is important for you to find harmony in your life and concentrate on your outside interests. The goal of promotion and tenure can easily consume you as an individual. Wanting to always be better, improve, publish, do service, and so on can be very stressful. At what price, however, is it worth?" Balance between an academic career and the rest of one's life is not often easy to maintain. The price of NOT finding that balance is too high. It is a measure of time, focus, and attention. Finding the balance is a constant and conscious choice, and often a difficult one.

I join with the authors in welcoming you to the demanding, joyous, and maddening world of higher education. Few other lifetimes are as fulfilling or as important as that of the life of the mind and its practical applications in teaching, research, creative expression, and public service. This volume will provide you with many of the important practical hints and directions for mastering the work ahead of you. Best wishes.

CHARLES R. McGUIRE
Associate Vice President for Academic Administration
Illinois State University

PREFACE

The need for a reference guide for doctoral students and new faculty working at institutions of higher education is apparent and critical for their success after graduation. While completing school and after graduation new faculty need to immediately start thinking and preparing themselves for promotion and tenure. Achieving promotion and tenure is a process that needs to be planned and new faculty should be aware of the many requirements involved in this process. *A Survival Guide for New Faculty Members: Outlining the Keys to Success for Promotion and Tenure* focuses on all aspects of becoming a new faculty member including the various expectations in completing a successful journey toward promotion and tenure. We believe it is essential for new faculty to understand the specific requirements involved in the promotion and tenure process. Understanding this process and being proactive will help faculty members achieve success in the tenure and promotion process.

A Survival Guide for New Faculty Members: Outlining the Keys to Success for Promotion and Tenure discusses critical promotion and tenure topics for this day and age. This book is comprised of three sections which include "The Basic Fundamentals" (Chapters 1–3); "The Nuts and Bolts of Success" (Chapters 4–6); and "The Final Steps" (Chapters 7–9). In this book, Chapter 1 discusses "Choosing the Right Institution"; Chapter 2 focuses on "What to Do Prior to Arriving at Your New Institution"; Chapter 3 addresses "Learning About Your New Institution Once You Are There"; Chapter 4 explains "Teaching"; Chapter 5 provides information on "Research and Scholarly Activity"; Chapter 6 explores "Service"; Chapter 7 discusses "Documenting Your Progress"; Chapter 8 focuses on "Promotion and Tenure"; and Chapter 9 addresses "Creating a Harmony for Being Successful." Each chapter describes a part of the process new faculty need to consider, as well as offers suggestions for effective planning and additional resources that can be useful when working toward promotion and tenure.

Upon completion of a comprehensive literature search, we found very limited resources available to assist new faculty in the tenure and promotion process. This book is an innovative way to provide thought-provoking content to doctoral students and new faculty to prepare them for promotion and tenure. It covers all of the essential components that need to be considered and it is unique in that it not only is very informative, but provides new faculty feedback and tips within each chapter.

The text is written in a style that readers can comprehend and understand and is supported with many examples. In addition, the information can be easily applied to new faculty at various types of institutions of higher education. In preparing this book, we wanted to explain and provide a detailed and comprehensive analysis of all the different components a new faculty member must consider when preparing for promotion and tenure. On the whole, this book will be an added resource to doctoral students and new faculty as they travel on their journey toward promotion and tenure. We are confident that readers will find it helpful and useful regarding all the aspects associated with promotion and tenure. We have found that this book is an excellent required or supplementary text for doctoral-level programs as well as a resource for new faculty as they enter higher education.

This book would not be possible without the support of family, friends, and colleagues. We thank Dr. Charles R. McGuire of Illinois State University for writing the Foreword of this book, and our many colleagues for allowing us to share your experiences with the tenure and promotion process.

J. P. B.
C. G. S.

CONTENTS

APPENDICES

A SURVIVAL GUIDE FOR
NEW FACULTY MEMBERS

Part I

THE BASIC FUNDAMENTALS

Chapter 1

CHOOSING THE RIGHT INSTITUTION

In most cases, you have probably spent three to five years or more completing your doctorate. You have probably worked harder than you ever have before to reach this point in your life and career. You have been taking classes, teaching classes, and conducting research, in your program of study. In addition, you may have had personal events and possibly family issues to deal with along the way. However, if you have selected this book, we assume that you made it through and you will begin to embark on your next venture. The first step in this stage of your career is to start searching for a faculty position that meets your qualifications and expectations. In the field of higher education, the job market is very tight (especially in times of economic instability) and it is possible that the number of graduates exceeds the number of jobs available to you.

What is a current or future graduate to do? How will this person market himself/herself to the best of his/her ability? What is the best way to get onto a faculty that will support and develop your skills? The answers to these questions and many more can be found in this chapter.

I think the scariest part of graduating for me was not defending my dissertation, but facing the reality that once I graduated I might not be able to find a job. I knew I had to start looking quickly but didn't even know where to begin my search!

Searching the Chronicle of Higher Education

The first place to begin looking for a possible faculty position is in the *Chronicle of Higher Education.* The *Chronicle* is a weekly publication and a great resource for information on current topics affecting students, faculty, admin-

Table 1.1
SAMPLE *CHRONICLE OF HIGHER EDUCATION*
BOTTOM PAGE ADVERTISEMENT

Psychology/Counseling: Mental Health Provider. 4/Counselor/Psychologist position. The Center for Health and Counseling at the University of Alaska Fairbanks (UAF) seeks to fill a full-time Psychologist position to begin no later than August 2009. This is a regular, full-time, 9-month position with benefits. Salary is grade 82, depending on experience. Relocation expenses may be provided. Job code 0057044. Contact: University of Alaska Fairbanks, Human Resources, http://www.uakjobs.com/applicants/Central?quickFind=66020; Fairbank, Alaska 99775; 907-474-7700.

Note: Taken from April 3, 2009, *Chronicle of Higher Education,* Volume LV, Number 30. Copyright 2009, the University of Alaska Fairbanks, Reprinted with permission.

istrators, and institutions of higher education. Most importantly, however, the *Chronicle* publishes job listings throughout academia. The actual publication is available in two formats: a newspaper-type format and a web-based, on-line version. Individuals can use the paper and on-line versions to read about current affairs at institutions of higher education and search for possible faculty positions. In the paper version, there is a separate section dedicated to job postings/listings and within this section of the paper there are three different ways you can systematically search for a possible faculty position. First, you can search job postings by topic (e.g., school psychology, education) at the bottom of the page, which are listed in alphabetical order. Many times a small description is provided and the reader is referred to a website for more detailed information. See Table 1.1 for a sample advertisement from this section.

The second and third ways to search for a faculty position in the paper version of the *Chronicle of Higher Education* are to use the indexes. These indexes are used to find possible faculty positions located in the one-eighth to full page advertisements. To save money and increase visibility, many different academic departments within one institution may place a larger ad representing multiple departments or listings together in the *Chronicle.* For this reason it is important to search the bottom page ads as well as use the indexes. One index can be used to search for potential faculty positions listed by the state in which they are located in, and the other is to search by topic area of the job (e.g., special education). See Tables 1.2 and 1.3 for sample indexes. These topics are listed in alphabetical order as are the states. There are two kinds of advertisements in the chronicle-individual advertisements and broader university or college advertisements. Make sure to check both kinds to see what faculty positions are available.

Table 1.2
SAMPLE *CHRONICLE OF HIGHER EDUCATION*
JOB LISTING GEOGRAPHIC INDEX

Geographic index of positions available

United States and U.S. Territories

Alabama	A35, A40, A44, A51, A54
Alaska	A34, A43, A50
Arizona	A54
Arkansas	A36, A41-A43
California	A33-A34, A42, A47-A49, A52-A55
Colorado	A34, A37, A42, A50, A53
Connecticut	A33, A38
Delaware	A33

Note: Taken from April 3, 2009, *Chronicle of Higher Education,* Volume LV, Number 30. Letters and numbers after each listing refer to page numbers. Copyright 2009, *The Chronicle of Higher Education.* Reprinted with permission.

When using the web-based version of the *Chronicle,* there is a specific job search section on the main home page. Here you can search by a specific type of job (e.g., accounting), or by categories (e.g., faculty positions, administrative positions, executive positions, and positions outside academia). Jobs are listed in the order they were submitted meaning that the most current listings are listed first. In our opinion it is easier to search by the specific type of job that interests you. However, either type of search will work. You can also sign-up for posts to be emailed to you. You can sign up for a specified frequency (1 time a week) or any time a job is posted in your category. See Tables 1.4 and 1.5 for a sample web-based advertisement, and the main search listing.

In addition to the *Chronicle* there are other internet-based sites for you to look for a faculty position. In a society where technology guides the workforce and often offers a means to communicate information in a less expensive format, universities have begun to place job postings on various internet job sites. Two of the most popular sites are Higher Ed Jobs at www.highered jobs.com and Academic 360 at www.academic360.com. Each of these sites allows universities to post positions at any time and provides immediate opportunities to update positions. Many sites such as these allow applicants to directly upload employment documents and submit them to the institution.

Table 1.3
SAMPLE *CHRONICLE OF HIGHER EDUCATION*
JOB LISTING POSITIONS AVAILABLE INDEX

Index of positions available in display ads

Dean	A34-A35, A46, A53-A54
Design/graphic arts	A37-A38, A42
Development/advancement	A51-A52
Digital media	A38
Economics	A33, A42
Editing/publication management	A51
Education/other	A35, A40, A42, A54

Note: Taken from April 3, 2009, *Chronicle of Higher Education,* Volume LV, Number 30. Letters and numbers after each listing refer to page numbers. Copyright 2009, *The Chronicle of Higher Education.* Reprinted with permission.

In addition to newspapers and internet listings, one of the main ways that a university advertises positions is on its own website. Typically job listings are found on the Human Resource page. If you are seeking a position in a specific region or area you might want to determine which colleges or universities are in that area and look directly at their own employment listings. It is important to not only know what type of job you are seeking but to also determine the type of university where you want to work.

Type of University

Research 1, Teaching, Research and Teaching

When seeking a faculty position consider the different types of institutions that are available. Many new graduates are unaware that universities are classified in various ways. One such classification is by Research levels. A Research 1 institution has a primary focus on research. It includes publications, presentations, and grant writing as requirements for tenure, but publications and grant writing are the major focus at these types of institutions with less importance placed on presentations. A typical teaching load at a Research 1 institution varies. It may consist of one class (maybe two) per semester with the rest of your time focused on research. These institutions are many times referred to as "publish or perish" institutions. At these institutions, the focus is on research; publishing scholarly works, and obtaining funding through federally funded grants. Of course, state, local, and organizational grants (e.g., The Council for Exceptional Children) are credited, but a strong emphasis is placed on securing larger, federally funded grants. Some professors indicate

Table 1.4

SAMPLE *CHRONICLE OF HIGHER EDUCATION*
ON-LINE EDUCATION

Position: Assistant/Associate Professor–Special Education
Institution: University of _____
Location: Wisconsin
Date posted: 3/23/2009
Application deadline: 4/1/2009

Assistant/Associate Professor Special Education

The University of _____ Department of Educational Studies invites applications for full-time academic year tenure-track Special Education Assistant/ Associate Professor, beginning August 2009. **Qualifications:** Ph.D./Ed.D. in special education or related field (Ph.D. or Ed.D. by date of appointment), and a minimum of three years of preK-12 special education teaching experience. **Desired qualifications:** experience with assistive technology/augmentative communication strategies, professional development schools, an interest in online instruction, and graduate/undergraduate research. Responsibilities: Teach undergraduate/graduate courses in special education, advise students, supervise field experiences, perform research, and participate in service activities. Application screening begins April 1, 2009 until position is filled.

As an Affirmative Action, Equal Opportunity Employer, the University of _____ is committed to increase diversity and inclusiveness. Women, persons of color, and individuals with a disability are encouraged to apply. If you have a special need/accommodation to aid your participation in our hiring process, please contact the individual above to make appropriate arrangements.

Employment will require a criminal background check. A pending criminal charge or conviction will not necessarily disqualify an applicant. In compliance with the Wisconsin Fair Employment Act, _____ does not discriminate on the basis of arrest or conviction record.

Send application letter, Vitae, transcripts, research goals, teaching philosophy, evidence of effective teaching, and names and contact information for three references to: Dr. _____, Chair Search and Screen Committee Special Education, University of _____, Department of Educational Studies, 240B _____ Hall, _____ State St., _____, WI _____. See our web page for program information. For other information contact Dr. _____ at ____-_____-____ or by email.

Note: Taken from http://chronicle.com/ on April 22, 2009.

Table 1.5
SAMPLE *CHRONICLE* WEB-BASED SEARCH LISTING

Chronicle Careers

Jobs from more than 1,050 institutions–222 new listings.

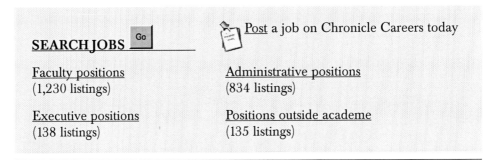

Note: Taken from http://chronicle.com/ on April 22, 2009. Copyright 2009, *The Chronicle of Higher Education*. Reprinted with permission.

that the work environment at a Research 1 university is often competitive with promotion/tenure based primarily on an individual's research productivity. However, it is important to note that this assumption does not apply to all universities. Other faculty members at Research 1 institutions would argue that professors work more closely with one another and instead of forming a competitive relationship, a strong collaborative relationship exists. Although in a Research 1 university, faculty members are expected to teach and engage in service, the weighting of teaching for tenure and promotion is often lower in these areas than scholarly activity. If you are looking for a faculty position at this type of institution, you need to be aware of the expectations to be successful and have clear understanding of the criteria needed to obtain promotion and tenure. A few examples of this kind of Research 1 institution include the University of Wisconsin–Madison, Vanderbilt, George Mason University, University of Texas, and Purdue University.

> *When I first started to apply for jobs I had no idea that some universities weighted scholarly activity and service differently. I guess I assumed that since all of these things were expected of me, they would carry equal weight. I probably would have saved a lot of time applying for jobs that didn't have a strong focus on service since that is truly my area of strength. I knew that research was important but at some institutions, services was a minimal part of the tenure and promotion criteria.*

Another type of institution is one that focuses solely on teaching. This type of institution is the polar opposite from the Research 1 institution. Teaching institutions often have a larger teaching load with less emphasis on research activity. A teaching load would typically be four courses per semester with the major emphasis being on teaching. It is not to say that research would not be conducted here, but in this type of institution, research is not a primary focus. In addition, promotion/tenure is based primarily on teaching, with some credit awarded for research and service activities. When applying for a position, it is perfectly acceptable to ask what percentage of credit is given based on student,s evaluations toward tenure. Again, if looking for a faculty position at this kind of institution, you need to be aware of expectations to be successful and criteria needed to obtain promotion and tenure. Examples of this kind of institution include Ball State University, the University of Wisconsin-LaCrosse, and Bowling Green University.

The last type of institution available is one that focuses on research and teaching. This type of institution falls in the center of the other types of mentioned institutions. Here teaching and research are equally important with an emphasis on service as well. The teaching load at this type of institution might consist of teaching two or three courses per semester with the rest of the time devoted to scholarly activities (i.e., publications, presentations, and grant writing). Obtaining promotion/tenure at this type of institution is based on an examination of the individual as a "well-rounded faculty member" who is successful at teaching (possibly based on scoring equally or above the department and/or college average on teaching evaluations), producing research products (in peer-reviewed journals), and is actively participating in service activities. Being aware of expectations at this type of institution is critical towards becoming promoted and tenured. Examples of this kind of institution include Illinois State University and Sam Houston State University. It is important to note that each institution, regardless of how they might be classified, has its own unique culture. You need to research and investigate institutions in which you might be interested to find out what kind of institution it is and which one best matches your knowledge, interests, and skill set. When investigating institutions, be thinking about questions you could ask someone when on an interview for a possible faculty position.

What to Look for Regarding a Faculty Position

What will be the right fit for you? Where do you hope to be in five or ten years? In what type of environment would you be successful? What are your goals? What skills do you have? Where do you need guidance or support? All of these questions are important for you to answer when considering a new faculty position. Are you primarily interested in research, with some teaching, or just teaching, or a combination of the two? Maybe you don't know. If you do know, your search is easier as you can target those types of institutions that fit your passion. If you are unsure of your preference, maybe you should think about applying to different types of institutions and "test the water." You might not end up where you start because it is not an exact science, but any planning you do might be helpful. Recent graduates should discuss options with their major advisor (dissertation chair) and obtain his or her input. Another option is to call friends at various institutions (and possibly even their friends) to see what kind of institution they are employed at and if they enjoy it. Make sure to find out "why" they enjoy working at their institution. You can also talk to your classmates and see what they are thinking and why they are leaning towards a specific type of institution. This is a difficult decision to make and often people find that what they originally thought they wanted out of an institution is not what they ended up finding in terms of satisfaction.

For example, a good friend of ours graduated from a Research 1 institution and felt that research was his calling. He worked on research projects for four years doing doctoral work with various faculty members within his department and loved every minute of it. It stimulated his development, got him back into the classroom, and paved the way for him to publish and begin grant writing. He honestly had not foreseen teaching as a critical part of his future employment. In his last year of graduate school, he taught an undergraduate course and worked more closely with college-aged students in a teaching role. He planned lessons, activities, student field experiences, assignments, and assessments (e.g., quizzes and exams); provided classroom instruction; worked collaboratively with classroom teachers where his college level students were placed; graded student work; and assigned final grades. Even though the learning curve was steep and the workload was intense, he found that he liked the teaching aspect of the university. Teaching and research both intrigued him and he decided to apply for a position at an institution that focused on both research and teaching. He secured this type of position and started as an assistant professor. His original plan was to be there for a maximum of three years and then move on to a larger institution. However, in the course of these three years, he found out something he did not know as a graduate student—he loved teaching and research and wanted to do them both. He actually interviewed for other positions at different institutions, but even after receiving job offers, realized that none were as good of a match for him as where he currently is employed. The support, people he worked with, culture, and many other aspects make his university a great place to be. He just began his sixteenth year at that same institution where he secured his first job and has moved up the ranks from assistant, to associate, to full professor and recently was chosen as the chair of his department. Who knew this would happen? It is not an exact science, but you should be aware of the institution's environment and philosophy before you apply so you know "exactly" what you are getting into.

Application Materials

After you have searched for open faculty positions and have decided which institutions might be a good fit for your needs and skill sets, the next thing to do is send them application materials. Make sure you carefully read the advertisement and send the institution exactly what they are looking for, and by the date that they request it. Speaking from experience, if your application is incomplete or even if your application is late, it may not be considered. Be prompt and follow the directions established in the advertisement. Usually, the institution will contact you and let you know they received your materials and alert you if something is missing. If they do not contact you, it is suggested that you contact them to make sure they received your application materials and that they are in order. The last thing you would want to happen is to not be considered because of a technicality. Typical materials to send include a letter of application, a curriculum vitae, transcript (s), a list of three to five references or actual reference letters, and sometimes sample publications or written work.

The letter of application is often the first thing that the search committee chair reads. This letter is very important as it is used to request consideration for the faculty position you are interested in and explains to the search committee why they should consider you for this position. You need to highlight your skills, knowledge, and experiences and directly tie them to the job description/advertisement that was posted. When search committee members finish reading your letter they should have a strong opinion as to whether you would be a prospective colleague. See Table 1.6 for a sample letter of application.

Another important document typically requested along with application materials is your curriculum Vitae. The curriculum Vitae is a document that highlights your degrees, knowledge, experiences, research accomplishments, awards/honors, organization affiliations and additional information that make you marketable or qualified for the faculty position you are trying to acquire. The job market is very tight and it is possible that you will be competing with many other well-qualified individuals. With this in mind, think of your curriculum Vitae as a means to shine in the eyes of the reviewers (search committee). In our opinion, the organization of your Vitae is critical. It needs to be concise and specific, but at the same time capture everything you have done and accomplished that will make reviewers see that your

Table 1.6
SAMPLE LETTER OF APPLICATION

Date

Name of Search Committee Chair
Address

Dear Dr. _____:

I am writing to express my interest in the position in the area of Low Vision and Blindness at (university name). In August 2008, I completed my Doctorate of Education degree in educational psychology with a specialization in visual impairments. During my doctoral studies, I was one of 19 National Center for Leadership in Visual Impairment (NCLVI) Doctoral Fellows. My areas of emphasis are education of children with visual impairments, orientation and mobility, and quantitative research methodologies. Additionally, I have certification as an Illinois school administrator and highly specialized expertise in assistive technology for people with visual impairments.

As my resume indicates, I have a wide variety of experiences at both the direct service and university level. Of particular interest is my:

- experience as a certified teacher of the visually impaired working with a wide range of students from birth through twenty-two years of age with and without multiple disabilities.
- certification as an orientation and mobility specialist that enables me to work with and conduct research pertaining to children, youth, and adults of all ages and degrees of visual impairment.
- university teaching experience in visual disability education programs.
- completion of 18 hours of specified graduate-level coursework in advanced quantitative methods for conducting and interpreting research.
- participation in the NCLVI, a one-of-a-kind added-value doctoral enrichment program emphasizing leadership development in the field of blindness and visual impairment and involving face-to-face seminars, fieldwork, internships, group listservs, and on-line discussion boards.

In addition, I have had the opportunity to review for professional conferences, supervise student teachers, and write highly competitive federal grant proposals. My experience is closely aligned with many of the principal responsibilities entailed in this employment opportunity.

I welcome the opportunity to talk with you further about my qualifications and the position in the area of Low Vision and Blindness at (university name). Enclosed please find the requested application materials. Letters of support will be sent separately by the individuals submitting them.

Sincerely,

Name
Address

(Note: Permission obtained from faculty member to reprint, October 6, 2010.)

achievements, knowledge, and accomplishments exceed those of other competing for the same position. How you organize this document is very important. It is suggested that you begin building your Vitae throughout your doctoral program and then update it biannually. See Table 1.7 for an example of an organizational structure you can use. If you do not have items that fall under a particular category then it is advised to not list that category.

The rest of the application materials are aimed to support your statements and comments in your letter of application. When sending your materials, remember that they are a reflection of your abilities as a future colleague. Make sure everything is complete, organized, and edited. A well-written organized application will be noticed by the committee. Application materials are typically reviewed by a search committee of representatives from the department to which you are applying. The search committee generally consists of three to five people. If your materials meet the qualifications needed for the position and you appear to be a strong match for the position, you might be contacted to participate in a phone interview. Not all institutions employ phone interviews as an initial interview phase, but it is becoming more common in the field.

Phone Interview

Once you have made it through the initial screening of applicants, the next step in the application process might be a phone interview. This step of the process is implemented by the search committee to gain more specific information about a candidate, narrow down the possible list of candidates, and to help the committee decide whom they might want to schedule an on-site interview with. Usually, someone from the search committee (or a departmental secretary) will contact you to set up the phone interview. Some institutions have replaced the phone interview with a more advanced internet based conferencing program. For example, some institutions are using the program SKYPE to conduct screening interviews. This allows the search committee to see you and for you to see them instead of just auditory responding. Regardless of whether the screening interview is an internet-based interview or a phone-based interview, make sure you write down the date and time of the interview. Second, make sure you give the person scheduling the phone interview a correct number that would be good to reach you. In some cases, you may need a special code to access or participate in the interview call. Make sure to place this code in a secure place and have it ready on the day of your interview.

Table 1.7
ORGANIZATIONAL STRUCTURE OF A CURRICULUM VITAE

Vitae
NAME
ADDRESSES

Home Address   Work Address

EDUCATION

Ph.D.
M.S.
B.S.

TEACHING CERTIFICATIONS (if applicable to your discipline)
PROFESSIONAL EXPERIENCE
    Public School Experience
    University Experience
    Related Experience

ACADEMIC AWARDS/HONORS
PUBLICATIONS
BOOKS
CHAPTERS
JOURNAL ARTICLES
MONOGRAPHS
WEBSITES
CONFERENCE PROCEEDINGS
BOOK REVIEWS
AUDIOVISUAL MEDIA
MANUALS
NEWSLETTERS
REPORTS
SUBMITTED

RESEARCH PRESENTATIONS
INTERNATIONAL/NATIONAL
REGIONAL/STATE

SPONSORED RESEARCH PROJECTS
NATIONAL
STATE
INTERNAL
GRANTS WRITTEN
GRANTS REVIEWED

ADVISOR/LEADERSHIP ROLES
EDITORIAL ACTIVITIES
COMMITTEES
UNIVERSITY COMMITTEES
EXTERNAL COMMITTEES

WORKSHOPS
PROFESSIONAL AFFILIATIONS

Common Errors Found in Application Materials
- *Cover letter addressed to wrong institution*
- *Mistyped/misspelled words in letter of interest*
- *Failure to include area code in phone number or contact information*
- *Addressed cover letter to the search chair and misspelled that individual's name*
- *Failure to include all materials requested*
- *Not meeting qualifications of job*
- *Inaccurate materials or materials that are difficult to decipher*

For the actual screening interview, you might consider your home environment which may be more limited in the number of distractions that might occur (of course, this may not ideal if you have young children at home or vocal pets), but regardless of the setting, choose a place where you feel comfortable and will have limited distractions. Typically, the committee will be in a room with a speaker phone and/or computer and will ask questions to which you will respond. It is very difficult to prepare for this type of interview as the committee could ask you an array of questions. One thing we would recommend, if you have not already done so, is research the institution to which you applied. Use the internet and the institution's web page to find details about the programs they offer, size of the programs, current faculty, and the goals and philosophies of the department, college, and university. We would also recommend that you review the faculty members who are currently employed in the department to which you are applying. Find out if their research interests are similar to your own and what their areas of interest are.

There is nothing that is more exciting for a search committee member than a candidate who has researched the institution and has a basic understanding of the operation of the institution and can reference university or program-specific information. Also, be prepared to answer questions about your philosophy (in relation to your area of study/expertise) and why you chose the institution you are applying to. The committee might also ask you questions in relation to teaching, scholarship, and service and your experiences in all three areas. You might want to write down the names of people as they introduce themselves and take notes of specific comments to reference later. See Table 1.8 for a sample of phone/internet interview questions.

Campus Visit

After the phone interview, the committee will determine whether or not to extend you an invitation for an on-campus interview. The department you

Table 1.8
SAMPLE PHONE/INTERNET INTERVIEW QUESTIONS

1. What do you feel are some of the most pressing issues in the field of [your specific area of study] today? How do you feel you can make a difference and how might that be realized?

2. Describe your most significant professional accomplishment to date. Why do you feel that it made a difference either in the lives of specific individuals or the discipline?

3. Tell us about your philosophy as it relates to the [specific field of study].

4. Tell us about an instance when you felt you excelled as a teacher. What was it about the teaching process and/or the outcomes of the teaching experience that you felt was unique?

5. What would you say are the strongest and weakest aspects of your scholarship activities to date?

6. Describe a recent time when you successfully collaborated with a university colleague or with public school personnel and there was a favorable outcome.

7. What contribution/s do you feel you could make to our department and university in the areas of teaching, research, and/or service?

8. Where do you see yourself in 3-5 years?

9. What questions do you have for us? (Make sure you have some. It shows you are prepared and interested in the position.)

are applying to will request that you come to the campus to meet everyone and partake in some activities. Frequently, the institution will reimburse you for any expenses incurred during your visit including travel, lodging, and food. If you are within driving distance, they will probably reimburse you for mileage to and from the institution. Ask what type of documentation you will need to submit to be reimbursed. It is also important to find out if there is a maximum allocation for hotel or airfare. Some institutions will only reimburse hotel charges at the current state rate.

A typical campus visit might include a research presentation on your line of research (or a recent research study you were involved with); demonstrating your teaching skills by teaching a class to university students; meeting with the search committee members; meeting with the department chair, dean, students, new faculty, and possibly the institution's Vice President of Academic Affairs. Most on-site interviews are also designed to provide you

Table 1.9
SAMPLE ON-SITE INTERVIEW SCHEDULE

January 12–14, 2010

Tuesday, January 12–Arrive at 5:27 p.m.
(Greeted by faculty member)

5:30 p.m.	Take to Hotel
7:00 p.m.	Dinner with Faculty

Wednesday, January 13

10:30–11:30	Campus Tour
11:30–12:00	Center for Teaching, Learning, and Technology Tour
12:15–1:30	Lunch with Faculty
2:00–3:00	Teach University Course
3:00–3:30	Department Evaluation Committee
3:30–4:30	Community Tour and return to hotel
6:00 p.m.	Dinner with Faculty

Thursday, January 14

8:00–9:00	Breakfast with Current New Faculty at hotel
9:15–10:00	Meet with Student Organization Representatives
10:00–10:30	Interview with Dean
10:45–12:00	Research Presentation
12:00–1:15	Lunch with Faculty
1:15–1:45	Search Committee
1:45–2:15	Interview with Department Chair
2:30	Leave for airport
	Flight at 4:05

with the opportunity to tour the community and the institution's campus. If there is something you specifically would like to see or do during the visit, make this known prior to arriving. For example, if you are interested in international studies, you might want to request a meeting with that department so you can obtain information about your interests in this area.

This experience helps department and faculty members decide if you would make a good colleague and become a contributing member in their department and institution. Faculty members will be watching, listening, and asking you questions as they try to get to know you as much as they can in the relatively short time you are on campus. Typically, a campus visit is one and a half to two days long and can be quite exhausting. See Table 1.9 for an example on-site interview schedule. For you, the visit offers the opportunity to determine if this environment in conducive to your needs and if the people you meet are ones with whom you will want to work. Ask yourself several questions during your visit such as: What is the environment like? Is the environment supportive? Is the environment competitive or collaborative? Are resources available for you to be successful? Are procedures in place to help you get acquainted with different programs such as a mentoring program? Also, what are the current faculty members like? Are they communicative? Were faculty generally interested in what you had to say? Did you feel welcomed during your visit? Were these people the kind of people you want to work with? Were administrators helpful, supportive, and accessible? What is the level of interaction between colleagues? What is the level of interaction between professors and students? What is the level of interaction between students?

The decision as to where you will work is a life-changing one, so you want to be sure to get as much information as you can. You might also request to meet with other new or junior faculty members to get their feedback on working at that institution. You will gain information through direct experience and observation while on your campus visit as well as through the questions you ask while on campus. Remember, you as a candidate are also interviewing the institution.

Questions to Ask while on Campus

While on your campus visit you will be meeting with faculty, staff, and administrators and they will be asking you a variety of questions ranging from your philosophy on teaching and research to classes you might like to teach. Most on-campus interviews have time built in for you to ask questions. Make sure you take the opportunity to ask questions that will give you the most useful information you can get about the institution and the faculty position so you are able to make a more educated and informed decision. See Table 1.10 for some possible questions to ask when interviewing on a university campus.

This is just a sampling of possible questions, but be sure you ask any questions you may have. Asking the right questions might prevent you from accepting a faculty position at an institution that does not meet your expectations.

You may also want to ask questions about local schools (if you have children), the housing market, and local activities as well as other questions regarding your potential new community. It is very important that you have as much information as possible about all institutions you visited so you can make the most informed decision about your new career.

Table 1.10
POSSIBLE QUESTIONS TO ASK WHILE ON CAMPUS

- What is the environment like here?
- Do faculty across departments collaborate?
- What is the support like for the department from the Dean's Office?
- How much support is provided to new faculty?
- Are new faculty included in department decision making?
- What are expectations for new faculty in the areas of teaching, scholarship, and service?
- What are the specific guidelines for tenure and/or promotion?
- What percent of faculty members that apply for tenure/promotion are granted it?
- What technological support is provided to faculty?
- What is course load like?
- Is there any course load reduction for new faculty?
- How are faculty evaluated?
- Are there any moving expenses included?
- What is travel support like in this department?
- Is there any kind of grant support through the department or the college?
- Does a formal mentoring program exist?
- Does the university provide any internal grants for new faculty?
- What is the relationship between the institution and local school districts?

One of the questions that I wish I would have known to ask was about publications, I did not realize that at the university in which I accepted a position, if I collaborated on a publication, the weight of that publication toward tenure would be weighted very low. The institution that I am at has a very strong opinion on writing as a sole author. Collaborative efforts are not highly regarded.

Job Offer/Negotiations

After the search committee interviews all of their candidates, they will then determine whom they want to recommend to the department chair for their new hire. Sometimes the committee makes the decision, but typically the committee makes the recommendation as to whom they think will be the best fit for the open position to the department chair, and then he/she makes the final recommendation to the Dean of the College. The Dean of the College will often make the offer to the applicant. However, this varies across institutions.

In most cases, the search committee will elicit feedback from anyone who interacted with the candidate and then they will analyze all of the data. They will use all of the information obtained to determine who would be the best fit for their department and the specific faculty positions they are hiring for. Once a decision is made, the individual name of the applicant, or list of names, will be forwarded to the department chair (or some other administrator) to make the final decision. In addition, he or she is also the one who makes the job offer to the applicant. This offer will usually be made over the phone with a formal offer letter to follow when details are worked out.

As a candidate for a faculty position, you should research the salaries of new assistant professors (or other rank) across the country, at the institution you applied, and in other comparable (similarly sized) institutions. When searching for this information, be sure to look at fields that are comparable to your own. Salaries across disciplines (even within the same departments) may vary. Besides salary, there are other possible elements to discuss with your offer. These include: an office with a desk, book shelves, file cabinets, a computer desk, a computer (typically a laptop so you can be more mobile), a printer, an additional monitor (so you can view two documents at once), any specific software or hardware you might need for teaching or research, assistance from a graduate assistant, a specified amount for travel, possible course release time, summer teaching opportunities, and additional support for moving expenses. This is not a cumulative list, but a good place to begin when you are thinking about what you need. It is a good idea to have your list prepared to communicate to the department chair (or whoever makes the offer to you) so the process can be expedited as quickly as possible. Negotiating salary is often overlooked when accepting a job. Many people shy away from talking about salaries in fear that they may not be offered the position. Negotiating salary is typically done after the position is offered to you and is relatively common in higher education.

If you accept the verbal offer, a formal offer letter will then be mailed to you so you can sign it and return it to the institution. Without a signed offer, the institution may not be at liberty to craft your formal contract. If you are interviewing at multiple places, be prepared to get more than one offer. It is also a very good idea to make a list of the places you visited and list the pro's and con's of each institution. Think about what you value as a person, teacher, researcher, and colleague and be sure the institution you select has similar values. This will be very beneficial to you when it is time to make your choice of where you would like to be a faculty member.

You should also know that when an offer is made to you, the timeframe to accept the offer is typically quite short. In our experience it is shorter than a week and usually falls into the three to four day timeframe. Sometimes it is longer, but this is very unusual and only in special circumstances. You were not the only person that interviewed for this faculty position (there are usually two to three people invited for each faculty position opening). This means there are other possible contenders for the same position you are interested in. The timeframe is usually short because if you turn down the job offer, the institution does not want to lose another good candidate. Being able to make a rather quick decision is very important for both you and the institution. See Table 1.11 for a sample offer letter.

Table 1.11
SAMPLE OFFER LETTER

February 15, 2008

Name
Address
City/State

Dear Name:

Upon the recommendation of the Department of _____ Search Committee, it is my pleasure to invite you to join the faculty of the Department of _____ in the College of _____ at _____ University. This is a probationary tenure-track appointment, which begins August 16, 2008. Listed below are conditions of your appointment.

The standard contract dates for nine-month faculty appointments are August 16 through May 15.

Your rank will be Assistant Professor.
Your employment is contingent upon us receiving your transcript conferring your terminal degree by December 31, 2008.

Your annual salary will be $_____, distributed as a nine-month salary of $_____ per month.

Summer employment opportunities. You will be given at least one course to teach each summer for the next two years.

Equipment needs provided. We will provide an office with a desk, book shelves, file cabinets, a new computer, a new printer, and Microsoft Office Suite software.

Graduate Assistant. For the first two years you will be given a full time graduate student (20 hours per week) to work with you on scholarship, teaching, or both.

continued

Table 1.11–*Continued*

Travel. For first two years we will provide complete reimbursement for registration, travel, and accommodations (hotel) at one program related national conference.

Job expectations–Course load for first year will be teaching three courses (3/4 time) and working on scholarly activity (1/4 time). It is expected that you participate in department faculty meetings and work closely with course teams.

The University will reimburse you one-half of your moving expenses up to a maximum of $2,000, consistent with the limitations of the relocation policy. See the Moving Expense Reimbursement form at http://www_____

Appointments during the probationary period are made on an annual basis and an annual evaluation of your professional performance will be conducted. The tenure decision is made no later than the sixth year of probationary status, sooner if prior full-time service credit is allowed.

For information on Faculty, Salary, Promotion and Tenure policies see
<u>Promotion & Tenure (ASPT): Resources: Office of the Provost</u>

If you require any accommodation(s) in order to perform the essential functions of your new position, please contact our Office of Disability Concerns at (___) ____-____ or TDD (___) ____-____ to outline your needs. The Office of Disability Concerns will hold any information you provide in confidence.

All academic appointments are contingent upon the receipt of certain documents and forms including official transcripts conferring the terminal degree/ highest degree. An official transcript bears the official signature of the Registrar, may have a raised university seal, and/or is printed on secured paper. A photocopy cannot be accepted as an official institutional document. Please see that official transcripts are sent immediately to: Human Resources, (University Address).

In addition, all appointments are contingent upon proof of eligibility for employment in the United States. The Immigration and Control Act of 1986, Public Law 99-603, requires all new employees to file an <u>I-9 in person and no later than three days from the beginning of employment</u>. This may be accomplished within our department or through the Office of Human Resources. A list included on the form indicates the types of documentation you will be expected to provide and can be obtained at http://www.uscis.gov/graphics/formsfee/forms/files/i-9.pdf#search= %22uscis%20I-9.pdf%22. Failure to comply with this law will result in cancellation of your appointment.

Table 1.11–*Continued*

If you are not a United States Citizen, State of _____ employee benefits for medical and retirement eligibility is contingent on visa status and on your meeting the Internal Revenue Test of "Substantial Presence." The website http://www_____ outlines in more detail this contingency and the names of the individuals available to discuss your situation and to outline any procedures you need to take.

Completion of additional employment forms are part of this offer and will be completed in person upon your arrival.

As verification that you accept this offer, please sign the enclosed copy of this letter and return it to me along with all other completed forms by February 27, 2008. A contract will be sent following your acknowledgement and acceptance of the terms set forth in this letter.

Again, it is a pleasure to welcome you as a faculty member of _____ University. If you have any additional questions, feel free to contact me at (___) _____-_____ or the Office of Human Resources at (___) _____-_____.

Sincerely,

Name
Title
Address
City/State

Enclosures

cc: Office of Human Resources

I accept the offer as described in this letter dated February 15, 2008.

_____   _____

Signature   Date

_____

Conclusion

Hopefully the information in this chapter will provide you with some guidance when looking for a new faculty position and the processes involved in getting hired at an institution of higher education. You have worked long and hard to get where you are and getting a new faculty position is the next step in your career path. It is evident that finding a job and going through the interview process it is not an exact science and can be very stressful and disheartening. Remember to remain positive and try to be as prepared as possible in your faculty position search. If not fully prepared, you may have a less than fulfilling experience. The information provided in this chapter has been developed to help new and future graduates find an appropriate faculty position that meets their needs and expertise. The remaining eight chapters will address other key issues. Use this book as a quick reference guide or "survival guide" for you towards acquiring a new faculty position and successfully obtaining promotion and tenure.

Faculty Tips on Getting Started

• Relax! We hired you because you were skilled; enjoy using those skills and don't worry about being "evaluated."

• You can do it! Your institution wouldn't have offered you the job if they didn't think you could do your new job.

Chapter 2

WHAT TO DO PRIOR TO ARRIVING
AT YOUR NEW INSTITUTION

You have accepted an offer to become a new faculty member at an institution of higher education, now what? What do you need to do to finish up where you are? What do you need to do to prepare yourself prior to your arrival at your new place of employment? The answers to these questions and more will be discussed in this chapter.

Finish Your Dissertation

The first order of business, if you have not done so already, is to complete your dissertation. It is very common for individuals to search for a faculty position and accept an offer prior to the completion of their degree. It is also common that individuals start a new position with the status of "All But Disseration" (ABD). From two professionals who have come down the same road you travel, we suggest you complete your dissertation and graduate, if at all possible, before you begin your new role as a faculty member. The extra burden of not yet having your dissertation finished while beginning your life as a new faculty member can be very difficult and stressful. You must remember that you will most likely have relocated to be closer to your new job and are taking on a new role with new responsibilities (which come along with certain expectations). Working on your dissertation can take up a great deal of your time, limiting your ability to focus on university related work. We strongly recommend and encourage you to finish your dissertation and earn your degree prior to arriving as a new faculty member to make your life a little easier and far less complicated. You will also be able to focus all of your energy on your new work in the areas of teaching, research, and service.

Finishing your dissertation and graduating should be your primary focus, especially after having formally accepted an offer for a new faculty position.

We suggest you lay out a plan, or timeline, that is manageable and reasonable and will help you achieve this goal. List the tasks that still need to be completed, the timeline for which they fall, and exact due dates that everything must be finished by.

> *I had no idea when I accepted this job that I might run into problems finishing my dissertation. I waited until the last minute to defend and then found out that my committee wanted more data pulled. I ended up in a situation where I had to take a lower salary for one semester and had to work on completing my dissertation. It was a nightmare. I worked days on the job and then stayed up all night working on my dissertation. If at all possible, get it done before you start work. It will pay off in the long run.*

Things tend to come up unexpectedly in the dissertation process, but developing a plan will help you achieve your goal and stay on the right track. We suggest you implement backward planning. First, create a complete list of everything that needs to be accomplished in order for you to complete your dissertation and graduate. After creating a complete list of tasks that need to be completed, write down the last possible date to complete your dissertation prior to beginning your new faculty position. Once you have that, work backwards with the selected dates to make a plan for the completion of all tasks. You may want to seek advice from your dissertation chair or other faculty members to help set timelines. Having some type of plan will hopefully make you more accountable and help motivate you to finish. Following this timeline is critical as it is not uncommon for individuals to find themselves in a situation where their "university created deadline" to defend their dissertation comes and goes, leaving them without employment and without a degree. See Table 2.1 for an example plan.

After creating a similar timeline to the one shown in Table 2.1, the work process begins. If you have not yet completed the data collection phase of your research it should become a priority. You may want to begin to think of ways you can elicit the involvement of others. Sometimes, hiring people to help with data collection is possible (and frees your time to move ahead on the timeline). After completing data collection, you will need to analyze the data, complete chapters four and five of your dissertation, and get feedback. Remember that it is essential to work closely with your dissertation chair and committee members so there are not any unexpected problems or situations that might delay your progress. Each university has a slightly different process so make sure you are aware of the specific requirements that your university requires. Finally, you will need to prepare for your dissertation defense. Your defense should be well organized and clearly depict the results of

Table 2.1
SAMPLE TIMELINE TO COMPLETE THE DISSERTATION

Tasks	Timeline	Due Date
Complete Data Collection	Jan-March	March 1
Analyze Data	March	March 20
Write up Chapter 4	April	April 20
Elicit Feedback for Chapter 4	April	April 30
Write up Chapter 5	April-May	May 10
Elicit Feedback for Chapter 5	May	May 20
Set up Defense Date	June	June 18
Defend Dissertation	July	July 8
Graduate	December	December 15

your research. After your defense you will probably have some corrections or edits that need to be made. After making the edits, you will need to deposit a formal copy and accompanying paperwork to the graduate school on your campus. Lastly, you should receive the final approval to graduate. If you choose, attend graduation ceremonies and realize the next graduation you will be attending will be one as a faculty member, not a student.

We recommend you attend your graduation ceremony if at all possible. You worked hard for your degree and should be recognized for your accomplishment. We have spoken to many professors who say one of their regrets was not attending their doctoral graduation ceremonies. In addition, it will put closure on one piece of your life and catapult you into the next chapter. This is also a great time to thank family and friends for their support. When going through this process make sure you know your current institution's policies, procedures, and dates regarding dissertation defenses and graduation. Often timelines become the reason why students do not graduate. See Table 2.2 for an example of due dates.

What if You Don't Finish?

At many institutions, you can still start a new faculty position without the completion of your dissertation and degree, but there will be a contingency on your contract. This contingency will state that you need to complete your degree by a certain date. If the degree is not completed, you could lose your faculty position and we have seen this happen. At some institutions, the salary for the first year may change if your degree is not conferred before your employment start date. It is difficult for the faculty member, as well as

Table 2.2
EXAMPLE INSTITUTION GRADUATION DUE DATES

	December 2009 Degree Completion	May 2010 Degree Completion	August 2010 Degree Completion
GRADUATION Degree Audit due in Graduate School	September 1, 2009	January 13, 2010	May 12, 2010
Application for Completion of Degree or Certificate and $30.00 fee due. Note: Applications for students who fail to meet completion requirements for a specific session are cancelled, and students must reapply for a later session. Reapply by contacting the Graduate School.	September 1, 2009	January 13, 2010	January 13, 2010 For students intending to march in May May 12, 2010 if not marching
Incomplete grades from previous semesters must be completed and grades submitted to Academic Records.	December 11, 2009	May 7, 2010	August 6, 2010
THESIS/DISSERTATION			
It is strongly suggested that all thesis/dissertation proposals involving living human, animal subjects or biosafety issues be submitted early in the semester prior to anticipated graduation in order to be reviewed by IRB/IACUC/IBC and assigned a protocol number.	Submit early in the semester prior to anticipated degree completion	Submit early in the semester prior to anticipated degree completion	Submit early in the semester prior to anticipated degree completion
Continuous Registration - *All students for whom continuous registration applies (thesis/dissertation audit hour) must notify Graduate School to iniate registration.*	August 16, 2009	January 11, 2010	May 16, 2010
Thesis/Dissertation Proposal Approval Form-For all students completing degree, proposal form with protocol number (if applicable) due in Graduate School.	September 1, 2009	January 13, 2010	May 12, 2010
Format Check Deadline-Last possible date to deposit Thesis/Dissertation in Graduate School for format check for degree completion.	Dissertation: October 19, 2009 Thesis: November 16, 2009	Dissertation: March 15, 2010 Thesis: April 12, 2010	Dissertation: June 14, 2010 Thesis: July 12, 2010
7 Days Before Oral Defense-After being tentatively accepted by the Graduate School Thesis/Dissertation Examiner, two examination copies of the Thesis/Dissertation must be filed in the academic unit office at least one week before the oral examination. *(Students should check with their advisor for discipline-specific dates.)*	7 Days Before Oral Defense	7 Days Before Oral Defense	7 Days Before Oral Defense
Last Date for Oral Defense - FOR DEGREE COMPLETION	Dissertation: November 5, 2009 Thesis: December 3, 2009	Dissertation: April 1, 2010 Thesis: April 29, 2010	Dissertation: July 1, 2010 Thesis: July 29, 2010
Thesis/Dissertation Filing Date - *2:00 p.m. deadline* for filing final Thesis/Dissertation copies in Graduate School for degree completion.	Dissertation: November 6, 2009 Thesis: December 4, 2009 2:00 pm deadline	Dissertation: April 2, 2010 Thesis: April 30, 2010 2:00 pm deadline	Dissertation: July 2, 2010 Thesis: July 30, 2010 2:00 pm deadline
Master's Comprehensive Examination *Academic units must submit results to the Graduate School.* Masters students must check with their academic unit for testing information and dates.	November 30, 2009	April 26, 2010	July 26, 2010
Degree Completion Date Diplomas are mailed approximately 8-10 weeks after this date.	December 12, 2009	May 8, 2010	August 7, 2010

Note: Illinois State University Graduate School Important Dates and Deadlines for Completion of Degree. (n.d.). Retrieved September 9, 2010, from: http://www.grad.ilstu.ed/downloads/datesanddeadlines10_11.pdf

for the other members in the department, when a colleague is completing a dissertation. Having your dissertation completed and your degree will be one less thing to worry about as you begin your life as a new faculty member.

Finding a Place to Live

One very important event that often occurs with a new job is relocating. The relocation process can be made easier by tapping into resources such as a realtor, the newspaper, the internet, or a combination of these. The institution you work in may have a case manager for relations. Not all institutions do, but check with the HR department. This individual helps to coordinate your move and assists you in finding a new home.

When searching for housing, you may want to contact your new department chair to see if he or she knows of any available homes in the area. If you are new to the area, a realtor may also be a good option. This is a person who knows the area and can show you around the community as well. Remember, however, a realtor's job is to sell houses and earn money. They may do a very good job of meeting your needs and show you homes you might actually consider purchasing or they may do exactly the opposite and show you homes you would not consider buying. It is important to note that you might even pay more for the house than it is worth because of realtor fees. We are not discouraging you to use a realtor by any means but want you to be aware of the advantages and disadvantages of this process.

Another option is to just use the newspaper. Either obtain an actual newspaper or access on-line newspaper listings. Homes might be more affordable as the seller is the person you will be dealing with instead of a realtor. If you go this route, remember to elicit the services of a lawyer to go over final documents and to help you with any paperwork. The last option is to use a web-based house listing service. For sale by owner (fsbo, www.fsbo.com) is one web-based listing service that offer a nationwide service. There are also local web-based listing services like for sale by owner local (fsboLocal-www.fsbo local.com). Here you can begin your search by state, specific city or all cities, distance, new or existing homes, prices, number of bathrooms, and number of bedrooms.

Available homes will show up based on the descriptors you use. What is nice about this method is that pictures of the home (inside and out) are available for you to view. Before you spend the time and effort to go view a home you will already have an idea if you want to see it in person or not. With the other two options, this is usually not available. This is also a great first step if moving from a distance. You can look at pictures and make arrangements to see several homes on your next trip. Of course, the choice is yours so you may use any one of the three suggested options or a combination of the three. Renting may be another option. Renting an apartment or house for a year will allow you sufficient time to find a place where you really want to live. Some individuals opt to go this route if they are unsure if the job they accepted is really the best match for them or if they are using this first job as a stepping ground for future employment.

In regards to searching for a new place to live, you may want to negotiate some funds during the negotiation phase of your salary and contract that will help support your travel during the relocation process. There is not a guarantee that relocation or moving funds are available, but it is a guarantee that if you don't ask, you may not get it. Depending on where you currently live and where you will be moving, this could be an unexpected expense you may not have planned on. When considering a place to live, you will want to consider whether you want to live in a local or nearby community in relation to where you are employed. If employed in a large city, you might want to consider a nearby community which will require a commute, but housing might be more affordable. If in a smaller community you might choose to live locally, given the housing market, cost of living, and what is available in the community. When deciding on a place to live, we urge you to consider several criteria. These include: school options for your children (even if you do not have any yet, but plan to), transportation, athletic events, community and cultural events, distance to the university, medical facilities, and children's programs.

School Options

What are possible school options for your children? Are schools rated well according to school report card data? See Table 2.3 and Figures 2.1, 2.2, and 2.3 for sample school report card data from Illinois and Table 2.4 for an Adequate Yearly Progress (AYP) table from Texas. Typically, all states have this data available on-line that you can access. You can also ask some of your new colleagues who have children about the local schools. Other questions to consider include: Do students have a lot of academic and nonacademic opportunities (e.g., swimming, band, foreign languages, plays, and outdoor education)? Are schools within walking distance of your new home? If not within walking distance, do schools provide transportation? Are school breaks the same as your new institutions breaks? Is the school population diverse? Does the school incorporate technology into its curriculum? All of the above mentioned are things you may want to consider in regards to schools. If the university you are going to be employed at has a College of Education, it might be wise to visit with those faculty members that are in public and private schools and get their honest options about the schools they visit.

Table 2.3
SAMPLE SCHOOL REPORT CARD DATA

School: PEPPER RIDGE ELEMENTARY SCHOOL (K–5)
District: MCLEAN COUNTY USD 5

School Enrollment (2009): 519
State Status: <u>AEWS</u>
All Subjects Meets and Exceeds (2009): 77.70%
U.S. Status:
Made Adequate Yearly Progress (2009): <u>No</u>

Administrator
Sarah Edwards
2602 Danbury Dr
Bloomington, IL 62705
(309)452-1042

Avg. Teacher Salary:	$55,072
Avg. Teacher Experience:	13.2 Years
Instructional Expenditure Per Pupil (2006–07):	$5,030
Operational Expenditure Per Pupil (2006–07):	$8,391
Low Income:	47%

Note: Interactive Illinois Report Card. (n.d.). *Interactive Illinois Report Card.* Retrieved September 9, 2010, from: http://iirc.niu.edu/School.aspx?schoolid=170640050262015

Transportation

Transportation in your new community might also be an area you investigate. What are transportation options in this community? Is there an efficient bus transportation system? Is there an effective train transportation system? Is there a local airport for when you have to travel? Can you access larger cities, if need be, with transportation options from this new community? If you are living in an area that is populated by university faculty members, inquire about whether or not shuttles or carpooling is already established. Often, a shuttle service will save a great deal of money in gasoline. One critical question to ask if living away from the university community is what the traffic patterns are like when commuting. Take this time and what the parking situation on campus looks like when weighing out the distance from work you want to travel.

Figure 2.1. County location of school within the state.

Note: McLean County, Illinois. (2010, July 7), In Wikipedia, The Free Encyclopedia. Retrieved July 26, 2010, from: http://en.wikipedia.org/w/index.php?title=McLean_County,_Illinois&oldid=37215 8887

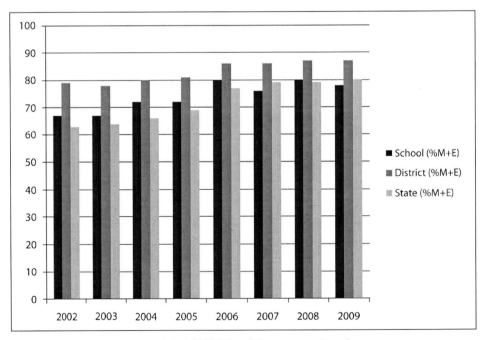

Figure 2.2. ISAT School Assessment Results.
PEPPER RIDGE ELEMENTARY SCHOOL-MCLEAN COUNTY
USD5.Composite Percent Meets and Exceeds–ISAT Assessment

Note: Interactive Illinois Report Card. (n.d.). *Interactive Illinois Report Card.* Retrieved September 9, 2010, from: http://iirc.niu.edu/School.aspx?schoolid=170640050262015

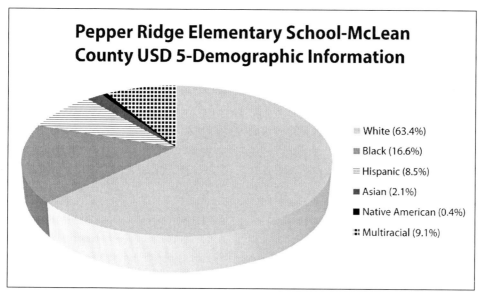

Figure 2.3. School demographic information.

Note: Interactive Illinois Report Card. (n.d.). *Interactive Illinois Report Card.* Retrieved September 9, 2010, from: http://iirc.niu.edu/School.aspx?schoolid=170640050262015

Athletic Events

Another area of interest may be athletics, either to play or to watch. Are there athletic events in this community or nearby that you can attend? Does your institution have sporting events you could attend? Are there any professional sports teams locally or nearby? Does this community have any health clubs available? We know the major focus is on your new faculty position, but we feel where you live and what is available or accessible can be very important in your decision-making process. Developing a balance between work and home life is essential for your health and well-being.

Community and Cultural Events

Community and cultural events is another area or topic you may want to consider. Are there other things to do in the community or nearby that you and/or your family can become involved with or do? Are there community and cultural events in this community or nearby? Is there a performing arts center where one can go see performances (e.g., singers, musicians, and musicals)? Is there an art facility in the community or nearby? Are there museums locally or nearby to visit? Are there festivals locally or nearby that you could attend? This might be important to you and it may not, but we feel it is definitely something to consider when making your move.

Table 2.4
ADEQUATE YEARLY PROGRESS DATA TABLE

Texas Educational Agency
Adequate Yearly Progress Campus Data Table
Final 2008 AYP Results

Campus Name: FT SAM HOUSTON ELEMENTARY (015914101) FT SAM HOUSTON
Status: Academically Acceptable, Meets AYP

	All Students	African American	Hispanic	White	Econ. Disadv.	Special Education	LEP (Measure)	LEP (Students)
Rdg./LA								
2007–2008								
Met Std.	259	81	46	121	101	18	10	n/a
Num Tested	291	95	53	130	114	31	14	14
% Met Std.	89%	85%	87%	93%	89%	58%	71%	n/a
Student Group %	100%	33%	18%	45%	39%	11%	n/a	5%
2006–2007								
Met Std.	333	113	57	148	130	53	10	n/a
Num Tested	362	128	`64	154	145	59	13	13
% Met Std.	93%	88%	89%	96%	90%	90%	77%	n/a
Change 2007 to 2008	–3	–3	–2	–3	–1	–32	–6	
Math								
2007–2008								
Met Std.	240	71	40	118	87	15	8	n/a
Num Tested	289	95	52	130	113	30	14	14
% Met Std.	83%	75%	77%	91%	77%	50%	57%	n/a
Student Group %	100%	33%	18%	45%	39%	10%	n/a	5%

Table 2.4– *Continued*

	All Students	African American	Hispanic	White	Econ. Disadv.	Special Education	LEP (Measure)	LEP (Students)
2006–2007								
Met Std.	306	93	52	144	117	42	10	n/a
Num Tested	362	362	128	64	153	145	58	13
13% Met Std.	85%	73%	81%	94%	81%	72%	77%	n/a
Change 2007 to 2008	–2	2	–4	–3	–4	–22	–20	
Attend 2006–2007								
Days Present	113,438	39,023	20,884	48,818	45,280	16,901		5,140
Days Member-ship	117,881	40,285	21,771	50,945	47,331	17,857		5,323
Att Rate	96.2%	96.9%	95.9%	95.8%	95.7%	94.6%		96.6%
Student Group %	100%	34%	18%	43%	40%	15%		5%
Attend 2005–2006								
Days Present	102,865	35,759	22,284	40,347	38,155	16,195		6,773
Days Member-ship	106,117	36,777	23,006	41,771	39,578	16,925		6,992
Att Rate	96.9%	97.2%	96.9%	96.6%	96.4%	95.7%		96.9%
Student Group %	100%	35%	22%	39%	37%	16%		7%
Change	–0.7	–0.3	–1.0	–0.8	–0.7	–1.1		–0.3

Note: Academic Excellence Indicator System. (n.d.). *Welcome to the Texas Education Agency.* Retrieved October 9, 2010, from: http://ritter.tea.state.tx.us/perfreport/aeis/

Children's Programs

If you currently have children or are considering having children in the future, this is an area you will probably want to consider. Are there children's programs available in this community such as school year and summer programs? Are there sports-related programs available (e.g., golf, football, soccer, softball, baseball)? Are there performing arts programs available (e.g., music, plays, dance, and theatre)? Are there local swimming pools in the area? Is there a children's museum locally or nearby? Are there movie theaters locally or nearby? These would all be important questions to answer if children are involved in your life. If you have a child with special needs or medical conditions, do not forget to spend time investigating the services available in the community to assist you in this area.

Visiting the Community

Another thing to do is to visit the community or communities you are considering in your move. Before purchasing a home, look around the community and try to spend some time there. We urge you to get a feel for where you might be moving. Collect data on the pros and cons of houses you are considering as well as their location. What is important to you? Are there places you would rather live? What is the housing market like where you are looking? What shape is the house in that you are considering and others around it? If you move, what will the resale value be? All of these questions and many others should be considered when undertaking the purchase of a home. You may ask your new colleagues about housing, the community, and things of interest to you. If they have lived around these communities for some time, they may have some valuable information that you could use to your advantage. You may also consider talking to potential neighbors and just surveying the neighborhood (observing what goes on) on a weekend day for a couple of hours to see if that is a place you could comfortably and safely live.

Shopping

Shopping is another area to consider. What can be accessed in or around the community you are considering? Where are the grocery stores? What stores are available? What are prices like on groceries, clothes, and furniture? How accessible are the stores? If the stores you like to shop at are not available, what are other options? Are there other stores in nearby communities? Although this is not as important of a topic as compared to others we have previously discussed, it is something you might consider. Again, you may ask your new colleagues about shopping and what is available. If they have lived in the area for some time, they may have some valuable information that would benefit you.

Nightlife

Nightlife in the community or surrounding areas might also be an important factor when considering a place to live. What restaurants are available? Is there some place to go dancing or to listen to live music? Is there a comedy club in the area or nearby? What kinds of entertainment are available? These and other questions are ones you may ask your new department chair or faculty colleagues. You could also look through the local yellow pages, search on-line, or contact the local Chamber of Commerce for pertinent information on these topics.

Parks

The last area we will discuss is parks. Are there parks in the neighborhoods? Are there parks in the community? Are there state parks nearby? Do the parks have playgrounds or swimming pools? Are there any walking, running, or bike trails? If you like to be outdoors and enjoy nature or have children, this may be of interest to you. Again, this is a topic you may think about asking your new colleagues. If they have lived in the community for some time they may have some valuable information that would benefit you.

Discuss Class Load

Another very important topic to discuss prior to your arrival for your new faculty position is class load. How many classes will you be teaching each semester or quarter, depending on the system in place at your new institution. Typically, a full-time load is 100% with each three-credit course counting as 25% of that load. At a Research 1 institution, a typical teaching load could be 50% (two courses) with a 50% research load per semester or it might even be 25% (one course) with a 75% research load per semester. At a Teaching institution, a typical teaching load would be 100% (four courses) per semester, while an institution that is a combination of the two might have a 75% teaching load (3 courses) with a 25% research load. Teaching load is something that we recommend you discuss prior to your arrival at your new institution and during the negotiation and offer process.

If there is a preferred type of schedule that you want, you need to make this very clear before you arrive. Some things to consider are how many preparations (preps) you will have. For example, when assigning classes to a new faculty member with a 75% teaching load, if possible, the preferred schedule developed by the chair should be two sections of the same course and one section of another course. Even though the faculty member has three courses to teach, they only actually have two preparations because they are teaching two sections of the same course. This makes the first year of planning easier and will free up some of your time to focus on other job responsibilities such as committee work and research activities.

In addition, it is important to find out if your time can be bought out by a grant. Grant buy-outs refer to using monies from a grant you secure to buy-out some of your teaching time, giving you ample time to complete the proposed grant project. For example, if you had a 75% teaching load with 25% devoted towards research and were released for one course per semester (based on your grant buy-out), your load would change to 50% teaching and 50% research. The grant would actually pay one-quarter of your salary and the department could then use the salary it would be paying you to teach one class to hire another qualified individual to teach your previously assigned course. This is very important to know because it could have a direct impact on you as you move towards promotion and tenure. If your institution promotes grants and grant writing, but wants you to conduct the grant on top of your other commitments, the likelihood of you being overwhelmed and not successful are high, especially as a new or junior faculty member. The buy-out time will allow you to continue with your grant-funded research while still teaching and preparing for your courses.

Another important issue to examine is summer teaching opportunities. You may want to inquire about the possibility of teaching in the summer and what types of classes are offered during summer sessions. Summer teaching is not for everyone. Some individuals need the summer break to recoup and prepare for the upcoming fall semester. However, as a new faculty member, you may want to teach in the summer if you are in need of extra income. A typical contract is for nine months spanning the academic year (fall and spring) and does not include summer teaching or summer pay. The amount of summer pay and summer teaching loads should be discussed prior to your arrival and during the negotiation of your employment contract. The amount of pay per summer will vary across institutions. Some universities offer a flat rate per course hour you teach while others offer pay based on a specific percentage of your salary. For example, if you teach four courses in the summer and the institution you work at offers one-third of your salary for a full load during summer, you will be able to take your yearly salary and divide that by three to determine your summer pay. Although this added income is a benefit, prior to accepting a summer teaching position, weigh out the time contratints that will be placed on you. Summer is an excellent time to focus on your writing and research. However, it is possible that you may want to do both. Knowing what types of classes are offered and the length of these classes will help you with your decision.

Table 2.5
SAMPLE TEACHING AND RESEARCH LOADS

Teaching	Research	Total
25% (1 3-credit course)	75% (50% for grant, 25% load)	100%
50% (2 different 3-credit courses)	50% (25% for grant, 25% load)	100%
50% (2 sections of the same 3-credit course)	50% (25% for grant, 25% load)	100%
75% (3 different 3-credit courses)	25% (load)	100%
75% (2 sections of the same 3-credit course) (1 section of another 3-credit course)	25% (load)	100%
75% (3 sections of the same 3-credit course)	25% (load)	100%
100% (4 different 3-credit courses)	0% (no time devoted to research)	100%
100% (2 sections of the same 3-credit course) (2 section of another 3-credit course)	0% (no time devoted to research)	100%
100% (2 sections of the same 3-credit course) (1 section of another 3-credit course) (1 section of another 3-credit course)	0% (no time devoted to research)	100%
100% (4 sections of the same 3-credit course)	0% (no time devoted to research)	100%

In the summer, classes could be offered over three, four, six, or eight weeks. The shorter the length of time teaching, the longer you would have to write and conduct research. However, the shorter the teaching time, typically the more intense it is because it is basically a 16-week course condensed into three or four weeks. All of this should be considered and as a new faculty member you should advocate for the schedule that best meets your needs. See Table 2.5 for sample teaching and research loads.

Another aspect to consider in regards to teaching load is the class schedule. Most faculty members prefer to only teach on two days, three at a maximum, so they can allocate time during each week to devote to writing. If your class schedule is spread out over the five-day week, you might begin to feel like your writing opportunities are limited and little is accomplished because your entire week is broken up with teaching responsibilities (e.g., preparing for class, teaching class, and working with students). You will need to advocate to your new chair or whoever is in charge of scheduling instructors (often program coordinators) for classes so you can request a favorable schedule. This is especially important in your early years as you progress towards promotion and tenure. If you do not have time to conduct research, you may not produce many publications, thus weakening your chances for promotion and tenure.

Related to course load and the specific classes you are assigned to teach are materials. As a new faculty member, it is important to know what resources are available to you including materials. You will want to request any teaching materials that might help in your preparation for teaching the courses you are assigned. Materials you will want to ask for would include previous syllabi, textbooks, sample projects, sample exams, and anything else that might benefit you as you prepare for your classes. You will want to know if the institution has on-line course systems (i.e., Blackboard, e-college) available. You might also ask if a copy of each of the current textbooks used in the the classes you are teaching can be sent to you so that you can start working on your classes prior to your arrival.

Another item to ask about is whether or not there are course instructional teams on your campus. Many times when institutions have multiple sections of a course taught by different people, they frequently get together to discuss and prepare for the course; a course instructional team. This team would discuss items such as what is effective and what needs to be changed or modified, the sequence of the curriculum, assessments, projects, and standards. These teams are important so students taking the course get the same content knowledge and experiences regardless of the instructor they have. Be sure to ask for contact information on the individuals on the instructional team so you can speak with directly with them, email them, or both. A simple conference call is one method you could suggest to speak with them all at once. You may also suggest using technology via a web-based chat or instant messaging to communicate with the team. If an instructional team is not available at your university, we suggest you contact other instructors teaching the same course you do or visit with your mentor for clarification on your ability to change or restructure course content. This is especially important if working at a nationally accredited university. Often, universities that are accreditated have selected assignments used during the accreditation process that cannot be altered.

Faculty Expectations and Support

Finding out as much as you can prior to arriving at your new institution will be helpful in making you feel more comfortable as well as helping to reduce stress and anxieties. It is believed that some of the biggest stressors in one's life are a death of a family member, moving, and starting a new job. You might be experiencing two of these stressors (moving and starting a new job) so the more information you can find out prior to your arrival, the better.

Other things you may want to find out about include time spent on campus, office hours, and committees. As you start to plan your life, which we recommend you do very carefully, you will want to consider time spent on campus. Is there a requirement or departmental policy as to how much time you are expected to spend on campus? Even if there is not, you should plan to be on campus as much as is possible so you can learn about the department, college, and university as well as the program you are teaching. It is also easier to get to know your colleagues if you are on campus, which may help you get involved in collaborative writing or research teams. One of the often "hidden" rules of the university is that you are visible to tenured faculty. Remember, it is the tenured faculty that will eventually vote on your own tenure status. If they do not know who you are or what you contribute to the department, it will be difficult to secure their vote. On the other hand, you may find you get more writing completed off campus so it will be important your first semester that you try to establish what gets done where, and where you are the most productive while not hindering your ability to establish strong working relationships with your colleagues.

Office hours for students will also come into play. Find out if there is a required amount of office hours, how often they need to be held, and if it is required to post office hours. It is important to have office hours so students have consistent days and times that they can come and speak with you regarding class-related items. We suggest you plan these office hours on the same days that you teach so that you can try to build in big blocks of time on other days to focus on writing and scholarship activities. We do not want you to think that every spare moment needs to be spent on writing and scholarship, but what we do know is that you need to be careful and carve out large periods of time to devote to writing and scholarship.

Another area to investigate is information related to committee work. Will you be required to serve on committees as a new faculty member? If so, what is the expectation? Will your committee assignments be limited to the department or will you need to serve on college and university committees as well? Do you need to serve outside the university? As evidenced, your days can be easily filled and you will need to be careful to balance your time so you are successful moving towards promotion and tenure.

The last thing you might want to determine is what kind of supports are provided by the department, college, and university to prepare you for your new faculty position. This could range from specifics on teaching, research and service, to benefits, to training. Where will your office be located? When can you get access to keys for your office? How do you get an email account? What do you need to do so you get your first paycheck on time? When do your benefits begin? Are there available workshops or professional development opportunities available to prepare you for your new role as a faculty member? Can you be shown around by a newer faculty member? Is there a mentoring program? The answers to these questions and more will better prepare you for your arrival. We feel you should be very proactive and prepare yourself as much as possible for your new role as a faculty member. Do not just show up on campus the week before classes and think you will be prepared and be able to get up to speed with everything. Obviously, you cannot learn everything there is to know before your arrival on campus, but the more you can learn and find out, the better prepared you will be and the more positive experience you will incur.

Conclusion

The information in this chapter highlighted different aspects you should be aware of prior to your arrival as a new faculty member in an institution of higher education. We believe that the use of this information and proper planning will make your transition from a doctoral student to a faculty member easier by reducing elements which often cause stress and anxiety. This chapter discussed finishing your dissertation as the most critical step in starting your new career. It also discussed finding an appropriate place to live and things to look for in a community; the importance of visiting the community and spending some time there; clarifying your class load; and determining faculty expectations and supports across the department, college, and university. We hope the information in this chapter provided you some insight and guidance to help you become successful on your journey as a new faculty member.

Faculty Tips about Relocating

- Take advantage of what the community has to offer. Find out about shuttles and carpools, it will save a lot of money on gasoline!

- Don't buy a home on a whim. Sometimes you get a job offer a few weeks before classes start and rush to buy a home that you may not be happy with down the road. Rent while you find the perfect home!

Chapter 3

LEARNING ABOUT YOUR NEW INSTITUTION ONCE YOU ARE THERE

You have accepted a job as a new faculty member at an institution of higher education, prepared yourself for your arrival, and now it is time to learn about your new place of employment. We don't just mean learn about the physical environment (although very important especially on large campuses), but rather about policies and programs at your institution of higher education. We feel this is one of the basic fundamental things you should do in order to prepare yourself to be an effective faculty member and recommend that you learn as much as you can about your workplace as it will ultimately be a benefit to both you and your students. Know that you cannot possibly learn everything and it may take years to understand daily operations at a comprehensible level, but gaining as much information and knowledge as possible will get you off on the right foot towards success in your new position.

Core Curriculum

The first thing you might want to learn about is the general education program. If at an institution with an undergraduate population, it is common for there to be some sort of general education program or curriculum. Typically, the general education or core curriculum has a fundamental goal. For example, courses identified as core curriculum may develop communication skills and/or skills and abilities related to the following four areas: (a) Critical Inquiry and Problem Solving-Students will develop and communicate a range of interests and curiosities, engaging those interests and curiosities through critical thinking, reasoning, and problem solving; (b) Public Opportunity-Students will identify the resources and articulate the subsequent value of civic and community engagement; (c) Diverse and Global Perspectives-Students will be exposed to diverse and global perspectives by developing and communicating an appreciation for the impact made in personal and professional lives; and (d) Life-Long Learning-Students will utilize the skills indicative of an effective life-long learner actively pursuing knowledge and applying new information and skills in interdisciplinary approaches (http://www.gened.ilstu.edu/students/).

The core curriculum is comprised of a combination of required and elective courses that all students must take outside of their major. Some required courses may include specific courses in English (writing), math, communication, and a foreign language, while elective courses may fall in general areas with different possible choices being available. Outside of the United States, a general education curriculum may not be as prevalent. Many universities such as European countries are more discipline specific and deviate from the traditional four-year undergraduate program offered in the United States.

At the graduate level, students typically also have these options, but are not required to take as many courses because they already have an undergraduate degree. They are still, however, required to take certain types of courses (i.e., statistics, research methodology, curriculum development) as well as electives that they choose that are of interest to them and relate to their course of study. Things to learn and questions to ask would include: What are the general education requirements for undergraduate students? What are the requirements for graduate students? When do students take these courses in their plan of study? What courses are required? What are different course options that students can take as electives? How many core hours are required? These questions will hopefully get you started in learning about your new institution and are imperative to ask if you will be assuming the role of advising in your new position. See Tables 3.1 and 3.2 for a sample of general education program requirements and a complete plan of study with general education and specific program requirements included.

Programs Offered

Another way to learn about your new institution is to investigate what types of programs are offered on your campus. What programs does the department offer? What is available at the Undergraduate, Master's, and Doctoral levels? Are there any teacher certificate programs offered? What is unique about the programs your department offers? We suggest you learn as much about the department as possible. Ask for materials about your department and thoroughly read them. This might include undergraduate and graduate course catalogs, departmental faculty meeting minutes, and other related materials. Go to the department website and peruse everything there because it is beneficial for you to learn as much as you can about the department in which you will be working. This will help you in your basic under-

Table 3.1
SAMPLE GENERAL EDUCATION PROGRAM
(CORE CURRICULUM) REQUIREMENTS

The General Education Program consists of an integrated set of courses (14 total) including:

Inner Core
(5 courses with 22 total course options)
- 2-course sequence integrating composition, communication , critical thinking, and information literacy:
  Composition & Critical Inquiry (ENG 101)
  Communication & Critical Inquiry (COM 110)
- Mathematics
- Natural Sciences or Natural Science Alternatives

Middle Core
(5 courses–one from each course category with 139 total options)
- Quantitative Reasoning
- Language in the Humanities
- United States Traditions
- Individuals and Civic Life
- Individuals and Societies

Outer Core
(4 courses–one from each course category with 92 total options)
- Science, Mathematics, and Technology
- Fine Arts
- Humanities
- Social Sciences

Note: Gen Ed Program Structure–Information for Faculty–General Education . (n.d.). *General Education Program–Illinois State University*. Retrieved August 9, 2010, from: http://www.gened.ilstu.edu /faculty/structure/

Table 3.2
COMPLETE PLAN OF STUDY WITH
GENERAL EDUCATION INCLUDED

Coursework equals 119 hours. For details concerning a given course, please visit Illinois State University's Undergraduate Catalog.
*Admission to Professional Studies Required (APS)

Semester 1
ENG 101 (Inner Core) (3)
Science (Inner Core) (3)
Math (Inner Core) (3)
SED 101–The Exceptional Learner (3)
Complete Basic Skills Test–State of Illinois
Total: 12 hours

continued

Table 3.2–*Continued*

Semester 2
COM 110 (Inner Core) (3)
Science (Inner Core) (3)
Middle Core (3)
Middle Core (3)
Middle Core (3)
Total: 15 hours

Semester 3
See Department of Special Education advisor for plan of study early in semester.
SED 201–Effective Collaboration and Teaching Exceptional and Diverse Learners I (3)
PSY 215–Educational Psychology (3)
Middle Core (3)
Middle Core (3)
Outer Core–SS–PSY 113 (3)
Total: 15 hours

Semester 4
SED 202–Effective Collaboration and Teaching Exceptional and Diverse Learners II (3)
CI 208–Literacy I (3)
Math Elective (3)
Outer Core (3)
Outer Core (3)
Total: 15 hours

Semester 5
SED 203–Measuring and Affecting Student Academic and Social Behavior I (3)
SED 379–Assistive Technology for Individuals with Disabilities (3)
SED 377–Communication Strategies for Individuals with Disabilities (3)
CI 209–Literacy II (3)
Outer Core (3)
All APS requirements completed by mid-semester for advanced registration for following semester.
SED 203 and CI 209 concurrent registration
Total: 15 hours

Semester 6
Practicum semester
* SED 204–Measuring and Affecting Student Academic and Social Behavior II (3)
* SED 383–Developing and Implementing Alternative Curriculum (6)
* SED 245.12–Fieldwork in Special Education: Alternative Curriculum (4)
EAF 228 - Social Foundations (3)
Take LBS1 Content test at end of semester
SED 204,383, and 245.12 concurrent registration
Total: 16 hours

Table 3.2–*Continued*

Semester 7
Field-based semester
TB Test
Criminal Background Check
* SED 382–Challenging Behavior: Analysis and Intervention (3)
* SED 384–Strategies for Accessing the General Curriculum (3)
* SED 373–Family-Professional Collaboration (3)
* SED 245.13–Fieldwork in Special Education: Accessing General Curriculum (4/4)
Take APT test at end of semester.
All concurrent registration
Total: 17 hours

Semester 8
STT 399–Student Teaching (14)
Total: 14 hours

Note: Specialist in Learning and Behavior Native Student Sample Schedule. (n.d.). *Illinois State University.* Retrieved October 9, 2010, from: http://www.specialeducation.ilstu.edu/planofstudy/ibs nativesamplesschedule.pdf

standing of what offerings your department has and in addition, it will also help you develop questions to ask when you actually join the department as a new faculty member.

We also suggest that you learn about your college as much as possible to try and understand what each department does and how they all fit together. Are there possible opportunities for you to work across departments or even colleges? For example, if you are a special educator interested in the rates of obesity among children with disabilities, you may want to collaborate on grants, research, or publications with individuals in the Health or Kinesiology Departments. Your faculty mentor or your department chair, as well as other faculty, might be good people to talk with in regards to these topics and more. As a last step, you might also investigate what your university has to offer in the area of programs and degrees for students. Are they well-known for any certain programs or degrees offered? Although not necessary, it may give you a better idea of what kinds of students attend this institution. See Table 3.3 for a sample of Undergraduate Degree programs available at Illinois State University.

Table 3.3
LIST OF POSSIBLE UNDERGRADUATE DEGREES AVAILABLE

A	D
Accounting	Dance Education
- Accounting Information Systems	Dance Performance
- Career Specialty	
- Financial Accounting	E
- Integrated Bachelor of Science Master of Professional Accountancy	Early Childhood Education
Actuarial Science	Economics
Agribusiness	Elementary Education
Agriculture	- Bilingual/Bicultural Education
Agriculture Education	English
Agriculture Industry Management	- Publishing and the Nonprofit Literary Arts
Agricultural Science	English Teacher Education
Apparel, Merchandising and Design	Environmental Health
Anthropology	Exercise Science
Art	
- Art History	F
- Graphic Design	Finance
- Studio Arts	Food Industry Management
Art Teacher Education	- Food Industry Science
Arts Technology in Art, Music and Theatre	Food, Nutrition and Dietetics
Athletic Training	French
Audiology	French Teacher Education
B	G
Biochemistry/Molecular Biology	German
Biological Sciences	German Teacher Education
- Organismal Biology and Public Outreach	Geography
Biological Sciences Teacher Education	Geography Teacher Education
Business Administration	Geology
Business Information Systems	- Earth and Space Science Education
Business Teacher Education	
	H
C	Health Education
Chemistry	- Community Health Education
Chemistry Teacher Education	- School Health Education
Clinical Laboratory Science	Health Information Management
Communication Studies	History
Communication Studies Education	History - Social Sciences Teacher Education
Community Health Education	Horticulture
Computer Science	Human (Child) Development and Family Resources
Criminal Justice Sciences	

Table 3.3– *Continued*

I
Information Systems
- Information Assurance & Security
- Systems Development/Analyst
- Web Application Development
Insurance
- General Insurance
- Business Information Systems
Interior and Environmental Design
International Business

J
Journalism
- Broadcast Journalism
- News Editorial
- Visual Communication

L
Languages Literatures & Cultures
- French
- German
- Spanish

M
Management
- Entrepreneurship and Small Business
  Management
- Human Resource Management
- Organizational Leadership
Marketing
-Integrated Marketing Communication
-Professional Sales
Mass Media
- Interactive Media
- Radio
- Television
Mathematics
Mathematics Teacher Education
Middle Level Teacher Education
Military Science
Music
- Band & Orchestra Instruments
  Performance
- Classical Guitar Performance
- Composition
- Keyboard Performance

- Music Therapy
- Voice Performance
Music Education
- Choral - General - Keyboard
- Choral - General - Vocal
- Instrumental - Band
- Instrumental - Orchestra

N
Nursing
-Prelicensure/BSN
-RN/BSN

P
Philosophy
Physics
-Computer Physics
-Engineering Physics
Physics Teacher Education
Physical Education
Physical Education Teacher Education K-
  12
Political Science
- Global Studies
- Leadership & Social Justice
- Public Service
Psychology
Public Relations

R
Recreation and Park Administration
- Recreation Management
- Therapeutic Recreation
Renewable Energy
- Technical
- Economics and Public Policy

S
Safety
Social Work
Sociology
Spanish
Spanish Teacher Education
Special Education
- Specialist Deaf & Hard of Hearing
- Specialist Learning & Behavior

continued

Table 3.3–*Continued*

- Specialist Low Vision & Blindness Speech Pathology **T** Technology - Construction Management - Graphic Communication - Industrial Computer Systems	- Integrated Manufacturing Systems Technology Education Telecommunications Management Theatre - Acting - Design/Production - Theatre Studies

Note: Undergraduate Programs: Academics: Illinois State University. (n.d.). *Illinois State University.* Retrieved October 9, 2010, from: http://www.ilstu.edu/home/academics/undergraduate.shtml

New Faculty Training

Another area to inquire about regarding your new institution is the area of "faculty training." As a new faculty member, you will want to determine if there are any training opportunities available at the department, college, and/or university levels. How can you prepare yourself for your first semester? What would be good to know? How can you get support from all levels and constituents? If teaching technology is available, who gives support with technology? Specific departmental information can be obtained from the department chair or veteran faculty. For university guidance and assistance, you can also ask these people or search the institution's website. Often universities will offer an orientation day where university specific information is dispersed. For example, at Illinois State University, there is help and support from the Center for Teaching and Learning (CTLT) and at Sam Houston State University, there is help available from the Professional and Academic Center for Excellence (PACE). These are valuable resources for all faculty who want to increase their knowledge and skills in the area of teaching. See Table 3.4 for one such possible opportunity.

Faculty Mentors

What are some other support options that will help you in your first year as well as in future years towards promotion and tenure? Hopefully, support will be provided to you at all levels: department, college, and the university. In the department, an effective model we have seen implemented is the use of an assigned faculty mentor to serve as a mentor to a new faculty member. Ideally, a faculty mentor is someone who has already earned promotion and tenure and also has some of the same content background or interests as the new faculty member. This person might meet weekly or every other week to

Table 3.4
NEW FACULTY ORIENTATION SAMPLE

New Faculty Orientation

Welcome to _____ University! The Center for Teaching Learning & Technology and the Office of Human Resources are committed to making sure your career at _____ gets off to the best possible start. The following experiences have been designed with that goal in mind.

Click here to register for one or all three.

New Faculty Orientation

New Faculty Orientation (NFO) will be Monday, August 11 in the Old Main Room at the Bone Student Center from 8:00 am–3:30 pm. Join us for a day-long introduction to _____ University's vision, values, culture, history, students, programs, resources, and more. It's an excellent opportunity to meet other new faculty and identify some of the people and services that can make your first year at _____ a smooth one.

Click here to see an agenda as well as information about parking and child care options.

New Faculty Reception

You and a guest are invited to a reception hosted by President _____ and Provost _____ at the University Residence, 1000 Gregory Street, from 4:00–6:00 pm on Monday, August 11. Relaxing with new friends and colleagues is the perfect end to a busy day.

New Employee Orientation

You can't miss this session! Sign up for your health, dental, and life insurance as well as other optional benefits. Also, learn details about your retirement plan. A Benefits Counselor will be on hand to guide you through your myriad choices.

We'll also introduce some of the technologies you'll need as you begin teaching, researching, and fulfilling other professional commitments at the University. A wide variety of session dates and times are available. If you have questions, contact Human Resources at (___) _____-_____.

Other Ways to Prepare for the Fall Semester

- JOIN CTLT's New Faculty Community.
  CTLT's New Faculty Community provides a virtual gathering place for those who will begin their teaching careers at Illinois State University in the fall of 2008.

continued

Table 3.4–*Continued*

- ATTEND CTLT's Summer Institute for the 21st Century Educator.
  Just because you haven't started teaching yet doesn't mean you're not eligible
  to join other ISU educators at CTLT's Summer Institute. We offer literally hundreds of hours of programming between mid-May and mid-August, each of
  them designed to help support high-quality teaching at our University!
- ATTEND CTLT's Fall 2008 Faculty Prep Week (August 11–15, 2008).
  Faculty Prep Week sessions offer an interactive, hands-on approach to classroom issues that affect us all. All sessions are offered in the Instructional
  Technology Development Center, the home of CTLT, 301 S. Main (just north
  of Jimmy John's).

Note: New Faculty Orientation. (n.d.). *Welcome to CTLT!* Retrieved October 9, 2010, from: http://www.ctlt.ilstu.edu/programs/nfo.php

just touch base with the new faculty member, provide support and guidance, answer questions, give feedback, evaluate written work, or a combination of things. The mentor is a person the new faculty member can count on to pro-vide honest answers and assistance on anything from teaching classes and dealing with students to travel procedures within the department.

Some universities have formal mentoring programs. For example, *Rising Stars* is a formal mentoring program at Sam Houston State University de-signed to assist junior faculty with reaching publication goals. Junior faculty are assigned to a tenured faculty mentor who has an established pattern of scholarly activities. The college provides scheduled meeting times where var-ious events occur that will support the junior faculty member. Examples of programming is meeting various editors, guest speakers on tenure and pro-motion, developing writing agendas, and seeking grant funding to support research. Participation in this type of mentoring program is always encour-aged as the accountability factor increases a faculty member's productivity. Each Rising Star mentee will receive special, targeted professional develop-ment related to research and publishing, a COE mentor for research, a cer-tificate of participation, and a $100 grant toward professional development related to research which can be used for conference attendance, workshop attendance, and research needs or books (Rising Stars–College of Education Graduate Programs–Sam Houston State University. (n.d.). Sam Houston State University, Huntsville, Texas. Carnegie Research Doctoral University. Re-trieved September 6, 2010, from: http://www.shsu.edu/~coegp/risingstars/risingstars.html).

If the college or department you are joining does not have an official men-toring program in place, you might request to be assigned an unofficial men-tor or find out if a similar program can be made available. Not having an established program in place might not change your mind about accepting a position as a new faculty member, but when weighed with other contributing factors, it may make an impact on your decision. Through our years of experience dealing with promotion and tenure, we have found that it is very important for a new faculty member to have direct and immediate support from a fellow colleague. This direct link is someone he/she can easily contact and build a rapport with to help him/her during their first year as well as future years. An important note is that the veteran faculty member should be willing to participate and work with the new faculty member. Over time, we have seen mentors not only give of their time and effort, but also receive support in the form of new teaching techniques, presentations, writing opportunities, and grant funding.

Another effective method in collaboration with the faculty member is for the department chair to meet regularly with new faculty. This type of program has been identified by many names including "Newbie Meetings," "Junior Faculty Support Meetings," and "Tenure Track Meetings." These types of meetings will help build a relationship between the new faculty member and department chair as well as provide an avenue for effective communication through dialogue and questioning. It is suggested that new faculty meet biweekly with the department chair four weeks after the new faculty member begins teaching. This timeframe allows the new faculty member to get situated and started without the pressure of meeting right away. Again, if the department you are joining does not have a similar program, you might ask if something like this can be established. If the chair is unwilling, maybe he can suggest someone else to whom you could speak.

At the college level, you should see if other new faculty meet regularly or meet at least once a semester. We have found that these types of meetings are good for providing support and for all new faculty to share their feelings and opinions. In more structured settings, there are actual agendas with specific topics new faculty can discuss, and sometimes there are even short presentations from promoted and tenured faculty and those working towards promotion and tenure. We have found that these college-based meetings also provide opportunities for new faculty to make connections across departments and that sometimes they end up collaborating on coursework, service, and research related projects (i.e., writing for publication, presentations, and funding opportunities).

The last level of support we would like to discuss is university support. Some universities have centers on campus that provide training and professional development to all faculty, but especially focus on new faculty. The university understands that a new faculty member is a large investment and through these centers provides support and assistance that will hopefully support this new faculty towards promotion and tenure and a successful career at the institution. Two examples of things a center might provide are Early-Career Professional Development Circles and Teaching-Learning Communities. See Tables 3.5 and 3.6 for explanations of both of these opportunities.

These opportunities and many others just like them are provided on many university campuses. We urge you to look for these when you investigate institutions and visit campuses during your interviews. You will find that university-level support like this, as well as the department and college support previously mentioned, will be very beneficial as you work towards promotion and tenure, and a healthy balanced lifestyle.

Faculty Evaluations

Since you will be teaching and possibly developing your own course for the first time, you may want to get a clear understanding of the evaluation system used at your university. Typically, institutions require pretenured faculty (if not everyone) to be evaluated by their students for every course that they instruct. You will want to find out if this is a mandatory process, what is implemented, and when it occurs during the semester. Most institutions conduct these teacher evaluations during the last two weeks of the semester. You will also need to find out how the evaluations are conducted. Is it Scantron with forced choice questions using a type of Likert scale, a paper and pencil open-ended response sheet, or maybe even on-line through a service such as Survey Monkey? It will be important to know this so you can plan in-class time for students to complete an evaluation. You will also want to learn the procedures for implementation. It is very common that another instructor or graduate student implement the teacher evaluation with the instructor absent from class so no bias is involved. It is a good idea to ask for a copy or copies of evaluations to see how you are going to be evaluated. At some institutions there are set questions that are asked and that is it. At others there are set questions and the instructor can also add other pertinent questions to their evaluation.

A third evaluation design is for the instructor to hand pick all of the items that will be on the teacher evaluation. See Table 3.7 for a list of some possible questions found on a university teacher evaluation. It is also of great importance to find out how the results impact you as a professor. For example, some institutions tie student evaluations of instructor performance to merit pay or to salary increases.

There is not a question as to whether or not conducting student evaluations on professors adds additional stress to the professor. However, we have found that if the data is properly used then the evaluations of professors can serve as a way to redesign curriculum, direct attention to areas identified as weakness, and to evaluate whether your own instructional delivery is effective for the students in your courses.

Table 3.5
EARLY-CAREER TRAINING

Early-Career Professional Development Circles

Launching an academic career is a daunting challenge, especially if you try to do it alone. Join your early-career peers (faculty in their first three years of teaching at Illinois State University) in a program designed to reduce your stress and increase your success. You are warmly invited to join CTLT's Spring 2009 "Early-Career Professional Development Circle." Here are the basics:

Who is invited?
  Anyone in his/her first, second, or third year of teaching at Illinois State University is welcome.

Where do we meet?
  The Circle meets in the CTLT Instructional Resource Commons in the ITDC Building, 301 S. Main, just north of Jimmy John's.

When do we meet?
  The Circle meets from 2:00-3:00 on the following dates. Thursday sessions repeat the content from Wednesday sessions, so pick the day that's most convenient:
  Wednesday/Thursday, January 28/29, 2:00-3:00 pm
  Topic: What do the best college teachers know about student learning?

  Wednesday/Thursday, February 4/5, 2:00-3:00 pm
  Topic: What do the best college teachers expect of their students?

  Wednesday/Thursday, February 18/19, 2:00-3:00 pm
  Topic: How do the best college teachers conduct class?

  Wednesday/Thursday, March 18/19, 2:00-3:00 pm
  Topic: How do the best college teachers treat their students?

  Wednesday/Thursday, April 8/9, 2:00-3:00 pm
  Topic: How do the best college teachers evaluate their students and themselves?

END OF SEMESTER LUNCHEON Friday, May 1, Noon-2:00 pm

No need to attend all five meetings. Just come whenever you can!

Why should I come?
  The Circle is designed to achieve two important outcomes:

  • to provide early-career faculty with the social support they need to counter the stress of beginning a teaching career in higher education
  • to provide early-career faculty with answers to their questions about teaching and learning in an effort to help them accelerate their success in the classroom

continued

Table 3.5–*Continued*

Who will facilitate the Circle?

The Circle facilitator is Dr. _____, CTLT Associate Director. ____ has almost three decades of teaching experience-most of them in higher education, almost two decades of experience in teacher preparation and professional development, and a career-long interest in working with students and faculty at "points of transition."

Note: CTLT-Early-Career Professional Development Circles. (n.d.). *Welcome to CTLT!* Retrieved October 9, 2010, from: http://www.teachtech.ilstu.edu/programs/pdCir.php

Table 3.6
TEACHING LEARNING OPPORTUNITY

CTLT-Sponsored Teaching-Learning Communities

Spring 2009

Under the CTLT Teaching Community Enhancement Grant program up to $200 is available to groups of 5–i2 faculty members who wish to strengthen a community of teachers by starting a TLC. The funds can be used for books or other materials related to the topic of the TLC. Several departments have already started Teaching-Learning Communities. If you or your department would like to join them, contact

_____.

Who:

Faculty members committed to a collaborative model of professional growth.

What:

Teaching-Learning Communities (TLCs) of 5–12 faculty membes who read, write, and talk about teaching-related topics of mutual interest and benefit.

When:

1 hour every other week during spring semester

Where:

A location decided upon by the TLC members

Why:

Research on teacher cognition indicates that teachers can be energized by this kind of interaction to refine their thinking and instructional choices

Join an Existing TLC . . .

Blank reflective teaching journals and/or TLC selected books on pedagogy available.

- Reflection on Teaching (current group is full, but may start new group by checking below)

Table 3.6–Continued

- Professional Development Circle for Early Career Faculty
- Internship/Profesional Practice Program Coordinators
- Preparing for Tenure: Before and After
- Grad Students as Future Profesors
- Social Networking Tools in Instruction
- Second Life
- Online Teaching
- Effective Use of Clickers in Classrooms
- Teaching and Learning in Large Classrooms
- Universal Design in Instructional Planning
- **. . . or Start Your Own!**

- **Professional Development Circle for Early Career Faculty**
  This Circle is designed to offer faculty in their 1st, 2nd, or 3rd year of service at ISU a combination of professional development and peer support in the hope that those who participate will feel better prepared to meet the teaching challenges faced by faculty early in their careers. Identify a network of supportive peers with whom you can candidly discuss both the challenges and rewards of teaching. Topics for the Spring 2009 series are based on chapters in the award-winning book, "What the Best College Teachers Do" (Harvard UP, 2004). Groups begin meeting on Wednesday, January 28, or Thursday, January 29.

- **Internship/Professional Practice Program Coordinators**
  The Professional Practice Coordinators TLC is a networking opportunity for faculty and staff who coordinate internship and professional practice activities for students. This TLC is designed to identify a network of supportive peers with whom coordinators can candidly discuss both the challenges and rewards of leading internship programs. It will also provide an opportunity to collaborate with colleagues to help meet challenges in recruitment, organization, logistics and resources, and create a supportive group while respecting the uniqueness of individual leaders in diverse programs with diverse priorities.

- **Preparing for Tenure: Before and After**
  Is the tick-tock of your tenure clock prompting a bit of stress? The tenure and promotion process can be challenging even for faculty with outstanding credentials. This TLC is for pre-tenure faculty 1–3 years out who want the ASPT process to be as smooth as possible. With the support of pre-tenure peers from across campus, we will try to reduce stress through thorough and early preparation of materials guided by campus regulations and advice from higher education experts.

- **Grad Students as Future Professors**
  Conversations will center on topics and issues brought forth by the group that deal with any and all issues related to teaching. From course planning to issues

continued

Table 3.6–*Continued*

in the classroom, this group will discuss strategies and share experiences. Even if you have not taught in the classroom, you are welcome to join us for stimulating conversation with your peers.

TLCs Based on TOPICS

- **Social Networking Tools for Teaching**
  Explore a variety of social networking tools that help you connect with students and create collaborative environment for your class. At each meeting, we will look at different tools and discuss how we can make the best use of tools for your teaching.

- **Second Life**
  Second Life is a virtual reality environment where you can interact with students, scientists, and scholars from all over the world. In this TLC, we will meet in real life and/or second life and exchange ideas about using simulation in classroom and teaching in a virtual environment. We will also help each other to learn more about this technology. Beginners are welcome as we can help you get started in Second Life.

- **Online Teaching**
  So, you're teaching a fully online course . . . or at least thinking about it! And you're wondering, "How do other online instructors deal with _____" (fill in the blank here with your area of interest). In this TLC, we'll explore the successes and challenges associated with teaching online and the many ways that your colleagues are addressing knowledge acquisition, communication, assessment, student engagement, and any other topics of interest! We'll also discuss promising practices for teaching and learning online found in the literature. Whether you're a novice or a veteran of online teaching, you'll find something valuable in these informal discussions.

- **Effective Use of Clickers in Classrooms**
  How do you know that your classroom clickers use is promoting effective learning? Learn what others are doing that's receiving praise from students, as well as put together your own plan with information on Best Practices, a copy of "Clickers in the Classroom" by Douglas Duncan, and a prepared worksheet. All levels of clicker users are welcome.

- **Teaching and Learning in Large Classrooms**
  Yes you CAN get your students involved in discussion and keep them engaged in the large classroom! Join the conversations with colleagues facing similar challenges, and leave with new ideas. Already got it figured out? Come share your experiences and maybe pick up a few new tools! Research and Planning worksheet provided.

Table 3.6–*Continued*

- **Reflection on Teaching (current group is full, but may start new group)**
  Discuss and reflect with colleagues what is working and not working for you in facilitating learning for your students. This group meets informally to share and compare what is going on with their students and in their classrooms. No teaching topic is off-limits. Start your own group and invite your colleagues.

Note: CTLT-Sponsored Teaching-Learning Communities Provide Support and Learning. (n.d.). Welcome to CTLT! Retrieved from: http://www.ctlt.ilstu.edu/programs/tlComm.php

Funding Opportunities

Learning about funding opportunities at your institution could be instrumental in helping you grow and develop towards successful promotion and tenure. Funding can help you develop your teaching, research, or a combination of the two. It can also help to establish your name in the field and help you expand your area of expertise. You will want to learn about the different kinds of funding opportunities on and off-campus. These are often referred to as internal and external funding opportunities.

Internal Funding Opportunities

There is a very good possibility that your new institution will have many different types of internal funding opportunities. Some of these may include: (a) University Research Grants, (b) Professional Development Grants, (c) Travel Grants, and (d) Material Grants. University research grants are small competitive grants that faculty can apply for on your campus. This money is funneled through the institution to promote research and support new and veteran faculty in the development of their research interests and agenda. Typically, a faculty member will write a proposal, based on university guidelines, and it will first go through a department committee, then to a college committee, and finally to a university committee. If accepted, the faculty member can use the funds to support his/her on-going research projects. These types of grants typically offer funding from $5,000 to $6,000 for individuals and $10,000 to $12,000 for teams, and many institutions have separate competitions for newer (less than four years at the institution) and veteran faculty (greater than four years at the institution). Along with the proposal, an outcome form is also submitted. If funded, this form must be completed and the outcome has to be documented before the faculty member can apply for another grant in the future. See Appendix A for a sample University Research Grant application.

Table 3.7
SAMPLE OF TEACHER EVALUATION ITEMS

For items 1–16 a 5-point Likert scale is implemented where D=Disagree, MD=Moderately Disagree, N=Neutral, MA=Moderately Agree, and A=Agree.

1. The instructor communicated the importance of the subject matter.

2. The instructor clearly communicated the course objectives.

3. There was considerable agreement between the initially announced objectives of the course and what was taught.

4. The instructor modeled language, attitudes, and behaviors that demonstrated sensitivity to cultural differences and diversity.

5. The instructor provided meaningful answers to questions that were asked both in and out of class.

6. The instructor's assessments correlated to course objectives.

7. The instructor's feedback regarding my performance in class was provided in a timely manner.

8. The instructor was available for consultation with me.

9. The instructor encouraged student participation in class.

10. I gained some new knowledge as a result of taking this course.

11. The instructor utilized technology appropriately, when needed.

12. The instructor clarified difficult aspects of the course, when asked.

13. The instructor demonstrated a thorough knowledge of the subject.

14. The instructor was enthusiastic about the course content.

15. The instructor set high standards for student performance.

16. This course provided me opportunities to expand my knowledge and experiences with aspects of diversity as they relate to the course content and objectives.

17. On the back of this opscan form please provide any comments (a) concerning the instructor, and (b) concerning the course that are helpful in improving the course or instructor's teaching.

Note: Questions Obtained from Department of Special Education, Illinois State University, permission to reprint obtained.

Professional development grants might also be a source of funding available to you as a faculty member. These types of grants often generate funds of up to $1,000 per faculty member and support faculty with professional development. Professional development could include attendance at a conference, workshop, specific technical training on software, or even grant writing/skill based events. Typically, it is expected that a faculty member receiving a professional development grant be able to use the newly acquired information. Examples of this might include improved classroom instruction, the development of a web page, implementing a new classroom activity or new technology into instruction. It might be expected that the faculty member share the information obtained with other faculty members through brown bag luncheons or mini-workshops.

Travel grants may also be available on your campus. We urge you to check around and see if there are additional opportunities for travel support. This support could be very helpful for you as you make presentations locally, regionally, and nationally to disseminate information and make connections in your field of study. Sometimes campuses have small travel grants available to help support your travel needs above and beyond the allocated travel funds you receive from your department.

Material grants are also sometimes available through your college. These grants are made available to support faculty in obtaining materials needed for their research. This could include materials such as software, recording devices, and flash drives. It must be noted that in most cases, grants will require some type of outcome to measure your performance toward reaching the goals proposed.

Another form of funding that may be available is Recruiting Funds. Typically, a college will allocate a percent of the budget to cover costs of recruiting new students to the institution or college. Knowing if this funding is available can impact the way you request funds. For example, if you are going to be at a conference to learn more about legal updates in the field and you will be hosting a recruiting table at the same conference, you might want to request recruiting funding and save your other travel funds for a conference where you are not presenting, but attending for professional development. The graduate studies office at your institution will often have a budget for recruiting graduate students.

External Funding Opportunities

Another type of support is through external funding opportunities. These could be federally funded, or funded from organizations, or agencies. This type of funding is more complicated and will be thoroughly discussed in Chapter 5, but it would benefit you to know what kind of support is provided at the university to assist with writing a federal grant or securing private foundation funds.

Is there support at the department, college, or university level? Is there help with developing ideas for grants? Is there help with the writing of these grants? Is there help with developing the budget for these grants? Is there help monitoring these grants once they have been awarded? All of these questions and many more are very important to find out. The last thing you want to do is spend a lot of time and effort with no possible outcome. We truly believe some type of support system would be very beneficial in the area of external grants, especially for new faculty.

University Culture

The last thing we want to discuss is university culture. We feel it is important for you to learn as much as you can about the culture of the institution where you will be working. What is the culture on teaching (i.e., number of courses typically taught, load, emphasis, importance, undergraduate versus graduate level classes, and value compared to research and service)? What is the culture on research (i.e., importance, quality versus quantity, grants, individual versus collaborative research, journal articles versus chapters versus books, and what is really valued)? What is the culture on service (i.e., department versus college, versus university versus external service, importance, and value compared to teaching and research)? What is the culture on office hours (i.e., length, amount, how often, and required or not)? What is the culture on responsibilities (i.e., time spent on campus, teaching your classes, holding office hours, participating on course teams, holding a final exam, setting high standards for students, grading papers promptly, and providing prompt feedback to students)? Although you will not learn about all of this prior to your arrival on campus, these topics may help guide you on things you may want to learn about in order to be successful. Sometimes, the culture of the department is not printed or documented. Often, it is the unspoken rules of the culture that you will need to learn. Again, a very good resource person may be your faculty mentor or your department chair as well as other colleagues in your department and/or college.

Conclusion

The information in this chapter highlighted different aspects we believe are important for you to learn about your new institution. We believe that you should be aware of this information and being proactive in regards to these topics will make you a more successful faculty member. This chapter discussed learning about the general education program and all degree programs at your new institution. It also discussed finding out about new faculty training, faculty mentors, faculty evaluations, funding opportunities, and the university culture. We know you will not be able to address or learn everything highlighted in this chapter before you arrive on campus, but we hope it serves as a guide for you as you prepare yourself for your new role in academia. You were probably not hired if the department did not think you would be successful, but at the same time they also know a lot of support is needed in the development of new faculty. This chapter emphasizes some knowledge you should acquire, but also some supports you should look for in order to be successful as a faculty member.

> *Being successful and earning promotion and tenure takes a lot of time and effort on your part, but the department, college, and university are invested in you as well.*

Faculty Tips on Learning about Your Institution

- Budget your summer money well because there is a high probability that you won't get paid until 2–4 weeks into the semester.

- Treat the secretaries well; they usually have unspoken power in a department.

- Do not be afraid to say, "I am new and I don't understand the system."

- Find some "faculty buddies" with whom to collaborate on teaching and research—it's very stimulating and supportive.

- Get to know as many faculty as possible as soon as possible to get connected to the department.

- Engage with faculty, and become an active part of the community.

Part II

THE NUTS AND BOLTS OF SUCCESS

Chapter 4

TEACHING

One of your primary roles as a faculty member will be teaching. It may be at the undergraduate level, graduate level, or both, but regardless of what level it is, teaching should be a major focus for you. In fact, as a new faculty member beginning your journey towards promotion and tenure, teaching should be emphasized because it will comprise about one-third the importance (in those research and teaching institutions highlighted in Chapter 1), if not more, when being evaluated as successful or not at your institution. This next section, Part II, will focus on teaching, research, and service, which are the three areas most often identified as important and leading towards promotion and tenure. At some institutions, collegiality is also addressed as a measure for tenure and promotion.

Class Load and Schedule

Your class load and schedule will be the determining factor in other endeavors you want to participate in. Class load was previously discussed in Chapter 2, but because it is so important we want to highlight this topic again. The number of classes you teach each semester or quarter, depends on the system in place at your new institution. Typically, a full-time load is 100% with each three-credit course counting as 25% of that load. At a Research 1 institution, a typical teaching load might be 50% (two courses) with a 50% research load per semester, or it could consist of a 25% teaching load (one course) with a 75% research load per semester. At a teaching institution, a typical teaching load is 100% (four courses) per semester, while an institution that is a combination of the two might have a 75% teaching load (3 courses) with a 25% research load. It is imperative that you know the exact expectations for teaching loads that your new university employs.

Course load is one part of the teaching puzzle and very important, but we feel your teaching schedule is something that is often overlooked and can greatly influence your success as a faculty member. Some questions to ponder over include: When is the schedule figured out and how are course assignments made? Is there any consistency in teaching load across semesters and the early years leading up to promotion and tenure for new faculty?

Typically, teaching schedules are figured out months before the semester begins and course assignments are made by the department chair, assistant chairperson, program coordinator, or another administrative person. You will want to make your feelings known to them about courses you would feel comfortable teaching and your actual teaching schedule. Your first year of teaching you should strongly advocate for yourself and try to teach courses in which your content base is strong and that you may have previously taught before as a graduate student or teaching assistant.

Consistency of classes is also important, in our opinion, because it allows the new faculty member to have at least one predicatable aspect of the job: the content and classes, they will be teaching. Once you get comfortable teaching a certain class or classes then you can branch out to other classes. If you are teaching three new classes each semester, it is difficult to keep up with the preparation of course materials and other items related to teaching while accomplishing research and service as well. It is often heard from new professors that they spend a lot of time their first year just trying to stay prepared and ahead of the progress of the students in their classes. This can be difficult for a new faculty member while trying to assure that the instruction you provide is a meaningful and relevant learning experience for the students. This also means that you will be grading and evaluating papers and projects with which you may have little experience.

If there is a preferred type of schedule and courses you would like to teach, you need to make this very clear before you arrive. In dealing specifically with scheduling, you might consider how many course preparations (preps) you will have. For example, you may request two sections of the same course and one section of another course or even three sections of the same course, if possible, to reduce the number of course preparations needed. Teaching multiple sections of a course makes preparations easier and allows you more time to allocate to other projects.

Class times are also relevant to examine. The days and nights you will be teaching may be important to your life at and outside the university. Another complaint we often hear from new faculty members revolves around a lack of time for outside activities and family. If you have outside obligations, such as family, you may find that teaching more than one night per week can cause additional stress for you. In addition, teaching five days a week often leaves limited time for research and writing. We believe, from experience, that a preferred teaching schedule would be two days a week, possibly three, because this then will free time up for your other university responsibilities.

Sometimes you cannot have an ideal schedule, so you will need to decide what is important to you and voice your request to the persons in control of these course scheduling decisions. Finding a balance between your personal and professional life is essential.

Course Teams

As previously mentioned, if more than one instructor is assigned to teach different sections of the same course, there may be an instructional course team that you can join. If there are no instructional course teams, but there are several different faculty members teaching different sections of the same course, you may want to initiate the development of such a team. Why would an instructional course team like this be important? What would be the benefits of an instructional course team or the development of such a team?

The use of an instructional course team offers many benefits. It gives instructors of the same course a chance to sit down and discuss the course itself. Topics that could be discussed would include: (a) course content, (b) course standards, (c) course schedule, (d) course texts or materials, (e) assessments, (f) course projects, and (g) grading standards. It does not mean that everyone has to teach in the same way or the same order, but it should be important that students have similar experiences regardless of the instructor they have for the course. Having an instructional course team can help with this consistency and make the students' experiences more comparable.

How often should instructional course teams meet? We believe these teams should meet at least three to four times per semester, if not more, especially for new faculty. This allows instructors to consistently share their experiences with each other as well as provide critical feedback to each other. We need to stress that the most important time to meet is at the conclusion of each semester. This time period is very important for instructors to discuss what worked well and should be kept unchanged, what went alright, but might need some modifications, and what should be eliminated all together. Sometimes no changes are needed, but this regular meeting at the end of each semester can be very valuable for curriculum changes and course improvements. It is ideal at this time to use student evaluations to help determine which assignments students found beneficial to their learning. During the semester, faculty involved on instructional course teams will need to coordinate their schedules to find a good time to meet. We urge you to get these meetings arranged at the very beginning of each semester before individual calendars fill up.

Another point to consider are the roles and responsibilities of the instructional team members and the decision-making process. Tied to this is the choosing of textbooks and materials. We believe the team must decide what their roles are and how decisions will be made. To us, it is quite simple; the team's role is to meet frequently and consistently to improve the delivery and content of a particular course and ensure that all students, regardless of the instructor, are receiving about the same experiences. Decision making is something that the team will have to discuss. What we have seen work very effectively is the notion that majority rules. This means that people can disagree with each other and offer differing viewpoints, but ultimately, whatever the team decides must be implemented for the purposes of consistency and uniformity. This works well when there is an odd number of instructors. If there is an even number of instructors then a tie, vote may occur. In the case of a tie the instructors can then go to the department chair or curriculum director to explain their cases and that person can suggest a solution to the situation. Although this situation may seem uncomfortable, it is important that it occurs so that students receive similar experiences.

Choosing the textbook or materials for a particular course can be accomplished either by an individual instructor or an entire instructional course team. We have seen both methods work very effectively. Sometimes the entire course team decides to use the same book and materials. Obviously, that would be the most effective way and make the most sense when multiple courses are being taught by different instructors. Faculty, however, may decide to use different textbooks and materials. This could also work as long as the same content knowledge and skills are being addressed. The choice is up to the instructional team and is a decision that the team should make as they begin meeting and planning for the future. Obviously, this is not a comprehensive list and there are other options to decision making, but we offer two examples here that will hopefully guide you in critically thinking about how to handle the decision-making process of instructional course teams.

Syllabus Development

An instrumental component part of the courses you will teach includes the course syllabus. The course syllabus will guide you and your students as you move through the semester. Who develops the course syllabus? Will you have to do it? Will you work on a course team to develop it? Are there samples available? Typically, syllabi for different instructors teaching a course are not the same. In all likelihood, instructors' syllabi will be different, even if just a few minor alterations exist.

A term frequently used at the university level is "academic freedom." Academic freedom allows faculty to put their own perspective into the course. Instructors should be careful to avoid controversial matter unrelated to the subject. When they speak or write in public, they are free to express their opinions without fear from institutional censorship or discipline, but they should show restraint and clearly indicate that they are not speaking for their institution. Academic tenure protects academic freedom by ensuring that teachers can be fired only for causes such as gross professional incompetence or behavior that evokes condemnation from the academic community itself. Further information regarding academic freedom can be obtained from the American Association of University Professors (AAUP).

As a new faculty member you will want to find out how syllabi are developed in your department and precede in syllabus development based on the information you obtain. Typically, every department maintains a copy of each syllabus used throughout the semesters for their records. In a nutshell, this means that there should be at least one syllabus you can look at as a guide to help you prepare your own course syllabus. Some departments have syllabi on their department website. In your first semester as a new faculty member, you may want to use someone else's syllabus and focus on the content and course delivery. After you have a semester under your belt, you can work on modifying your syllabus.

The syllabus will have many different component parts. At several institutions, especially those that are accredited, a standard syllabus format is used. Some of the component parts found on the syllabus might include: instructor contact information, the university's catalog course description, an expanded course description, the purpose of the course, course standards, required texts and materials, course requirements, standards for written work, late procedures, grading scale, other course standards, an academic integrity statement, a special needs statement, and a course schedule. We will highlight some of the more important sections next. One very important aspect of syllabus development is to determine the required content that the syllabus must contain. Many institutions are nationally accredited. Often within the accreditation process, specific requirements necessitate that the syllabus reflect certain elements such as alignment of course content to national standards in your field.

Providing your contact information on the syllabus is very important. How will students get a hold of you and when and where will you have office hours? From a student perspective, this is important so they can determine the best way to make contact with you outside of class time. It will also be important to include the course description and accompanying course standards. As many programs are standards-based, it is key to include what standards will be addressed in each course.

From a student perspective, additional items of importance to be listed in the syllabus include the texts and/or materials that will be needed, what do they (the students) have to do (i.e., assignments, projects, and exams), schedule of topics for each class session and assigned readings by date, and when is everything due (i.e., the course schedule with tasks and due dates). Make sure that you detail everything as clear as possible so the students know your expectations. If a student were to complain at the end of the semester, your chair would likely refer to your syllabus to try and resolve the situation.

> *My very first semester as an assistant professor I had a student challenge a grade I had given them in one of my classes. Although the student made an A in the course based on content, he exceeded the number of absences permitted before I dropped one letter grade. I had repeatedly told this to the students in my class. When the Dean called me in to discuss the appeal, we realized that this statement of action was not included on the syllabus therefore, I was asked to change the grade back. I know this was a difficult choice for the Dean and appreciated him discussing the situation with me before talking with the student. However, it would not have happened if my syllabus was correctly written.*

We also suggest you put "tentative" on your course schedule. This will allow you to be a little more flexible and extend time on a subject area that needs it and move forward faster for a subject area that does not necessitate as much time. See Table 4.1 for a sample course schedule and Appendixes B and C for a sample undergraduate and graduate syllabus.

Table 4.1
SAMPLE COURSE SCHEDULE

TENTATIVE Course Schedule
Tentative Schedule (Section 01). May be adjusted by the instructor if needed!
Mark your attendance (+, - for each class)

Date (Week of)	Topics	Readings to be completed before class
Aug. 24	**Syllabus & Course overview**	Text note: Cohen & Spenciner (C & S) Alberto & Troutman (A & T)
Aug. 31	Etic & Emic Placement issues Confidentiality	C & S, Chpt. 1

Table 4.1–*Continued*

Date (Week of)	Topics	Readings to be completed before class
Sept. 7	Norms & Test Scores RIOT Assessment Tool Box Review of Records	C & S, Chpt. 3
Sept. 14	Reliability & Validity *Study Guide*	C & S, Chpt. 4 ***Section 1 is due***
Sept. 21	Administering Tests Achievement Tests	C & S, Chpt. 6 ***Quiz 1***
Sept. 28	Observing & conferencing Target Behaviors Collecting Data	A & T, Chpt. 3 C & S, Chpt. 5 ***Section 2 is due***
Oct. 5	Graphing Data Writing Reports *Study Guide*	A & T, Chpt. 4 C & S, Chpt. 18 ***Test critique is due***
Oct. 12	Reading assessments	C & S, Chpt. 8 ***Quiz 2***
Oct. 19	Behavior & assessments FBA	C & S, Chpt. 15
Oct 26	Behavioral Objectives Families & Diversity	C & S, Chpt. 2 ***Section 3 is due***
Nov. 2	Performance/alternate assessments *Study guide*	C & S, Chpt. 7 ***Sections 4 & 5 are due***
Nov. 9	Oral language assessment	C & S, Chpt. 10 ***Quiz 3***
Nov. 16	Mathematics assessment	C & S, Chpt. 11 ***CEAR report is due.***
Nov. 23	**No Class– Thanksgiving Break**	
Nov. 30	Adaptive skills assessment	C & S, Chpt. 14
Dec. 7	Sensory & motor assessment	C& S, Chpt. 16 ***Corrected CEAR to your teacher***
Dec. 14	Signed CEAR form Final exam-as scheduled	Final Exam ***Signed CEAR form in to me***

Assessments

Assessment is another important area and major component part of teaching. How are you going to assess the progress of your students' learning? Will everything be based on the individual student in your class? Will there be group projects or activities? How often will you assess your students? When will you assess your students? These questions, and many more, should guide you in the assessment process. The first thing we recommend you do is lay out your schedule for the class. What content is going to be taught, in what order, and when will it take place during the semester? Now evaluate everything and try to decide how you want to assess the knowledge and skills of your students and how often. More assessment is typically better and a variety is suggested. Give your students many opportunities throughout the semester to demonstrate their knowledge and skills (versus a few assessments worth all of the points) and use a variety of assessment techniques (if possible) to try and assess students using their own personal strengths.

Obviously, we are not suggesting you have to use every different kind of assessment technique in each class you teach, but make sure you fully consider all of the alternatives and match the appropriate assessment to the knowledge or skills that need to be assessed. For example, if vocabulary is important, the assessment might be a matching exercise where the students match the word with the definition or a short answer exercise where students write out the definition of each word. A project on vocabulary might not be that appropriate given it is a knowledge-based skill. Consider what would be the most useful and efficient way to assess your students. Your options may include exams and/or quizzes which could either be scantron exams (easy to score), matching, short answer, essay, visual displays, presentations, or a combination of these. These could then be further broken down to in-class or on-line assessments.

In-class assessments are easier for an instructor to monitor, but they also take class instructional time away from you and your students. On-line assessments free up class time, but if not properly designed, the opportunity for students to possibly assist each other on the assessment exists. Ultimately, this decision is up to you, as the professor, as to what type of assessment you will use. We recommend you consider the advantages and disadvantages of each before selecting the form of assessment you will use. Remember that if things do not work out the way you intended, you can always change what you are doing for the next semester you teach this course. A very important item to note is that if you are at an institution where specific assignments and projects were designed for accreditation purposes, be sure to have those assessments thoroughly explained to you. Most often, the data collected from the assessments are used over a three to five year time period and the assessment instrument cannot be changed to assure accuracy of the data.

Another possible option could be the assessment of your students through projects and/or activities. These experiences can be used to assess knowledge and skills as well as the application of information learned in your course. Projects are a good way to have students show you what they have learned and take away materials that can be used later on in their program of study or in the future as a reference to their profession. You will need to decide if these will be individual or group projects. If implementing a group assessment, you will also need to consider how you will promote participation from all group members so that everyone is truly credited with the work that they do. Typically, when there is a project or activity, there is also an accompanying rubric that goes with it so the students know what is expected and how it will be graded and so the instructor can be consistent in their grading. See Table 4.2 for a sample rubric. In group projects, many faculty members find it necessary to include a self-evaluation and group member evaluation tool within the rubric.

When planning assessments you might also try to place them strategically throughout the semester where appropriate so that everything is not due at the end of the semester. When everything is due at the end of the semester, it not only puts additional stress on the students, but you as well. Grading several items at the end of the semester while trying to compute grades, finish up pending committee tasks, and develop final exams can be challenging. You will also need to find out if a final exam is required as part of your courses. This varies across institutions, but you want to make sure you follow correct institutional procedures regarding final exams, especially as a new faculty member.

Table 4.2
SAMPLE RUBRIC

CATEGORY	Outstanding	Very Good	Satisfactory	Poor	Unsatisfactory
Accuracy of Content	9–10 pts. All information presented is accurate and based on evidenced-based practices.	7–8 pts. Most of the information presented is accurate and based on evidenced-based practices.	5–6 pts. Some of the information is accurate and based on evidenced-based practices, but some of the information is incorrect.	3–4 pts. A few accurate details are present, but less than half of the information is not present.	0–2 pts. Information is not accurate nor based on evidenced-based practices. The presentation does not contain any accurate information.

continued

Table 4.2–*Continued*

CATEGORY	Outstanding	Very Good	Satisfactory	Poor	Unsatisfactory
Length of Presentation	9–10 pts. Presentation is 5 to 7 minutes long. Time is used wisely, substantially covering relevant information.	7–8 pts. Presentation is 5 to 7 minutes long. Time is used wisely presenting relevant information.	5–6 pts. Presentation is 4 to 5 minutes long. Time is used wisely presenting relevant information.	3–4 pts. Presentation 2 to 4 minutes long. Time is used by presenting relevant information.	0–2 pts. Presentation under 4 minutes long or 5–7 minutes long, but time is not used wisely and fails to present relevant information.
Topic Research	16–20 pts. The assigned topic is thoroughly researched and under-stood by the student. Student presents in-depth information over topic.	11–15 pts. The assigned topic is well researched and under-stood by the student.	6–10 pts. The assigned topic is somewhat researched, and student has a basic understanding of the topic.	1–5 pts. The assigned topic is limited in research, and therefore the student has little understanding of the topic.	0 pts. The assigned topic was not researched and the student does not understand his/her topic.
Presentation Style	5 pts. The presentation is creative, organized, and thoroughly developed.	4 pts. The presentation is creative, slightly unorganized, but contains well-developed ideas.	3 pts. The presentation demonstrates creativity, is organized, but information is not developed or ideas do not flow.	2 pts. The presentation is creative, but it lacks organization, development, and flow.	1 pts. The presentation contains no creativity, organization, flow, or development.

Note: Adapted from: Rubrician.Com. (n.d.). Retrieved July 10, 2010, from http://www.rubrician .com/

Teaching Style

You have created your syllabus and your course assessments, now you need to determine how to effectively and efficiently deliver all of the content information and skills to your students. What method will you use for your instruction of content and skills? Is one method preferred over another? Will you use different methods depending on the content and skills to be taught? Is there something new you need to learn so you can effectively teach your students? These are some of the questions you should consider when you are teaching.

It is highly likely that you already have a preferred teaching style, but you should not solely teach by a particular style or method simply because it is comfortable to you. If the content and skills warrant another method, you must be aware that you may need to teach differently than you are accustomed to and you might have to learn new teaching strategies. Some teaching options include lecture, demonstration, hands-on, on-line, in-class activities, and combinations of these. Lecture format is probably the most typical type of instruction but should be enhanced by other methods. This is where the instructor stands in front of the class and delivers content to the students. This can be implemented in front of a small class of 20 to 30 students or to a large class of 100 to 150 students. Typically, this format is implemented where general content knowledge is being delivered to students. The instructor delivers the information and the students receive it. Students in this case are treated as passive learners receiving information.

We know that learners who are more active in the learning process benefit more from instruction so if you use the lecture format, you may want to think about how to get your students involved in the content. This can be done by requiring students to read something prior to class, giving them questions to answer regarding class content, giving unannounced quizzes during class, or providing small group activities during class where you deliver some content (i.e., have the students break into groups for an activity or to discuss, and then have student groups report their findings back to the larger group). Small group activities get students involved, make them more accountable, and hopefully will help them become more actively involved. You must remember that if you do not initiate these types of activities to get students actively involved, most will just be passive learners.

Demonstrations are activities the instructor might do in front of the class to show the students something that was previously discussed in class, something to initiate a new topic, or something to verify content delivery. For example, an instructor in chemistry may show the students an experiment demonstrating a specific chemical reaction. Hands-on activities are those where the students actually interact with the materials. You, as the instructor, may deliver content and general information and then the students will experience it through a hands-on activity. For example, the instructor may discuss the advantages and disadvantages of some different computer programs that focus on problem-solving and then the students investigate the programs themselves to formulate their own ideas and perceptions about the programs. Students could come back to class as a large group and discuss their findings.

On-line instruction is another instructional option currently gaining momentum and popularity. This format can be synchronous (a planned and set time) or asynchronous (students get on-line whenever they want) and has many different options. The instructor can incorporate video clips, audio clips, content knowledge through Power Points, on-line discussions, on-line chats, virtual classrooms, and many other options. This format can be very useful and many classes can be effectively taught on-line. If using on-line instruction, it is imperative that the students are being assessed on the knowledge and skill content of the course not on the ability to use the technology (unless this is the course criteria).

The last option is to utilize a combination of the aforementioned methods. We feel that no one specific method is best, but rather that the content and skills drive the instructional method. The key in effective teaching is how to get students actively involved in their own learning and involved in experiences that will help them learn the content and skills to be taught in the class you are instructing. What you want to teach your students should be the foundation for how you teach them. Can it be learned by just listening about it? Do students need to experience it to learn it? We urge you to really think about how students learn best and the different instructional methods available when planning how you will teach your students. Numerous books are available that specifically deal with teaching methods. For additional information on specific teaching strategies refer to these books, observe other instructors who employ these techniques and/or attend professional workshops that focus on instructional methods.

Lastly, we would like to mention the importance of balancing time. Several faculty members indicated that teaching a class with a length of one and half hours was much easier for them as a new faculty member, than teaching a three-hour block class. Longer classes require that you are able to maintain the students' attention to the content for a longer period of time. This is a difficult issue for most new faculty. Varying the format of teaching seems to help address this challenge.

Available Technology and Support

Technology and support is another aspect to consider when planning your instruction. What platforms are supported? What hardware is available?

What software is available? What internal and external support is provided? These are questions you will want to consider and ask your mentor and/or department chair possibly during the interview process, but for sure once you accept a new faculty position at your new institution. In regards to platforms, you will want to know if your new institution is PC based or MAC based or a combination of these. You may also want to know the availability of these formats on campus and in computer labs on campus.

A new trend over the last few years has been to make the typical university classroom a "smart" classroom. A "smart" classroom is one that has been developed with technologies to aid the instructor in their teaching. A typical "smart" classroom has an overhead projection system that is hooked to a computer (usually with a MAC and PC option), a DVD unit, a VCR, a document camera (ELMO), and internet access. This system would also have the capability of hooking a laptop to it with minimal effort enabling you to access your own documents without logging on to an external system or using a memory stick. Software on the computer in this system would include Microsoft Office and any other instructional software.

Many universities offer university-wide systems such as Blackboard, E-College, or WebCT. These are programs designed to assist the instructor in delivering content, as well as providing a format that enables the instructor to develop discussion items, deliver on-line quizzes and exams, provide a communication system with internal email, and post scores/grades for projects, assignments, quizzes, and exams. In addition, many of these sytems allow the instructor to track the viewing of documents by individual students.

Technology is an important component in teaching, necessitating the need for strong internal and external support. What is available within your department, college, and university to help you learn the technologies available in order to optimize your experience teaching your students? Also, what is available in regards to classroom technical support if something goes wrong with the equipment while you are teaching? The use of technology can offer many surprises, both pleasant and unpleasant, so we recommend you always be prepared in case the technology fails and believe us, on occasion it will fail. Technology can definitely make your life easier and more effective and efficient, but you must make sure you properly prepare yourself to use the technologies. Many universities offer a computer lab or Help Desk that is accessible to both students and faculty.

Being Successful

Teaching students is a huge responsibility and in order to be successful, we feel we should provide you with a few recommendations. First of all, try to stay as current as possible in your area of study and on the content you are teaching. This may mean you need to conduct research in this area, constantly read the most current literature, make connections with organizations related to your content, and stay in touch with professionals in the your field. Being current will earn your students' respect and will also better prepare them for the future. Your courses will be more up-to-date and thus reflect the most current literature being presented in your field.

Another way to be successful is to effectively teach and assess your students. Making appropriate decisions in regards to instructional delivery options and the types of assessments implemented will be very important to you as the instructor and to your students. Were the assessments appropriate? Did the assessments yield the information you intended to get? Were the assessments fair and reliable? You will also want to evaluate your teaching based on your students. How your students perceive their experience in your class will ultimately factor in to how successful you feel. Are you an approachable person? Do students feel comfortable asking you questions and coming to you for help? We feel this is a very important characteristic of successful instructors.

Asking questions and receiving feedback is a large part of how we learn. If students cannot come to you as their instructor, you will be losing out on some very important teacher opportunities. When you are teaching, we also suggest you use real-life experiences and examples to help get your point across to your students. If possible, make your courses real and have a human component to them. Research to practice is another component you may want to consider communicating to your students. What is the value of this course and its content? How does the research fit with what is really happening in life and the world around us? The ability to help students make this very important connection is truly an art of a successful instructor. You must remember that you want your students to be problem-solvers and critical thinkers and unless you teach them how to do this, they may not learn these skills. Being able to connect theory with practicality is a true art. It is important for you to model as an instructor. The ability to make a connection with your students and provide them with real-life examples will help them to better understand the content.

> *I asked my students what they thought the most important piece of information for me to have was and their response was simple. . . . It is also important that your students know you want them to succeed and learn. Students who feel that they are supported in their learning environment will be more motivated to try their best and be successful.*

The last thing is to try to be innovative. This does not mean you have to make significant changes each semester, but you should evaluate your classes at the end of each semester to look at possible changes that could make the course stronger and more powerful for the students. Although change is difficult, and can sometimes be uneasy, it helps us grow and develop and ultimately makes our courses more valuable for the instructor and the students. Just remember that successes can be measured in many different ways such as student grades, student feedback, and self-evaluations. Teaching is a process that will steadily improve over time.

> *When I got my first set of student evaluations back I was devastated. I didn't perform nearly as well as I thought I should have. My department chair asked me if I had ever heard the term "life-long learner." I realized that in order to be an effective instructor you need to be a life-long learner and willing to try new things and then instill this same idea in your students.*

Student Issues

Students are the livelihood of the university and are needed for our classes and university to function. We have previously discussed being accessible to students so they can ask questions and get information clarified, but there are other things regarding students that you should consider. These include student feedback, student dispositions, grades, and grade issues.

Providing adequate and timely student feedback is very important to be a successful teacher. Students want to get feedback from their instructor and they want it in a timely fashion. They also want the feedback to be specific and to the point. To provide quality and productive student feedback, you need to give yourself adequate time to go through all of your students' work. You must schedule time to do this. One idea is to plan your daily schedule to include grading times. In addition, you should carefully evaluate the best time for assignments and projects to be due. This is especially important if a project is divided into parts where students turn the project in to you at different times of the semester and each part is related or based on the previous section submitted. For example, if students are turning in Part 2 of a project that is based on Part 1, but have not yet received feedback on Part 1, this could present a problem for you and your students. Without the proper feedback from you, the instructor, the students' work may not be the quality it would have been had you provided timely and specific feedback to them on Part 1.

Another student area to consider is that of dispositions. We find that many times students have behavioral challenges that need to be addressed. It is not the content knowledge that is the issue, but actually how students are behaving and sometimes these behaviors actually impact the students' grades. A dispositional concern could be poor attendance, poor quality of work, poor attitude, plagiarism, cheating, or a variety of other things. These are all things that we feel should be addressed with the student so they are made aware that there is an issue that could impact their future performance. In teacher education, we have had students who have the knowledge and skills, but the maturity level of the student is not acceptable in the classroom in order to be successful. When this happens, the instructor will sit down with the student to go over the concern and develop a remediation plan to provide support and correct the difficulties. The goal here is not to punish the student, but help them grow and develop as an individual and hopefully be successful. See Table 4.3 for a sample disposition form.

Table 4.3
SAMPLE DISPOSITION FORM

Disposition Concerns

Illinois State University

Disposition concerns are very important for teacher candidates as disposition becomes increasingly important to the development of collaboration skills and other professional behaviors. Concerns need to be identified early and problems need to be resolved as soon as possible. All teacher candidates will be evaluated on the following disposition indicators*, but only those candidates who have engaged in behaviors that suggest a negative disposition should be reported.

Disposition Indicators

Collaboration Issues: The ability to work together, especially in a joint intellectual effort.

Honesty/Integrity: The ability to demonstrate truthfulness to oneself and to others; demonstrate moral excellence and trustworthiness.

Respect: The ability to honor, value, and demonstrate consideration and regard for oneself and others.

Reverence for Learning: Respect and seriousness of intent to acquire knowledge.

Emotional Maturity: The ability to adjust one's emotional state to suitable level of intensity in order to remain engaged with one's surroundings.

Reflection: The ability to review, analyze, and evaluate the success of past decisions in an effort to make better decisions in the future.

Table 4.3–*Continued*

Flexibility: The willingness to accept and adapt to change.

Responsibility: The ability to act independently, demonstrating accountability, reliability and sound judgment.

Student's Name (please print)   Student ID Number   Major

Explanation of Concern(s):

This concern has been discussed with the teacher candidate. My signature verifies that I am aware of the document's contents and existence.

Faculty/Staff Signature   Student Signature

Faculty/Staff Name (please print)   Department   Date

Send a copy of this report to: CECP, Campus Box 5440

Rubric

Disposition Concerns

Indicator	Does Not Meet Expectation	*Meets Expectation*
Teacher candidate has appropriate disposition to work with children or young adults.	Teacher candidate has shown a pattern of behavior through three unresolved referrals and student's department has not notified CECP that the issues have been resolved.	Teachers candidate has no referrals or no referrals that have not been resolved by the student's major department (student's major department has notifed CECP of resolution.)

General Procedures: Teacher candidates must meet expectations for Admission to Professional Studies and for Admission to Student Teaching.

Faculty/Staff/PreK-12 School Personnel will report disposition concerns after discussing the concern with the teacher candidate. The faculty/staff member will complete the Disposition Concern form and have the teacher candidate sign and date the form. The original form is then sent to CECP.

The CECP office will send a copy of the concern to the student's major program coordinator. It is the responsibility of the department to investigate and resolve dispositional concerns with

continued

Table 4.3–*Continued*

the teacher candidate. Departments must notify CECP when they are satisfied that specific concerns have been resolved.

When a student has a record of three dispositional concerns in the CECP office that have not been resolved by the teacher candidate's major department, the student will have a "No" for meeting this disposition assessment and will not be admitted to Professional Studies and/or Student Teaching. CECP will contact the major department to verify that the 3 dispositional concerns have not been resolved.

Documentation of Student Conference
   (May be used by Program Coordinators to resolve disposition concerns.)

Student: _____   Other Participants: _____

_____

_____

_____

Concern:

Plan:

_____   _____
Student Signature   Faculty Signature

Date: _____

*Adapted from Department of Special Education at Illinois State University. Permission obtained to reprint.

In addition to meeting specifically with the students, many institutions are starting to employ a dispositions committee. This committee addresses those dispositions in students that the individual faculty member is unable to help the student resolve. This is a valuable committee as multiple members provide a larger pool of interventions for the student.

Student grades are also an issue that must be addressed. There will probably be a time in your career when a student disputes a grade you have given him/her. We urge you to keep good records and to make your grading scale and procedures, including late procedures, very clear in your syllabus. Not only should this system be in writing, but you should also make sure you follow what you stated in writing. When there is a grade dispute, one of the first things that will be questioned is your calculations and if you followed your syllabus. At most universities the procedure for a grade dispute is for the student who has questioned his/her grade to approach the professor first. If the situation cannot be resolved, then the situation is taken to either a grade dispute committee (student concerns) or to the department chair. You need to be aware that the department chair cannot typically change the grade nor will he/she for the student based on what the student says, but he/she will most likely ask you to verify the calculations and make sure you are confident with your final grade. If so, then the chair will tell the student that the grade stands. Do not be surprised if you then receive a phone call from a parent or an attorney regarding the grade.

Being aware that this situation may occur is very important. As a faculty member, you need to understand your institution's policies and The Family Educational Rights and Privacy Act (FERPA). As an instructor, you can only discuss course grades with the student, even if the parents are paying the tuition. To discuss grades with someone else other than the student, including parents, the student in question must sign a waiver signifying he/she gives permission to his/her parents to discuss grades. If parents call you about their child's grade, you are not at liberty to discuss anything about it unless a signed waiver is in place at an appropriate office (i.e., the Office of the University Registrar) on your campus.

If the student is not accepting of the decision, then he/she might appeal the grade following the university policy. An appeal of a grade can be a tramatic experience for a new faculty member. This holds especially true when proper documentation was not kept or when the student has valid information to support a lack of consistency in grading by the instructor. Many professional organizations exist which offer liability insurance to membership. For example, in Texas, the Texas Association of College Teachers offers a policy in which covers a limited amount of monies to cover legal advice. All universities also have legal representation for faculty. This is information you should be aware of in case you find yourself in situation which warrants legal support.

Faculty Expectations

How you figure out expectations in regards to teaching can be a tricky question to answer. Each department, college, and university will have different teaching expectations and some will be very clear (i.e., be in class when you are supposed to, hold office hours, and have a final exam) and others may not (i.e., policy on attendance and missing assignments). We urge you to hold conversations with your mentor, other colleagues, your department chair, and possibly even your dean. There may even be a department on campus like CTLT, previously discussed in Chapter 3, where you can go to discuss these issues. Go on a fact-finding mission to learn the teaching expectations. Often a hidden curriculum exists within the culture of the university. As a tenure track faculty member, knowing this culture is essential for your success. For example, university policy may state that you are to be in your physical office one day per week, but tenured faculty feel that junior faculty need to be more visible. You may not find this in writing, but it is important to know this information.

Conclusion

The information in this chapter highlighted different aspects we believe are important for you to think about and consider in the area of teaching. Teaching is one of the three main components you will be evaluated on for promotion and tenure. It is important that you perform well in this area and you continue to grow and develop. In order to be successful, there are many topics to consider. We hope this chapter helped to answer some the questions you may have had.

This chapter discussed some general teaching characteristics such as class load and schedule and course teams. It also addressed some fundamentally important aspects necessary to get the class going and these include choosing textbooks and materials, syllabus development, assessments, and teaching style. Lastly, this chapter addressed characteristics to consider once you begin your teaching and throughout your teaching career. These include available technology and support, being successful, student issues, and figuring out expectations. There is a lot of information related to teaching in this chapter and we realize that you will not know everything your first semester nor will you perfect your teaching skills right away; but if you use this chapter as a guide, we feel you will be on your way towards a successful career in the area of teaching. Being a successful teacher takes time and effort and is a process where you will improve over time. It is also a very instrumental part in the promotion and tenure process. We hope you take your teaching seriously and continue to self-assess your teaching to work towards being a successful faculty member in the area of teaching.

Faculty Tips about Teaching

- Always hold your students to high standards. Being too lenient isn't helping them in the long run! (Hold them accountable if it is a lack of effort, organization, or planning.) Although your students are adults, they are still growing. Help them to grow as students, teachers, and as human beings. Realize that they "bloom" at different rates. Help them to gain confidence and remember to ALWAYS keep this as your ultimate focal point to teach our students: The bottom line of teaching is STUDENT LEARNING at the fastest possible rate in the areas of social, emotional, and academic areas.

- Reflect 'til you die! :) Never think that you are too intelligent to make mistakes that you have to change in order to ensure OUR students are learning at the fastest possible rate! :)

- Access students needs mid semester—then act on their feedback—but be reasonable—dont's change what is not good instruction—then explain why you are not changing something and do your best to make sure you do a few things the students ask.

- Use other faculty as a resource. Find out whoever has taught the courses you are teaching and ask them for their materials. Sometimes several different views on the same course can be helpful. Don't feel like you have to invent everything to start.

- Build relationships with your students—Be sure to let them know that you are concerned about them as students, teachers, and as people.

- Be willing to let your students teach you something that they read about or learned in another class. Don't be afraid to admit that your were wrong or that you do not know (then correct the error or find out the answer).

Chapter 5

RESEARCH AND SCHOLARLY ACTIVITY

Depending on the institution you choose, you may find that one of your primary roles as a faculty member will be in the area of research or scholarly activity, which is comprised of publications, presentations, and grants. You may focus on one specific area of study or diversify to different areas of study, but one thing is for sure; to be successful you will need to focus your time on four primary areas within the scholarly activity component: teaching, publications, presentations, and grants. In order to be successful in each of these areas, developing a line of research needs to be a major focus of interest for you as a faculty member. In fact, as a new faculty member who is beginning your journey towards promotion and tenure, research will comprise about one-third the importance, if not more (in those Research I institutions highlighted in Chapter 1), towards your success. This chapter will focus on the topic of Research/Scholarly Activity which is frequently reported as the most significant area which impacts promotion and tenure.

Release Time

In an effort to balance your need to conduct research and still maintain your teaching expectations, you must plan your time wisely. One way to find additional time to conduct research is through acquiring release time. Release time is often considered part of your teaching load, but it is often dedicated to research and research-based activities. When you are interviewing and discussing job offers for a new faculty position, the topic of release time is one aspect you will want to obtain more information about. Sometimes institutions will give new faculty release time (for instance, they teach one less course) so they can focus on their research and research agenda.

For example, at a university with a four course teaching load each semester, the load with research release time might be a three course teaching load each semester or even a two course teaching load with the "released time" dedicated to research. You will want to ask if this is possible and if so, how often will it occur. If research is your primary interest (and even if it is not), you will want to make sure you have time built into your schedule to do this.

One suggestion is to make sure that the language in your contract guarantees a specified amount of release time even in the event that administration in your department changes. This should be placed in your contract, not because we believe that your new department chair will be unethical or that their word is not credible, but rather as a means to protect yourself. Administrators often change and if this occurs in your department and there is no evidence of the agreement, it may not be honored. We must also point out that if you are given release time for research, then you are expected to use that time efficiently and effectively, and thus be productive. When you are evaluated each year, the evaluation committee (often tenure and promotion committee) will be evaluating your work and your productivity. If you failed to use the release time for research, or have not been productive, you may lose that time and be given an additional course to teach. If it is in your contract and you are not being productive, this will not be looked at favorably as you move towards promotion and tenure. If you are given time off from teaching, specifically for research, there will be an expectation that you will use this time and make progress toward completing the research and publishing the results of the research.

You may have many works in progress, but unless the manuscript is published, the presentation is made, or the grant is funded, it may not be credited to your scholarly record. To make sure you are productive, we encourage you to develop a research agenda and a well thought out and detailed plan of what you are going to accomplish each semester, how you are going to do it, who you are going to do it with, what the products will be, and then try to stay focused and aligned with your plan.

Developing Ideas

If you have not already figured it out, research will be an important part of your life as a faculty member. It is customary that each year you will be evaluated within your department and will continue to be evaluated even after receiveing tenure and promotion. However, the first few years as you move toward tenure are more difficult to show progress in scholarly activity. It is not advisable to wait until the last year or two before promotion and tenure to get started on your research career. Most committees are looking for faculty who exhibit a consistent record of publication. It is not to say you will not be granted tenure if you wait and publish all items in the last year, but it may raise questions to the committee regarding the quality of publications, the reasons behind waiting to publish, or the apparent lack of dedication early on in your career. Publications take time from beginning (developing the idea) to the end (in published form) so it is important to get started immediately if you have not already done so.

What will you do? What are some good ideas? Where will you begin? Who will you work with? These are all questions you will want to answer so that you can begin your work. We believe that idea development is the key to a good start and your success as a faculty member. So where will you get ideas for research? If you do not already have some ideas (which some of you may have gained from graduate school, from professors, or from your dissertation advisor), a good place to begin is with your dissertation. If you have not already started, this could be a good first research task; attempt to get your dissertation research published. In order to accomplish this task, look in your future research section, and see what suggestions you made. How can you extend your dissertation research? What related projects can you begin? Where will you go next in the area of research? Quite often the data in your dissertation as well as the literature review can be used to create several publications. Of course, it will take work to fine tune and rewrite the material to match the needs of the journal in which you are submitting, but a little work up front could lead to many future rewards.

You can also think about your areas of interest as a beginning route. What research have you previously been involved with that you would like to continue? Are there opportunities available to you that already exist? We suggest you sit down and map out all that you have done, what you are interested in, and who you have previously worked with to get a list of workable ideas. This may give you a better indication of the route you should plan to take. We also recommend that you speak with your faculty mentor, other colleagues, and possibly even the department chair to help you flush out your ideas and maybe connect you with other faculty who may have similar interests, are currently working on similar projects, or who may be interested in working with you. At several institutions, the university library has staff that are assigned to work with faculty members. This is something you may want to investigate as well.

Research Agenda

Building upon the ideas you have generated will allow you to develop a two- to three-year plan (if not longer) of what type of research you will focus on. What will your major area of research entail? What path will your research take and where will it take you? How does everything you are planning to do fit together? These are questions you should think about when developing your research agenda. It is important to note the importance of your research agenda. Committees that evaluate promotion and tenure port-folios will be thoroughly reading your information as well as going through your documentation. They will be looking for a research agenda or a line of research that you have focused on.

Obviously, a large number of publications would be a great accomplishment, but if the topics and focus are broad and lack specificity or relatedness, there could be some issues with promotion and tenure. It is not only important to publish, present, and obtain grant funding, but it is also important to establish a line of research that is attainable, credible, and sustainable over time. It all begins with ideas and idea development which was previously discussed. After you have a list of ideas, you will then want to prioritize this list. When prioritizing your list, think about what ideas you are interested in, what are the ideas that are attainable, and what are the outcomes of each idea (i.e., publication, presentation, professional development opportunity, or grant application). You might also think about what items might be related so that you can capitalize on similar characteristics of projects. Now you should try to develop a timeline of what you want to accomplish and when it should occur. This will help you plan and set clear goals for yourself. It will also serve as a personal guide or action plan as you move towards promotion and tenure. See Table 5.1 for an example timeline with outcomes. As you can see, it is a long and sometimes complicated process so that is why we suggest you get to know your colleagues for possible collaborative projects. It is important that you conduct research as a new faculty member. We are suggesting you develop a research agenda and plan so that you begin with a strong foundation towards building a successful research career.

Human Subjects Process

At most universities, when working with human subjects in your research, you will need to develop a proposal that will be reviewed by a committee of faculty members to make sure that the participants' rights are protected. All universities are committed to protect the rights and welfare of human subjects participating in research investigations under the authority of the university. In addition, all research involving human subjects is to be conducted in accordance with relevant federal regulations. Federal regulation, *Title 45, Code of Federal Regulations, Part 46,* requires that all institutions receiving federal funds, which conduct research using living humans as subjects, establish and operate an Institutional Review Board (IRB). The purpose of the IRB is to ensure the protection of these human subjects. The IRB is guided by the ethical principles embodied in *The Belmont Report* and by additional local standards and expectations. Investigators who plan to use human subjects in research are responsible for obtaining written approval from the IRB

Table 5.1
SAMPLE TIMELINE WITH TASKS AND OUTCOMES FOR ONE IDEA

Idea	Tasks	Timeline	Outcome (s)
Reading Comprehension Study	Proposal Development	June, 2010	
	Material Development	July, 2010	
	Contact Schools	August, 2010	
	Contact Teachers	August, 2010	
	Human Subjects Proposal	September, 2010	
	Get Permissions	November, 2010	
	Conduct Study	January through March, 2010	
	Analyze Data	April, 2010	
		June, 2010	Manuscript Submission
		June 2010	Presentation Submission

prior to conducting research involving human subjects, taking whatever steps are deemed necessary to protect subjects, and abiding by reporting requirements of the IRB. See Table 5.2 for some frequently asked questions about human subjects.

It is very important that no research is conducted prior to the approval of your research proposal by the IRB. Typically, there will be a proposal forms you will need to fill out any time you conduct research involving human subjects. The proposal is often reviewed at the department level by an IRB Departmental Representative. This person reviews the proposal for any glaring errors or omissions. If the reviewer finds any information that needs to be modified, added, or deleted, he/she will commonly give the proposal back to the writer to correct. Upon receiving corrections, the IRB Department Representative will then fill out a reviewer form and send the proposal and reviewer form to the university's IRB. At this time they will also

Table 5.2
SOME FREQUENTLY ASKED QUESTIONS ABOUT HUMAN SUBJECTS

When do I need an IRB protocol?

You need an IRB protocol when you are doing research on human subjects. Research means any systematic investigation, including research development, testing and evaluation, designed to develop or contribute to generalizable knowledge. A human subject is a living individual about whom a research investigator (whether faculty, staff, or student) obtains: (1) data through intervention or interaction with the individual or (2) identifiable private information or records.

A protocol is not required for program review unless you intend to disseminate the results. Dissemination includes publication, presentation at a conference or seminar, or a thesis or dissertation.

All of the following research activities involving human subjects are subject to the review and approval of the IRB:

1. Sponsored by the university, or
2. Conducted by or under the direction of any employee or agent, including students, of the university in connection with his or her university responsibilities, or
3. Conducted by or under the direction of any individual or agent using the property or facilities of the university.

How long does a review take?

A protocol that has been reviewed by a department representative and designated as **Exempt** needs to be reviewed by the chair of the IRB Executive Committee. This generally takes one week.

A protocol that has been reviewed by a department representative and designated as **Expedited** needs to be reviewed by a member of the IRB Executive Committee. This generally takes two weeks. Then it must be reviewed by the chair, which generally takes one week.

A protocol that has been reviewed by a department representative and designated as **Full** needs to be reviewed by the entire IRB Executive Committee at the monthly meeting. Department reviewed protocols must be received at least two weeks prior to the meeting at which they will be reviewed. The PI will be notified of the committee's decision usually within 24 hours of the meeting.

Protocols may need revision by the PI before approval can be granted. The chair is usually able to review the revisions within a week of receiving them.

continued

Table 5.2–*Continued*

How do I submit a protocol for a class project? (Batch Protocol)

To aid in processing class-originated research protocols the IRB suggests a "batching" of the protocols together. There would be one, single protocol submission for all of the essentially identical projects. The instructor would complete one IRB Protocol Submission Form together with one protocol narrative. The instructor will also submit one informed consent document and/or script that will be used by all of the students doing the research.

The instructor would then attach to this basic protocol submission two additional elements. The first element would include descriptions of the particular variation(s) each student, or group of students, will take on the project. This typically will include: a listing of the questions to be asked (for interview-type research activities) or instrument to be administered (for survey-type research activities); a more detailed specification of the characteristics of the subjects to be recruited for that particular activity, if appropriate; and any additional conditions or design elements that will be used exclusively for that activity.

Does classroom work require IRB approval?

All student research is subject to IRB review following guidelines outlined in Illinois State University Policy for the Protection of Human Research Subjects. Class research projects (including independent studies) require review by the IRB only if they are intended for generalization (e.g., publishing, presenting, or archiving), contain more than minimal risk encountered every day, or involve a protected class of citizens (e.g., mentally incapacitated persons, children, prisoners, pregnant women, or economically or educationally disadvantaged persons).

Class-only projects that may be disseminated in the future must be reviewed (e.g., student research symposia). IRB review must occur prior to any data collection.

Class projects designed to "practice" systematic investigation techniques need not be reviewed when they involve supervised training of new members of a profession. Examples include teacher trainees practicing evaluation, clinical interns practicing assessment or diagnosis, and student journalism reporters practicing interviewing, etc. These activities should still communicate applicable or reasonable elements of informed consent (e.g., institutional affiliation, purpose of investigation, risks, benefits, voluntary participation, permission to withdraw, etc.)

Note: IRBFAQ. (n.d.). *Research & Sponsored Programs: Illinois State University*. Retrieved October 9, 2010, from: http://www.rsp.ilstu.edu/research/human_subjects/IRBFAQ.shtml

indicate the level of review that is needed. See Table 5.3 for IRB levels of review and Appendices D and E for an example human subject's proposal and reviewer form and Appendix F for a completed proposal. Once at the university level, the proposals are then reviewed depending on the specific institution's schedule, so it would be important to know the schedule if you are planning a certain timeframe to begin your research.

Once reviewed, the possible decisions by committee are (1) accept, (2) withheld pending (also referred to as pending with revisions), and (3) denied. It is very common to get a response of withheld pending so do not become alarmed if this is the decision you receive. This usually means you need to just make some adjustments to the proposal and address reviewer concerns. Typically once the concerns and adjustments are made, you will resubmit the proposal before it will be accepted. Once accepted, you may then begin your research, but not until official notice of approval is received.

The IRB process varies across institutions. The type and size of your institution will greatly impact the IRB process and the amount of university support that is provided to faculty during the process. It is common for the IRB process to be submitted via an on-line data process. An IRB proposal or application may also be submitted directly to the university committee rather than being reviewed by a department-level committee first. Often, the departmental committee step is replaced by a review from the department chair, and dean of the college.

Table 5.3
IRB LEVELS OF REVIEW

Exempt

Research conducted in established or commonly accepted educational settings, involving normal educational practices such as:

- research on regular and special education instruction strategies
- research on the effectiveness of or the comparison among instructional techniques, curricula, or classroom management methods.

Research involving the use of educational tests (cognitive, diagnostic aptitude, achievement), survey procedures, interview procedures, of observation of public behavior, unless:

- information obtained in such a manner that human subjects can be identified, directly, or through identifiers linked to the subjects

continued

Table 5.3–*Continued*

- any disclosure of the human subjects' responses outside the research could reasonably place the subjects at risk of criminal or civil liability or be damaging to the subjects' financial standing, employability, or reputation.

Research involving the use of educational tests (cognitive, diagnostic, aptitude, achievement), survey procedures, interview procedures, or observation of public behavior, that is not exempt under the above criterion, if:

- the human subjects are elected or appointed officials or candidates for public office
- or Federal statute(s) require(s) without exception that the confidentiality of the personally identifiable information will be maintained throughout the research and thereafter.

Research involving the collection of existing data, documents, records, pathological specimens, if these sources are publicly available or if the information is recorded by the investigator in such a manner that subjects cannot be identified, directly or through identifiers linked to the subjects.

Research and demonstration projects which are conducted by or subject to the approval of Department or agency heads, and which are designed to study, evaluate or otherwise examine:

- public benefit or service programs
- procedures for obtaining benefits or services under those programs
- possible changes in or alternatives to those programs or procedures
- possible changes in methods or levels of payment for benefits or services under those programs

Taste and food quality evaluation and consumer acceptance studies:

- if wholesome foods without additives are consumed or
- if a food is consumed that contains a food ingredient at or below the level and for a use found to be safe by the Food and Drug Administration or approved by the Environmental Protection Agency or the Food Safety and Inspection Service of the USDA.

Expedited

Research on drugs or medical devices for which an investigational new drug application or an investigational device exemption is not required.

Table 5.3–*Continued*

Collection of blood samples by venipuncture, in amounts not exceeding 550 millimeters in an eight-week period and no more than two times per week from subjects 18 years of age or older, who are in good health and not pregnant and who weigh at least 110 pounds. Or other adults and children, considering the age, weight and health of the subjects, the collection procedure, the amount of blood to be collected, and the frequency with which it will be collected. For these subjects, the amount drawn may not exceed the lesser of 50 ml or 3 ml per kg in an eight-week period and collection may not occur more than twice per week.

Prospective collection of biological specimens for research purposes by noninvasive means such as:

- hair and nail clippings, in a nondisfiguring manner
- deciduous teeth, and permanent teeth if patient care indicates a need for extraction
- excreta and external secretions including sweat
- uncannulated saliva
- placenta removed at delivery, and amniotic fluid at the time of rupture of the membrane prior to or during labor
- supra- and subgingival dental plaque and calculus, provided the procedure is not more invasive than routine prophylactic scaling of the teeth and the process is accomplished with accepted prophylactic techniques
- mucosal and skin cells collected by buccal scraping or swab, skin swab, or mouth washings
- sputum collected after saline mist nebulization.

Recording of data from subjects 18 years of age or older using noninvasive procedures routinely employed in clinical practice. This includes:

- the use of physical sensors that are applied to the surface of the body or at a distance and do not involve input of matter or significant amounts of energy into the subject or an invasion of the subject's privacy
- weighing or testing sensory acuity
- magnetic resonance imaging
- electrocardiography, electroencephalography, thermography, detection of naturally occurring radioactivity, electroretinography, ultrasound, Doppler blood flow, and echocardiography
- moderate exercise, muscular strength testing, body composition assessment, and flexibility testing where appropriate given the age, weight, and health of the individual.

continued

Table 5.3–*Continued*

The study of existing data, documents, records, pathological specimens, or diagnostic specimens that have been collected for nonresearch purposes.

Research on individual or group behavior or characteristics of individuals, such as:

- studies of perception, cognition, motivation, identity, language, communication, cultural beliefs or practices and social behavior
- research employing survey, interview, oral history, focus group, program evaluation, human factors evaluation, or quality assurance methodologies (some of this may be exempt)
- where the investigator does not manipulate the subjects' behavior and the research will not involve stress to subjects.

Full

All other studies, including those involving deception of subjects in ways that may lead to their distress or the collection of data in ways that may identify individual subjects.

Note: Laws. (n.d.). IRB Levels of Review: Human Subjects Research: Research & Sponsored Programs. *Research & Sponsosred Programs: Illinois State University.* Retrieved October 9, 2010, from: http://www.rsp.ilstu.edu/research/human_subjects/IRBLevelsofReview.shtml

Manuscript Preparation

Another major component of research is comprised of publications. Publications are defined in many ways; a publication could be a journal article, a chapter in a book, a monograph, a newsletter piece, an e-journal submission, or a variety of other products. The writing style of each person should be considered when determining which venue to submit your manuscripts to. In addition, your personal writing style should also match the format, the audience, and type of communication that the publication is seeking to share with the readers. We suggest you make a detailed list of possible publication outlets to which you might submit your work. If you know possible publication outlets, ahead of time, this may reduce time as you begin writing your manuscript.

It is equally important to find out which of the venues for publication will count towards tenure and promotion. For example, at some institutions, a newsletter will not be viewed in the same manner as a journal article in a referred journal. For the focus of this section, we are going to address manuscripts that will be submitted for possible publication as a peer reviewed, referred journal article. A peer-reviewed, referred article is one that goes through a blind review process. Typically, journals of this nature have editorial boards. Members of the editorial boards are experts in their area of expertise and review manuscripts that are related to this expertise area. All manuscripts are reviewed without any identifying information about the author (hence the name "blind review") and members of these boards review manuscripts to see if they have the quality to be published.

Manuscript preparation, in our opinion, begins with idea development. If you are considering doing a project that will have publishable results, you should make sure that your idea and research project will produce results that will add to the already existing literature base in your designated field of expertise or provide emerging ideas to the field. As a newly hired assistant professor, other than personal satisfaction, there is little purpose in developing an idea and conducting a research project that will not produce outcomes (i.e., publication, presentation, or future grant) that will advance your career and help you move towards promotion and tenure. When you begin your career, you should focus on conducting those projects that will directly or indirectly help you achieve success within the university framework.

An essential consideration in manuscript preparation is to determine whether you will work independently, collaborate with another individual, or possibly collaborate with multiple people. Collaborating on research projects is important for your career development, as you will get more involved, and the number of products you produce will probably be substantially greater. Be aware, however, that for promotion and tenure your institution may want to see what your leadership abilities are and, in many cases, will want to see you publishing manuscripts by yourself (sole author). If you fail to demonstrate the ability to produce articles in which you are the lead author, your record might not receive as much credit (even if you have more products) as someone who has completed projects by himself/herself and taken on a leadership role more often. We say this with caution as some universities encourage more collaboration as a means to increase grant opportunities to show cross-disciplinary involvement.

After you have developed your initial ideas and evaluated them to determine if they support your research agenda, it is time to conduct your research. Please refer to the previous section on the human subject's proposal for guidance. Remember, any research project with human subjects must receive institutional approval before anything can begin. Failure to do this could result in consequences for you and your institution.

Data collection is a large part of the research process and a piece that impacts your determined outcomes. What were the effects? Was there evidence of improvement or change? Did the study impact the population? Will the information you obtained be generalized across populations? If your study and assessments are designed appropriately, the data you collect will help you answer these questions, and many more. Many times faculty members have great ideas for research but need help designing the study. If this is a situation you find yourself in, make sure you access your resources. Find someone on your campus whose interests are the same as your own or someone whose area of expertise is research design. You may have to leave the confines of your department in seeking help. Other support personnel may be your department chair, faculty mentor, or a colleague. As you can already see, these individuals are often instrumental in your career and your progress towards promotion and tenure.

Once the data is collected it will need to be analyzed. This is another area where you might need to elicit help. If you are unsure about the procedures you implement to analyze the data or just want corroboration that you implemented the correct methods, you might find an individual who will be willing to offer feedback and guidance. Please note that we all have different strengths and areas we need to develop so asking questions is totally acceptable and even suggested. Just like our students, we are constantly growing and developing and we believe our world (higher education) truly has the mentality of "lifelong learners."

After the data is analyzed, you will begin to write up the results and the rest of the manuscript for possible submission to a journal. We suggest you go back to the list you created of possible publication outlets. What type of manuscript do you want to prepare (i.e., research focus or a practical focus)? Which journal might be most appropriate? What are your options? Once you have decided a possible publication outlet, obtain some sample issues to investigate format and appropriateness of your manuscript. For example, if the format of the journal is that of a research article, you will want to use a research format for your manuscript. See Table 5.4 for example components to include in a research-based manuscript.

If your manuscript idea seems to fit with the style and content of the publication, you can start developing your manuscript. Following the components presented in Table 5.4, fill in all of the appropriate information. It is important to note that most journal manuscripts have a limit of 20–25 double-spaced pages, but we urge you to consult the journal guidelines for exact parameters and guidelines. There are many journal databases in which you can obtain journal guidelines as well as acceptance rates. For example, Cabells is an online directory available at most institutions. When you have completed your manuscript we suggest you ask someone to go through it to edit and see if everything makes sense. This person might also offer suggestions for improvement upon reading it. Once you receive feedback and have made all edits and changes, it will be time to submit your manuscript to be considered for possible publication. Most manuscript submissions are now conducted through some type of on-line system so again, check with the specific journal guidelines

Table 5.4
SAMPLE COMPONENTS FOR A RESEARCH-BASED MANUSCRIPT

- Title Page
- Abstract
- Introduction
- Review of the Literature
- Purpose of your Investigation
- Method
  - Design
  - Subjects
  - Setting
  - Materials
  - Procedures
- Results
- Discussion
  - Limitations
  - Future Implications
- References

and procedures. Along with your manuscript you will also want to submit a short letter or email (depending on how the manuscript is submitted) indicating the manuscript is not currently under review by another journal nor has it been previously published in full or part. This letter should also offer a brief outline of the submission. See Table 5.5 for an example.

Table 5.5
EXAMPLE SUBMISSION LETTER

Dear Dr. _____,

I am submitting a copy via email, as requested, of the manuscript "The POWER to Write: Improving Written Products for Students with Disabilities" to *Beyond Behavior* for review. This manuscript has not been previously published and it is not currently being considered for publication elsewhere.

Please feel free to contact me at (____) _____-_____ or by email at _____ with any questions or if you need any additional information.

Sincerely,

_____, Ph.D.

If you submitted your manuscript to a peer-reviewed journal (which should be your preference), if the editor thinks it is appropriate for the journal, it will go out for review. Most journals elicit reviews of your manuscript from three to four reviewers who will have four to eight weeks to conduct the review. If the manuscript is not appropriate for the journal the editor will usually contact you and possibly suggest some other possible outlets. If not appropriate for the journal, it will not go out for review. When the editor receives all of the reviews, he/she will then contact you with the decision. Possible decisions could be: accept as is, accept with minor revisions, accept with major revisions, revise and resubmit, or reject. You should know that it is very rare to receive the decision of accept as is. Unless the review comes back as rejected, you should now read through the reviewer feedback and comments and decide if you want to make changes and resubmit it. We suggest you should complete this task regardless of the decision. If the decision is major revision and resubmit you may consider another outlet, but first consider all feedback and comments as they could help you develop your manuscript and make it considerably stronger. If you are sending it back to the original editor with changes you should also send a response as to what specific changes you made. See Table 5.6 for an example response.

Presentations

Presentations are another venue that can receive accolades, in the area of Research/Scholarly Activity, towards promotion and tenure as well as personal satisfaction. Typically, tenure and promotion credit can be earned for presentations of research made at state, regional, national, or international conferences. We believe that national and international conferences are more highly regarded, but all are important and will earn you valuable acknowledgments. Presentations are an excellent way to disseminate your research findings to others, get your name out in the field, and possibly create new opportunities for the future. Presentations, like publications and grants, can also be performed by you as the sole presenter or consist of multiple presenters. As you prepare for promotion and tenure, you should have presented your research at some presentations at local, state, regional, and national conferences.

Determining what information to present is often challenging. Ideas can come from your research interests and projects, from your teaching, or even from service-based activities. Obviously, if you are working on a grant or a research project, this is a way to disseminate your findings; it is really an extension of your research and a mode to disseminate your scholarly work. Your teaching, however, can also provide possible opportunities for you to present. Maybe you are implementing innovative teaching techniques, as-

Table 5.6
SAMPLE MANUSCRIPT REVISION RESPONSE

Dear Dr. _____,

Thank you for supplying me with the reviewer feedback and comments. Attached please find the revised manuscript with the requested revisions based on this feedback. Additions are specifically described below.

- Development of the problem under investigation and statement of the purpose.
  - Added text on the top of page 4.

- Summarize previous investigations in order to inform the reader of the state of current research.
  - Added table of research findings on pages 4–6.

- Identifies relations, contradictions, gaps, and inconsistencies in the literature; suggests the next step or steps in solving the problem; discussion and or interpretation of implications of the results.
  - Added text in discussion section on page 18.

- References started on new page.
  - References started on page 19.

If additional information or revisions are requested please contact me. I can be reached via email (insert email address) or by phone (insert phone number). I look forward to hearing from you.

Sincerely,

_____

sessments, or using technology in some way that would help others to become stronger in their respective fields. Presentations can then be an extension of these ideas.

Another possible area to build upon for presenting scholarly work is service. You may have ideas to disseminate based on your work in public schools or with local agencies. If this is the case, presentations can become an extension of your service activities. Presentations do not always have to be tied to specific research you are conducting, so make sure you consider all areas you are involved with for possible presentation ideas. Plan to discuss your ideas with your mentor, a colleague, or your department chair, and see if you can get some feedback from them. One note to consider is that many conferences are looking for completed proposals almost a year in advance. With this in mind, you might want to make a list of the conferences you are interested in attending and those you are interested in presenting at along with the dates of the conferences and the due dates for proposals. This list will help you organize what proposals need to be written and when they need to be submitted. This information can also be incorporated into your master plan leading towards promotion and tenure. This information is often available on the organization's website.

Another point we want to highlight is the importance of conferences. Besides presenting to others and disseminating important ideas, strategies, methods, and research results, there are other benefits to conferences. Conference attendance can help promote your own learning. At conferences you can make important connections, and formulate new ideas for future projects. It is also a nice opportunity to get off campus into another location to focus on your area of expertise. We highly recommend you attend conferences for all the above reasons. You will not only find that you will help others with the information you share, but it will be a very worthwhile experience for your own professional growth and development.

Grant Funding

The third area we will discuss that is influential in obtaining promotion and tenure is grant funding. Depending on the type of institution you are at, grant funding can highly influence the decision on your tenure and promotion. Grants can either be internal or external. Internal grants are funded by your institution and earn you merit is this area, but not as much as a state, agency, or federally funded grant. Internal grants could be for travel, professional development, or even a small research project. Sometimes these small research grants are available to help new and veteran faculty begin conducting their research projects with funds being paid to the individual. Please see Chapter 3 for a more thorough description of these small internal research grants (URGs) and Appendix A for a sample URG application.

In regards to writing external grants, you should seek out the type of grant support which is available at your new institution. Your faculty mentor, department chair, or other faculty members are great resources for you in this area. Is there college level support? Is there university level support somewhere on campus (maybe a Research and Sponsored Programs office)? Support at any level is critical for the development and implementation of grant funding. Is there someone available to help you organize your materials? Is there someone available to help you develop a reasonable budget? Is there someone available to help review your grant application package and give you feedback on your proposal? If you have never completed a federal grant application before you will definitely want to seek out support and guidance.

Some institutions offer grant writing workshops as a support for new faculty members. In these workshops, faculty members attend training on writing external grants and begin to prepare a proposal with the support of the presenters of the workshop. In some cases, the workshop provides the faculty member with specific feedback and support from previous grant awardees. Institutions that want to promote the writing of grant applications for outside funding typically have some type of support system in place for new and veteran faculty.

As previously mentioned, collaboration is on option in grant writing activities. You may consider submitting a grant proposal with one or more people so you can collaborate on getting the work completed. This is especially helpful if one of the members has previously written and obtained a grant. Preparing a grant application takes a lot of time, energy, and hard work. Because of the time commitment, most universities recommend documenting your efforts regardless of whether or not the grant was funded. It is very difficult to obtain a federal grant as the competition is often great; therefore, do not be discouraged if you do not receive funding on your first grant submission. Instead, view the grant writing process as a learning experience and critically review the feedback that was given to you. Take the information and apply it to your next grant application. There is a great deal of information regarding the grant writing process and this section only touches on the basic premise. There are many books available that specifically address federal grant writing, obtaining grant funding, seeking foundation grants, and even literature that specifically addresses various fields and specific agencies that fund projects within the identified field.

It is important to know that after the grant application is accepted, there is still a great deal of work to be completed prior to receiving the actual funding. Make sure you contact the project officer in charge of the grant you received and also the appropriate person on campus. The office of sponsored projects on most university campuses keeps records of all grants applied for and those received. It is important to follow the appropriate policies and procedures of the grant funding agency. Communication is essential to assure that this occurs.

Getting help with the grant writing and budget from the very beginning will assist you in making sure that agency and university policies and procedures are followed. We recommend that you call a meeting with everyone involved with your grant at your institution to get an understanding of what needs to be done and who needs to do it. You might also consider developing a timeline with all the events that need to take place and names of who is responsible for each task. When you plan a grant application be aware of what you are getting involved with and what is required of you and those you contract in the grant. Specifically, examine the amount of time you you will need to devote to this project. Planning and preparation will make this experience more feasible, attainable, and productive for everyone involved.

Being Successful

We have now discussed the three major components of the Scholarly Activity/Research area: publications, presentations, and grants. So how do they all fit together? How can you get the most benefit for the work you have done? What is the best way to organize your work? First, you need to understand that all three of these components can and should be interrelated. Whenever you conduct research, you should always consider how to disseminate your findings and receive credit for the work you have completed.

We feel it is very important to have a planning strategy for every research project you are involved with and then follow the plan. In the area of publications, it is important to always have multiple projects going in different stages of development (i.e., in print, in press, submissions, and in progress). Knowing it could take a full year from the time it was submitted just to get a manuscript in print will allow you to determine the timeframe to assure you have multiple projects in que. You cannot wait for a project to be published before you begin another project. If this is your plan, it will most likely not be effective. You will find this will limit your opportunities to show a pattern or history of publications. We highly recommend that you always have multiple projects underway. Depending on the field you are in, you may be able to get multiple publications from one research study. For example, in education, you might submit a data-driven (research-focused) manuscript to one journal and submit a teacher friendly "how to" manuscript to a more practical type of journal. These "how to" manuscripts are considered practitioner based and provide concrete instructional methods to teachers seeking to improve on their teaching or implement new instructional strategies.

Publications can also lead to presentations of scholarly work at conferences. This is another way to earn credit on your research record. Once more, we stress to always be thinking about how you can disseminate your findings. Other than publications, presentations are a very valuable way to reach this goal. Submit a conference proposal, and if accepted, you can report your findings. Not only do you get to attend a professional development conference and present your findings, but conferences also provide excellent networking opportunities.

Last year I presented at a conference some of my findings from a current study I was conducting. I was so surprised to find that one of the attendees at my session was currently studying a similar topic. After the session we spent a great deal of time discussing ways we might be able to collaborate and to strengthen each of our projects. Today, we have published a book about our findings. I always encourage others to use conferences as a time to not just learn new information but to network and develop new relationships.

The last area we mention is grant writing. Grants are not easy to obtain and they can be very time consuming, but remember that many products can be the result of grant work. Here you can actually get credit for acquiring the grant, completing the grant, and writing manuscripts and making presentations to disseminate the findings of the grant. What this means to you, as a faculty member, is that you can earn credit towards promotion and tenure at all three levels of Research/Scholarly Activity through a grant. This, however, sometimes does not happen as the principal investigator is sometimes consumed by the grant and fails to manage time to write up the research findings or to attend conferences to present these findings. We encourage you to find out from the Dean of your college as to whether or not the institution you are working at recommends that junior faculty explore grant-writing possibilities. If trying to obtain a grant, be sure you have the time and proper support to get it completed as well as furthering your career at the same time.

Collaboration/Outreach

When conducting research, many individuals explore two different options: work alone or work in collaboration with others. Most institutions allow you to receive credit for both types of research as you progress towards promotion and tenure, but you will want to check with your colleagues, department chair, and evaluation committee for specific information regarding this aspect of research. At some institutions, the only research that is favorably looked upon is that which you do by yourself, but those are very rare. If this is your case, you really need to develop a strong plan and good time management skills to get things accomplished.

At most institutions collaborative research is recognized and is promoted, but again you should clarify with others expectations and guidelines. Typically, as you move toward promotion and tenure, you should be taking more leadership roles. In the area of publications this means you should be identified as first or second author more often than later in the list of authors. The committee that will evaluate your research performance will look at your progress and determine if you are emerging into a leader. It is most important to seek clarification in this area and ask specific questions such as: Does it matter what author I am in a collaborative publication (i.e., second, third, or fourth author)? Do all authors in a collaborative piece get credit? What percentage of single author versus multiple authors is acceptable? Knowing this information will help you in your planning and development. You should be cautions of agreeing to participate/collaborate in a project that will take time and energy that ultimately will not be counted or earn you credit towards promotion and tenure. We often see new faculty say yes to every project offered to them for fear that they will never be asked again. You should closely monitor your projects so you do not become overwhelmed. It is worse to not complete something on time and with high quality than to just say no at the beginning. Also, you want to determine if you can fit the project into your research agenda. This might also help you in deciding whether to accept or reject an opportunity.

When it comes to collaboration, we suggest you look for individuals to work with both inside and outside your new institution. Obviously, you will have many new colleagues. These are all people you could possibly collaborate with in your department, college, or across campus. In addition, you might also think about working with former fellow doctoral students you went to school with. You will find that opportunities arise over time and a healthy relationship with former classmates might reap possible research opportunities. Another avenue to consider is attending professional meetings. Get involved in your subject areas professional meetings or conferences. Attend and make presentations and you will be surprised how many connections will foster. Over time, these might turn into possible collaborative research projects. You cannot just sit back and wait for projects to appear; you need to be a proactive in regards to your own career and future success in your field of study.

Faculty Expectations

The last thing we want to address is how you determine the faculty expectations in regards to research. Each department, college, and university will have different research expectations and some will be very clear (i.e., the number of publications, presentations, and grants needed for promotion and tenure and the value of sole authored versus co-authored works) and others may not (i.e., no specific number of publications, presentations, and grants identified for promotion and tenure), but one thing is for certain; to successfully be promoted and granted tenure you will need to conduct research and publish. We urge you to hold conversations with your mentor, other colleagues, your department chair, and possibly even your dean. You might even contact your department evaluation committee with questions and clarifications about expectations in the area of research. Go on a fact finding mission to learn the research expectations. Over time you should feel more comfortable conducting research and disseminating your findings to other professionals through publications and presentations.

Conclusion

The information in this chapter highlighted different aspects we believe are important for you to think about and consider in the area of research and scholarly activity. This is one of the three main components you will be evaluated on for promotion and tenure. It is important that you perform well in this area and you continue to grow and develop over time. Research is comprised of publications, presentations, and grants. The importance of each can be different at different institutions. In order to be successful, there are many things to consider and we hope this chapter will help you achieve success.

This chapter began by discussing release time for research and what that entails. It then discussed idea development, starting a research agenda, and following through on that, and the IRB process. It also addressed some fundamentally important aspects necessary to develop a manuscript for possible publication from idea development to the actual submission of the manuscript. Next, the chapter discussed presentations and grants and how they fit with your research agenda and the publication process. We discussed how a new faculty member can be successful in the area of research and provided examples of how this can be managed. Lastly, this chapter addressed how collaboration and outreach can benefit your research agenda and productivity as well as expectations for faculty in the area of research.

There is a lot of information related to research in this chapter and we realize that you will not know everything your first semester nor will you have time to jump immediately into research, but if you use this chapter as a guide, we feel you will be on your way toward a successful career in the area of research. Being a successful researcher takes time and effort and is an ongoing process. This is also a very instrumental component in the promotion and tenure process. We hope you take your research seriously and continue to self-assess your research agenda as well as having others evaluate your productivity as you work toward being a successful faculty member in the area of research.

Faculty Tips about Scholarly Activity

- Always keep your Curriculum Vitae updated.

- Set aside time for scholarly work. If you don't set aside the time for scholarly work, it will not appear. Once you set aside time for scholarly work, don't give it up for anything. Well, almost anything. Keep in mind that 99% of things that come up or need to be done should not get in the way of time scheduled for scholarly work. Your future depends on it!

- Even if you are not at a "research institution," there is support there. Look for it to support your research agenda.

- Budget time to write. Really—Do It! Put it in your calendar and do not use this time for anything else. If someone wants to meet with you, that time is committed, meet another day. Spend at least one day per week where you put everything else aside and write text. You can do it from home or do it from work—but do it. Self-monitor your own productivity.

- Team up with people to do work on writing and research.

- Find out what other people are doing, and if you have a good collaborative idea, pitch it.

- Always have research in the works—research is usually a one to two year process from initial idea to publication.

Chapter 6

SERVICE

Another one of your roles as a faculty member will be in the area of service. This is comprised of service to your department, college, university, outside agencies, and professional organizations. The focus or emphasis may be placed on one particular area, but typically faculty should be involved in many different levels within and outside the university. Although probably not as highly regarded or evaluated as teaching and research, service might still comprise about one-third the importance (in those Teaching and Research institutions highlighted in Chapter 1) of your work toward promotion and tenure. This next chapter will focus on service opportunities which is the third area discussed in Part III of this book.

Department Service

Within your institution, the department is the first level of service in which you will be expected to participate. Typically, you will probably not be involved in much service your first year, but after that, you should progressively become more involved each year as you progress toward promotion and tenure. Many times, elections in your department, college, and university for committees are held in the spring. If you are beginning your new faculty position in the fall, the opportunity to engage in committee work at the department level will not be afforded to you. If this should occur, see it as a benefit as the free time you will gain will result in more opportunities for you to focus on your research agenda and teaching. When an opportunity does arise in the department, college, or university, typically, you may choose to submit your name for possible consideration. Course instructional teams, as were previously discussed in Chapter 3, are committees you should attempt to be a part of as soon as you can. This will not only impact your relationships with colleagues, but will benefit you in the areas of teaching and service.

At the department level, there will be many service opportunities so there is little need to rush into everything that is presented to you. When an opportunity arises, it is important that you make calculated decisions regarding participation in service activities. It is very important that you pay attention to what service activities you commit to and how you will be spending your time. You need to remember that service activities are performed in addition to other commitments in teaching and research. We recommend that you ask your faculty mentor or department chair about the work the different committees perform, how often they meet, and the total time commitment of each committee. This information will hopefully help you with your decision-making in the area of departmental committees.

At some university settings, the option to select committees at the department and college level are not given to you. It is not unusual to receive a notice that you have been selected to serve on a specific committee. This decision is often made by the Dean or Chair of your department. If this should occur, carefully evaluate the appointment. In most instances, it would be best to accept these committee assignments unless you find that it would greatly affect your performance in other areas. If you cannot fulfil the appointment, you should put in writing a formal request to be removed from that committee stating exact reasons for such removal. For a tenure track faculty member, this can be a difficult decision and one that should be made with caution. It is acceptable to turn down committee assignments, but you do not want to be in a position where your colleagues or administrators feel you are avoiding performing your share of the work load. However, reasonable requests to be removed from a committee might incude a request to step down from an elections committee if you are running for a specific position that this committee will head. Another possibility is being removed from a search committee in which an acquaintance will apply for the position. It is of upmost importance to identify any conflicts of interest in committee work.

Some possible committees you might get involved with could include but are not limited to the following: (a) Curriculum Committee, (b) Scholarship Committee, (c) Elections Committee, (d) Department Research Committee, (e) Faculty Resource Committee, (f) Master's Committee, (g) Doctoral Committee, and (h) the Evaluation Committee. See Table 6.1 for a list of some of the possible department committees and their functions.

College Service

Within your institution, the college level is the second level of service that you can and should participate. Typically, you will not be involved in service your first year at the college level, just like in your department, but after that, you should become progressively more involved each year as the op-

Table 6.1
POSSIBLE DEPARTMENT COMMITTEES AND THEIR FUNCTIONS

Committee	*Function*
Curriculum Committee	Reviews curriculum proposals for new courses, program additions and deletions, and course name changes.
Scholarship Committee	Chooses the winners of scholarships offered through the department.
Elections Committee	Runs the elections and counts the ballots for faculty openings in the department.
Department Research Committee	Evaluates internal research grants such as the University Research Grant applications.
Faculty Resource Committee	Works on helping the chair with possible departmental resource allocations, such as departmental grants.
Master's Committee	Works on admissions, curriculum, and any other Master's program related business.
Doctoral Committee	Works on admissions, curriculum and any other Doctoral program related business.
Evaluation Committee	Evaluates yearly faculty performance portfolios and promotion and tenure portfolios.

portunities arise. Many times elections for such committees are held in the spring so if you are beginning your new faculty position in the fall, your opportunities to participate in these committees will be limited. This again is a benefit to you as it gives you time to begin your research agenda and focus on teaching. Typically, one or two representatives from each department serve on college committees. When an opportunity does arise, you need to submit your name for possible consideration. At the college level, there will also be many service opportunities so there is no need to rush into everything that is presented to you. When an opportunity arises, it is important that you make calculated decisions on what service activities you will participate in. It is very important that you pay attention to what service activities you commit to and how you will be spending your time. You need to remember that service activities are in addition to other commitments in teaching and research. We recommend you ask your faculty mentor or department

Table 6.2
POSSIBLE COLLEGE COMMITTEES AND THEIR FUNCTIONS

Committee	*Function*
Curriculum Committee	Reviews curriculum proposals for new courses, program additions and deletions, and course name changes for the entire college.
Scholarship Committee	Chooses the winners of scholarships offered through the college.
Elections Committee	Runs the elections and counts the ballots for faculty openings in the college.
College Research Committee	Evaluates internal research grants, such as the University Research Grant applications, that the college submits to the university.
Diversity Committee	Works on diversity-related issues and how they fit into the curriculum of the college.
Teaching and Learning Committee	Develops a teacher evaluation instrument for all college faculty to implement as well as best practices for instruction and learning.
College Council	Works on college-related issues that include college bylaws and monitoring the work of each department and all college committees.
Evaluation Committee	Evaluates promotion and tenure portfolios from all the departments in the college.

chair about the work the different committees perform, how often they meet, and the total time commitment of each committee. This information will hopefully help you with your decision-making in the area of college committees. Some possible committees you might get involved with could include the following: (a) Curriculum Committee, (b) Scholarship Committee, (c) Elections Committee, (d) College Research Committee, (e) Diversity Committee, (f) Teaching and Learning Committee, (g) College Council, and (h) the Evaluation Committee. See Table 6.2 for a list of possible college committees and their functions.

University Service

Within your institution, the university level is the last level of service that you can and should participate in if possible. Typically, you will probably not be involved in service your first year at the university level, just like in your department and college, and it may take a while as these opportunities are often few and far between. Many times only a few representatives from each college are asked to serve on these committees and often they are appointed by the dean of your college or recommendations could come from your department chair. When elections for these committees are held, they usually happen in the spring, like in the department and college. At the university level there will not be as many service opportunities so if you see something that interests you, we urge you to submit your name for consideration. When an opportunity arises, it is important that you make calculated decisions on what service activities you will participate in. It is very important that you pay attention to what service activities you commit to and how you will be spending your time. You need to remember that service activities are on top of your other commitments in teaching and research. We recommend that you ask your faculty mentor or department chair about the work the different committees perform, how often they meet, and the total time commitment of each committee. This information will hopefully help you with your decision-making in the area of university committees. Some possible committees you might get involved with could include the following: (a) General Education Committee, (b) Academic/Faculty Senate, (c) Athletic Council, (d) Council for Teacher Education, (e) Scholarship Committee, (f) University Research Committee, (g) Faculty Review Committee, (h) Parking Appeals Committee, (i) Benefits Committee, and (j) University Review Committee. See Table 6.3 for a list of some possible university committees and their functions.

Table 6.3
POSSIBLE UNIVERSITY COMMITTEES AND THEIR FUNCTIONS

Committee	Function
General Education Committee	Reviews curriculum proposals and monitors the general education curriculum for the entire student body.

continued

Table 6.3–*Continued*

Committee	Function
Academic Senate	The primary governing body to recommend the educational policy of the university and to advise the president on its implementation and provides for faculty, staff, and student participation in academic governance.
Athletic Council	Responsible for monitoring athletic program standards and quality related to NCAA requirements.
Council for Teacher Education	Responsible for developing requirements for teacher education and for providing avenues of communication among all areas of the University concerned with teacher education. It has the authority and responsibility to oversee academic programs leading to certification of teachers and other professional education personnel who work in prekindergarten through twelfth grade school settings.
Scholarship Committee	Chooses the winners of scholarships offered through the university.
University Research Committee	Evaluates internal research grants, such as the University Research Grant applications, and the university research awards.
Faculty Review Committee	Listen to appeals on promotion and tenure decisions.
Parking Appeals Committee	Assist in the resolution of university parking citation appeals.
Benefits Committee	To address concerns and provide advice on all fringe benefits for employees at the university.
University Review Committee	Review annual evaluation policies, to make recommendations for changes, and to review college guidelines for conformity with the university guidelines.

Public School Service

Outside your institution, or external service, there are other opportunities with which you might consider. For example, if you are in the field of education, one of those areas might be the public schools. External opportunities usually take a little longer to get involved with because as a new faculty member in a new community you usually need to make some connections before you can participate in these opportunities, especially in schools. This means that you will probably not be involved in much external service your first year until you get established in your institution and the local community. Once you have made some connections with school personnel, some service opportunities may develop. You may find service opportunities with school administrators, teachers, related personnel (i.e., school psychologists, counselors, and physical therapists), parents, and committees (i.e., curriculum, technology, and professional development). These opportunities could be in the form of workshops or continuing professional development. Over time you could find yourself working with more schools and possibly an entire school district. Again, just like with internal service, when an opportunity arises, it is important that you make calculated decisions regarding your participation in service activities. It is very important that you pay attention to what service activities you commit to and how you will be spending your time. You need to remember that service activities are on top of your other commitments in teaching and research. Also, you do not need to be doing every type of service, but as you progress towards promotion and tenure, it is important that you find your niche and capitalize on your interests and talents. Your service commitments should tie directly to your current research agenda.

Community Organization Service

Outside your institution, or external service, another opportunity you might consider becoming involved with would be community organizations. Again, external opportunities typically take longer to get involved with because as a new faculty member, in a new community, you usually need to make some connections before you can participate in these opportunities, especially in schools. This means that you will probably not be involved in much external service your first year. However, this will change once you get established with community organizations in your community or nearby communities. One way to get involved with community organizations would be to contact them over the phone and ask how you can assist them with current projects or forthcoming projects. We also suggest you visit their websites to gather background information on the organizations. You may find service opportunities in community organizations as a volunteer (i.e., helping out with the community organization on an as-needed basis), through special events (i.e., helping out with a fundraiser), as a board member (i.e., more of a time commitment helping the organization move forward), or even a board officer (i.e., extreme time commitment working with the growth and development of the organization). Many times starting out small, possibly as a volunteer, is an initial step in becoming involved with a community organization. It also provides you the opportunity to determine if this organization is a good match for you and your interests and skills.

Eventually you might find yourself working more in depth with these organizations or maybe not, but remember that the choice is yours and you must be very selective with your service choices. It is very important that you pay attention to what service activities you commit to and how you will be spending your time. You need to remember that service activities are in addition to your other commitments in teaching and research. Also, you do not need to be engaged in every type of service, but as you progress towards promotion and tenure, it is important that you find your niche and capitalize on your interests and talents. Community service offers an array of research opporunties and allows you to establish connections which might lead to collaborative grant projects. Many federal grants require that you partner with community service groups. Having a service history with a community organization provides a segway to working on such grant projects.

Professional Organization Service

Outside your institution, or external service, another opportunity you might consider becoming involved with would be professional organizations. This external opportunity might be a little easier to become involved with, compared with the previously discussed external service opportunities described above. This is partially because you may already be involved with professional organizations upon your arrival as a new faculty member. Professional organizations can be important in the areas of teaching, research, and service, so if you are not already involved, then you should consider becoming involved.

Being involved with an organization will not only provide you with multiple service opportunities, but will also provide you opportunities for your own professional development and advancement. You may find service opportunities in professional organizations such as a general member (i.e., you attend general meetings and conferences with no direct involvement with the organization other than attending events), a subcommittee member (i.e., you volunteer to perform a specific task with a more specific role), a subcommittee officer (i.e., you volunteer with a specific role and a leadership position), a general officer (i.e., you serve as a leader for the organization), a division member (you attend general meetings and conference themes related to the division with no direct involvement with the division other than attending events), a subcommittee member within the division (i.e., you volunteer to perform a specific task with a more specific role within the division), a subcommittee officer within the division (i.e., you volunteer with a specific role and a leadership position within the division), or a division officer (i.e., you serve as a leader for the division). Many times starting out small, possibly by just attending professional organization meetings and events is a good way to help you decide what would be a good match for you regarding your interests and skills. Over time you might find yourself working more in depth with these organizations and divisions within the organizations or maybe not, but remember that the choice is yours and you must be very selective with your service choices.

Again, it is very important that you recognize that the service activities you commit to will require a time commitment and that service activities are in addition to your other commitments in teaching and research. Carefully select the role you choose to take on in a professional organization as your role within the organization may carry different weights in being awarded "credit" towards tenure and promotion. For example, serving as a member on a subcommittee (i.e. publications committee member) at the state level will offer less credit towards tenure, promotion, and/or merit than serving as an officer (i.e., secretary or president) in a national organization. As previously mentioned, you do not need to participate in all types of service activities, but as you progress toward promotion and tenure, it is important that you find your niche and capitalize on your interests and talents.

Documentation of Service

When you are involved in service activities, regardless if they are internal or external, it is important that you acquire documentation of your participation. This documentation can be used for your annual performance portfolio as well as your promotion and tenure portfolio. This documentation could be in the form of a formal letter on letterhead or an informal letter, but it should come from either a committee chair or some type of administrator who can document your participation. Topics that can be included in the letter could include the number of meetings attended, important work accomplished, and any type of leadership responsibilities that were undertaken.

The more specific the letter the more it might impact the credit you receive for the service work you have done. We suggest you keep a log of the service work you have participated in, what you did, when you did it, and any other specific information that would be pertinent. After a year, a great deal of work can be done within a committee, at a public school or agency, and in a professional organization. When it is time to write a letter, the committee chair or administrator may have a difficult time remembering the exact role you placed in the outcome of the committee tasks. The log that you keep might help them to recall some of your strengths when they are writing your letter. This will provide them with a resource to turn to when determining the very specific and detailed information that will truly reflect all the time and energy you have devoted to the service activity. Certificates are often provided to you at the end of your term and these can be included in your portfolio as well. See Table 6.4 for a sample service documentation log that a faculty member might keep.

Table 6.4
SAMPLE SERVICE DOCUMENTATION LOG

Diversity Field Experiences Notes

Meeting Dates

1/28/09 (1 hour 30 minutes)

- Documentation forms vs. field placements–need to know early.
- What are possible options for programs?
- How do we track it?
- What can we do now?
- What do we have to figure out first to get the ball rolling?
- How much diversity is currently in courses?
- How do we begin the dialogue to find out what diversity is in the program?
- How will programs fulfill the needs?

How will we do it?

1. Educate on new standards.
2. Find out how programs incorporate diversity.
3. What are programs currently doing?
4. How does work programs are currently doing fit with the new guidelines?

Possibly develop a website to share what programs are doing.

Next Task: How to do it? Develop a set of questions to ask programs.

3/18/09 (1 hour 30 minutes)

Went over undergraduate survey data. Data for responses is in an attachment in an excel file. Data suggests many programs think they are supplying diverse field experiences for their students, but are not sure and are not systematically placing students in these environments. Other programs really have no idea.

Table 6.4–*Continued*

Next Steps?

1. Assessment and monitoring tasks
   a. CECP Forms-tracking
   b. Coordinators in programs-tracking
2. What are programs going to do?
   a. Where will placements be?
   b. How will requirements be met?
   c. When will placements happen?
3. Programs need to thoughtfully and purposefully plan these experiences.

Develop plan for programs and CECP

3/20/09 (1 hour 30 minutes)

Framework for Programs–All approved CTE Diversity documents were reworked into a more coherent and concrete document.

Worked on new data collection document.

Introduction-Rationale–You were previously given a survey to fill out that addressed the following 7 questions (list them). Now we would like you to focus on your program areas.

List sites or schools used for placements, alternative examples.

Although only 20 hours are required in a diverse setting according to CTE, we would suggest you investigate all of your clinical hours in regards to:

- what classes they are tied to (if any)
- when do students receive placements (sequence)
- are the field experiences tied to coursework (i.e., discussion) and how (list course number and title)
- list of activities–explanation and examples

Need to explain what we are going to do with the information-web page-resource for programs and others with contact information?

Being Successful

We have now discussed both internal and external service opportunities which can include service to your department, college, and university as well as service to the public school, community, and professional organizations. So how do they all fit together or do they fit together? How can you get the most benefit for the service work you have done? What is the best way to get

124   *A Survival Guide for New Faculty Members*

involved with service activities? First, you need to understand that service work is important, but not at the same level, in most cases, as teaching and research. Whenever you do any service-related work, you should always be thinking about how it fits with your teaching and research. Is there a way to get data that could be disseminated through presentations or publications? Could your service work lead to some type of grant funding? How can the service work you do for others benefit you as a faculty member working toward promotion and tenure?

We feel it is very important for you to make some type of plan for the service work you hope to do. Try to prepare yourself for future service-related projects by making a plan of action. This plan may also help you decide what opportunities are important and fit with the other work you are already involved with and those opportunities that do not fit with your existing work. This does not mean if the service work does not fit with what you are already involved with, that you should not do it, but you should have some type of plan or guidelines to help guide you in your service work. Find strengths and capitalize on those types of opportunities, but also consider areas that you need to develop. By performing service work in areas where development is needed, you can work on improving your own knowledge and skills as well as those of others. Service work, as was previously mentioned, can also lead to presentations at conferences as well as publications and future grant opportunities (i.e., many grants now focus on collaborative relationships like a university with a public school or community organization). This is another way to earn credit not only in the area of service, but also on your research record. Also be thinking how your service work may impact the courses you are teaching.

We mentioned, in the area of teaching, the importance of being current and implementing real-life examples and service work can help you do this in your teaching. You might modify course content, projects, or student opportunities because of your service work and here you could get credit in the area of teaching for this work you have done. We suggest you always be thinking about how every opportunity you are involved with can benefit you in all three areas (teaching, research, and service) in which you will be evaluated. Remember, however, to guard your time and not be overly involved in service where it takes you away from teaching and research. What this means is that you can possibly earn credit towards promotion and tenure at all three levels of teaching, research, and service by being involved with internal and external service opportunities. In one instance we say get involved, but at the same time, do not get too involved. Just be cautious in what you get involved with as a new faculty member, seek guidance from your faculty mentor, colleagues, and your department chair and over time you will figure out what opportunities will benefit your career as well as those constituents you are working with on the specific service opportunities you are involved. We highly recommend that you find out the "unspoken" rules that govern service at your institution.

Faculty Expectations

The last thing we want to address is how you figure out expectations in regards to the area of service. Each department, college, and university will have different service expectations and some will be very clear (i.e., the number of internal committees you should be on, the types of committees you should be on, and the type of external service you should be involved with) and others may not (i.e., no specific number of internal or external committees described for promotion and tenure), but one thing is for certain: to successfully be promoted and granted tenure you will need to be involved in the area of service both internally and externally. We urge you to hold conversations with your mentor, other colleagues, your department chair, and possibly even your dean. You might even contact your department evaluation committee with questions and clarifications about expectations in the area of service. Go on a fact-finding mission to try and figure out the service expectations, both internally and externally, and know that over time you should also learn about these and feel more comfortable participating in service activities.

Conclusion

The information in this chapter highlighted different aspects we believe are important for you to think about and consider in the area of service. Service is one of the three main components you will be evaluated on for promotion and tenure and it is important that you perform well in this area and continue to grow and develop over time. Service is comprised of your participation in many different areas and includes service to your department, college, and university at the internal level and service to public schools, community organizations, and agencies at the external level. Also considered is your involvement in external service in your profession with professional organizations or possibly state or national service activities. In the area of service, we want to highlight that this is an area that is developed over time and can consume your time if you are not careful. In addition to describing different opportunities and providing specific examples, this chapter also discussed how you can document your participation in service activities, how you become successful in this area, and faculty expectations. Service is an important area and some of your time needs to be devoted to this area. We hope this chapter will serve as a guide in the area of service as you move toward promotion and tenure. You need to understand that you will probably be evaluated in this area so over time your service record should show a progression of involvement. We hope you take your service seriously and continue to self-assess your opportunities as you grow and mature in this area, working toward being a successful faculty member at your institution.

Faculty Tips about Service

- Service can eat up your time and is not equal with teaching and research. Be careful what you commit to.

- Find out service expectations early so you are aware of what is expected.

- Make a plan regarding what service activities you will be involved with and then stick to it.

Part III

THE FINAL STEPS

Chapter 7

DOCUMENTING YOUR PROGRESS

Y ou will be very busy your first year as a new faculty member and each year after that as you progress towards promotion and tenure. Your time as a faculty member will be devoted to teaching, research, and service at varying levels depending on what type of institution you are at and what your interests and foci are. Whether you accept a position at a Research 1 University, a Teaching University, or a Teaching and Research University, one thing for sure is documentation of all the work you will be involved with will be instrumental for yearly evaluations and when you submit your portfolio for promotion and tenure. How will you monitor everything that you do? What is the best way to keep track of your professional activities? What materials will you need to submit with your documentation, if any? What all is important to document your activities? The answers to these questions and many more about documenting the work that you do can be found in this chapter.

Give yourself a little slack (all of the little things that will work themselves out as you get accustomed to your new job). I wish I would have been more realistic about my own expectations of myself, and less worried about "am I measuring up." No one put extra stress on me. I did that to myself. Everyone in my department was supportive. I just had to ask and they were there!

Keeping Track

You will likely be extremely busy your first year as a faculty member and every year after that. You will be involved in teaching (e.g., teaching courses, planning for instruction, meeting with students, and improving the cur-

129

riculum), research (e.g., publications, presentations, grant funding, and coordinating all three areas), and service (e.g., within the university at the department, college, and university levels and outside the university within schools and organizations) and need to make sure you keep track of your professional activities including who you engaged in these activities with and where the activities were performed. This information will be used to determine your yearly progress toward tenure and promotion. During your final semester prior to going up for tenure and promotion, you will need this information compiled so that the evaluation committee can clearly see that your performance meets the minimum expectations to receive promotion and tenure.

Organization will be one of the fundamental characteristics you will need to employ. The ability to be organized will not only allow you to be more successful in your day-to-day functioning, but it will also help you with keeping track of your activities. Organization, planning, having a research agenda, and selectively choosing projects you will be involved with, as well as other topics previously mentioned in the preceding chapters, will help to ensure that you do not overextend yourself.

In addition to being organized, another important aspect for success is the ability to keep effective and accurate records. Again, you want to make sure that you capture everything you do and have a record-keeping system in place to store your documentation. There are many different ways you can keep track of your activities. We will suggest three main ideas that have worked for numerous faculty members.

First, you can keep track of your professional activities through your vitae. Your Vitae should be updated yearly and submitted with your yearly evaluation papers. Keeping it current will provide a reference for when you are building your professional portfolio. One way to keep it current is to constantly update it as new entries (e.g., publications, presentations, and honors) are obtained.

Another way that faculty members track progress is through specific department documentation forms. Most departments/colleges have a set of forms you will need to submit each year to document your yearly progress. These same forms can be used continually throughout the year to document activities. An additional way to document progress is to keep a Microsoft Word or Excel file that simply lists the categories of teaching, research, and service, and each time you accomplish an activity in one of these categories, it can be added to your list.

A final way to document your progress is to develop a portfolio prior to the start of your faculty appointment. The portfolio can consist of the areas in which you will be expected to show progress as a faculty member. The use of large binders with clear sleeves inserted will allow you to keep your documents in one collective place for future reference. Some sample sections you may include are: student evaluation forms (to document teaching), copies of syllabi (to document course planning), published manuscripts/journals (to document scholarly activity), conference brochures (to document presentations at local, national, and state conferences), internal grants (demonstrates grant activity whether funded or not), external grant activities, community activities and professional organizations (minutes from meetings attended, etc.).

It is crucial that you stay current and continuously monitor what you have accomplished in the areas of teaching, research, and service. We know how busy you will become and if you do not consistently monitor and document what you accomplish, you may forget about it at the end of the year and not receive credit for the very important work that you do. Over time you could leave many things off your record that could possibly have an impact on your future success. We know it sounds a bit too excessive, but we recommend that you reflect as often as possible to see if anything needs to be added to your list of accomplishments. This constant evaluation will ensure you are current and that you receive credit for everything you are involved with. See Table 7.1 for a sample departmental document that could be implemented to help you keep track of everything you do each year. If you struggle with keeping up with documenting your activities, we suggest you find a simple method to store your artifacts from these activities. For example, one first year faculty member indicated that she was too overwhelmed to track her activities and simply placed any published manuscripts, service certificates, receipts from professional development, conference brochures, etc. into a designated file cabinet drawer. At the end of the year she sorted the items by date and completed her vitae and departmental forms. Although this is not a preferred method, it did accomplish the goal for this particular faculty member.

Table 7.1
SAMPLE DEPARTMENTAL DOCUMENTATION DOCUMENT

ILLINOIS STATE UNIVERSITY
DEPARTMENT OF SPECIAL EDUCATION
PROFESSIONAL DATA
FOR 2010
ANNUAL PERFORMANCE EVALUATION

Name: Rank:

The guidelines for evaluating faculty performance in the areas of (1) teaching, (2) scholarship, and (3) service are outlined in the *ASPT Policies and Procedures of the*

continued

Table 7.1–*Continued*

Department of Special Education. Refer to these guidelines for examples when completing this form. The period being evaluated consists of the **spring, summer and fall semesters in the 2010 calendar year** (January 1 to December 31).

As part of the DFSC procedures for the current evaluation period, you have an opportunity to supplement the information you have included on this form with a personal meeting with the DFSC members prior to their collective review of materials. If you would like this type of meeting, please so indicate by checking the appropriate blank below:

_____ Yes, I would like a meeting with the DFSC members.

_____ No, I do not wish to meet with the DFSC members.

This form, a current Vitae, and supporting documentation must be submitted to the DFSC by 4:00 pm on January 5, 2011. Electronic copies of this form and current Vitae must also be submitted to the DFSC by 4:00 pm on January 5, 2011. The electronic copies can be delivered by providing _____ a disk or a flash drive, or can be e-mailed as an attachment. If using e-mail, please send it to both the department secretary _____ (email address) and the department chair _____ (email address).

Load Assignment
(please list courses taught and/or other assignments)

SPRING SEMESTER

SUMMER SESSION

FALL SEMESTER

I. TEACHING

A. Student Course Evaluations

For each course you taught during the evaluation year, transfer your mean ratings for each of the 16 items on the SED course evaluation form onto this form.

Table 7.1–*Continued*

	SPRING					SUMMER				FALL				
Course No.														
Enrollment														
1.														
2.														
3.														
4.														
5.														
6.														
7.														
8.														
9.														
10.														
11.														
12.														
13.														
14.														
15.														
16.														

B. Are all original forms with written student comments attached for all courses taught? (Check one)

____ YES   ____ NO

If no, please explain.

C. Do you have any comments related to course evaluations?

continued

Table 7.1–*Continued*

D. Are copies of syllabi (includes related materials such as course outline, description of projects and evaluation measures) for each course taught during the evaluation period attached? (Check one)

_____ YES   _____ NO

   If no, please explain.

E. At least one additional artifact is required for documentation of teaching contributions. Please list the additional artifact(s) you are providing and please indicate the relevance of this artifact in relation to your professional development as a teacher.

F. List any teaching awards you received.

G. List any dissertation or thesis committees on which you have served. Please indicate if thesis or dissertation was completed during the past calendar year.

H. List dissertations or thesis for which you were the research director or committee chair. Please indicate if thesis or dissertation was completed during the past calendar year.

I. Provide any additional information related to your teaching contributions (e.g., any work with school partners related to teaching).

II. SCHOLARSHIP

A. List scholarly presentations made at a state, regional, national or international meeting. Provide appropriate documentation (e.g., copy of program).

B. List scholarly presentations proposed for future a state, regional, national or international meetings. Provide appropriate documentation (e.g., response to call for proposals).

C. List publications that were in print or in press during the past year. Attach copies of manuscripts for "in print" publications and attach letter of acceptance from "in press" manuscripts.

D. List publications that were submitted for publication during the past year. Attach copy of manuscript and letter of receipt from a publisher

E. List all grants submitted and indicate the funding agency, amount, and funding status (e.g., decision pending, funded, not funded).

Table 7.1–*Continued*

F. Summarize your research work in progress and indicate the status of each item on your agenda. Provide samples of any products resulting from your research activities.

G. List/describe any book reviews or manuscript reviews you conducted. Attach copies of published book reviews or other documentation.

H. List any research/scholarship awards you received.

I. Other

III. SERVICE

A. List ISU committees/task forces on which you served during the evaluation period.

1. Department Committees/Task Forces
2. College Committees/Task Forces
3. University Committees/Task Forces

B. List any offices you hold in professional organizations.

C. Describe any national/state/community service activities in which you participated (e.g., grant proposal review, participation on board)

D. List professional development workshops, clinics, demonstrations, etc. you provided to school/agency groups.

E. Describe consultation services you provided to school districts/agencies.

F. Describe any student advisement activities in which you participated.

G. List any service awards you received.

H. List other service activities in which you participated.

MISCELLANEOUS

Provide any additional information related to your accomplishments and contributions that are not included in the previous sections.

Note: Form used by Department of Special Education at Illinois State University. Permission to reprinted obtained.

Developing a Plan

To be successful documenting your yearly progress, we recommend that you develop a plan. If you want to be successful each year (in teaching, research, and service) and every year leading up towards promotion and tenure, you will need to be organized and capture everything that you have accomplished in all three areas. How will you document all that you do? How often will you document everything? The more often you monitor your progress on what you have done, the better off you will be. Will it be every week, every other week, or every month? The choice is up to you, but we suggest you develop a written plan so that when it is time to submit your annual performance portfolio, you have already documented the activities you have been involved in. If you use Outlook, or some other type of calendar system, you might put an entry in your calendar at the interval you have chosen (i.e., every week, every other week, or every month) and then every time it sends a reminder, it will prompt you to document what you have accomplished at that interval.

Another method is, as soon as you have completed an activity, received word about a publication, or when a significant event happens, you automatically document it. Regardless what type of documentation system you implement (e.g., departmental forms, your Vitae, or a Microsoft Word/Excel file), it is important that all your activities are documented and captured soon after they occur. If you do not capture what you have done, you might forget about a particular event and then fail to add it to your annual performance portfolio when you submit it. Typically, these annual performance portfolios capture a year's worth of work from January 1 to December 31 of a designated year. This includes all the work you have done in the areas of teaching, research, and service, over 12 months and/or three or more semesters (e.g., spring, summer, and fall).

Imagine trying to remember everything you did for an entire year. This would be an extremely difficult task to master without proper documentation. We have seen colleagues wait till the last moment before their annual performance portfolio is due and then scramble to try and get all the information they need in one place and then complete the required paperwork. When this occurs, the person typically forgets many different events in the three areas assessed and does not receive the credit that he or she deserves. This type of error will not only impact you in your yearly annual performance (which often leads to some type of salary increment or raise as well-merit pay), but if you do not stay current with your documentation, it could also impact a decision on your promotion and tenure. Of course, the development of some sort of documentation plan is important, but even more important is the ability to follow through with the plan you developed. If you do not follow through with your documentation plan, there is a good chance that you will not capture everything you are doing and you might not be successful in your quest toward promotion and tenure.

Constant Updates

We have already highlighted how important it is to successfully document all that you do and are involved with as well as the importance of developing a plan. A plan, however, will be of no use to you if do not adhere to it. It is important that the timeframe you have chosen (i.e., once a week, every other week, or once a month) is followed. If there has been no progress or nothing done in the areas of teaching, research, and service, then nothing has to be added to your documentation form (whichever you have chosen to use). If something has been completed, however, you can then easily update your record in one or more of these very important areas toward promotion and tenure.

If you begin this process in January and always add new information to the top of each category, when it is time to submit your yearly annual performance portfolio or your promotion and tenure portfolio all of your information will already be in chronological order. If you continue to follow this procedure throughout the year, then your materials will always be organized and ready for you to submit on the appropriate forms. If you fail to follow a process or choose to not constantly update your progress, you will find it much more difficult to fill out your paperwork and complete the appropriate portfolio to document your progress. See Table 7.2 for categories you might consider when keeping track of your progress.

Remember, if you constantly update your progress and keep track of everything you do and are involved with, it will be that much easier when it is time for you to go up for promotion and tenure.

Documenting your Work

In order to be successful with your yearly annual performance portfolio as well as your promotion and tenure portfolio, it is important to not only keep track of everything in some type of written form, as was previously mentioned, but you will also probably need some type or form of a hard copy of everything. See Table 7.3 for types of materials you might collect.

Given all of the information listed in Table 7.3, you can see how important it will be to be organized. You will be involved in many different projects with colleagues and others and it will be important to effectively keep track of everything. As previously mentioned, you can either keep track using a file system or you can use an on-line system. For a file system, it is as easy as

Table 7.2
CATEGORIES FOR KEEPING TRACK OF YOUR PROGRESS

Teaching
    Courses Taught
    Course Evaluations
    Course Revisions
    Innovations Tried
    Professional Development Opportunities

Research
    Publications
        In Print
        Manuscripts "in press"
        Manuscripts Submitted
        Manuscripts "in preparation"
    Presentations
        Presentations Made
        Presentations Submitted
    Grants
        Funded
        Not Funded
        Submitted

Service
    Department
    College
    University
    Public Schools
    Agencies
    Professional Organizations

keeping a drawer in your file cabinet or some type of accordion-type folder in your desk drawer. The first thing we suggest you should do is to make separate areas within the file cabinet drawer or accordion file folder labeled teaching, research, and service. Then every time you have a product or something in one of the three related areas, you can add it to your files. This is the method addressed earlier that worked very well for several first-year faculty members. For example, after the spring semester in the area of teaching, you could put a copy of all of your syllabi and corresponding course evaluations in the teaching section. For research, you could put a copy of your most recent publication or copies of the pages of the conference program indicating you made a presentation at the conference. In the area of

Table 7.3
POSSIBLE DOCUMENTATION MATERIALS

Teaching
     Course Syllabi
     Teacher Evaluations
     Reflections of your Teaching Progress
     Documentation of Professional Development Activities attended

Research
     Copies of your Publications
     Letters recognizing manuscripts submitted
     Copies of work in progress
     Copies of presentations made (copy of program)
     Copies of grant letters signifying funded or not funded proposals

Service
     Letters of Support from
          Committee Chairs
          School Administrators, or
          Organizational Leaders

service you could put letters of support for the work you have done with a community organization. If you continuously do this all year, at the end of the year, you will have everything you need to submit for your portfolio. The products themselves will also help you remember all that you have done throughout the year. It will be important for you to communicate with your faculty mentor, colleagues, and department chair about what is important to document, how you should document your work, and the specific process that is implemented in your department.

Another way to document your progress could be using some type of an on-line system. Many universities are moving toward the implementation of on-line documentation systems. With this system, all information is added on-line in a virtual portfolio instead of a hard copy portfolio. This means that all copies of information are put online as Word documents, pdf's, or direct internet website links. These on-line documentation systems can also help in the evaluation of your portfolios as many people can access your work at the same time (or at any time during the day–very early or very late) versus a paper copy where only one person can view it at a time and it is usually only during business hours. Although an on-line system may have more advantages versus a paper system, it is still necessary to be organized and keep track of everything in order to be successful with your yearly portfolio as well as with your promotion and tenure portfolio. We urge you to talk with your faculty mentor, colleagues, and department chair early in the process (prob-ably almost as soon as you arrive) to find out exactly what you need to do and exactly what is required each year in regards to documentation of the work that you do. The last thing you want to be doing is scrambling at the end of the year trying to capture everything you did. Remember, in many cases, you will be beginning your new role as a faculty member in the fall semester which begins in August or September so you will not have much time (about four months) before your first annual performance portfolio needs to be turned in to be evaluated.

Conclusion

The information in this chapter highlighted the importance of document-ing your progress and how you can keep track of everything you do in the areas of teaching, research, and service. We believe it is important for you to be organized and stay current with your documentation so you can be suc-cessful with promotion and tenure. This chapter discussed how you can keep track of all the work you are involved with to be as successful as possible. It also discussed how you should develop some sort of plan to document your progress as well as how you should constantly monitor and document all that you do. Lastly, this chapter discussed the importance of following through with your plan and how to keep either hard or electronic copies of every-thing you do for documentation in your annual performance portfolio as well as your promotion and tenure portfolio. We hope the information in this chapter provided you some insight and guidance to help you successfully document your work in the areas of teaching, research, and service toward successfully becoming promoted and tenured at you current institution.

Faculty Tips on Documenting your Progress

- Update your materials as soon as you complete something. If you don't, you might miss something at the end of the year when it is time to be evaluated.

- Keep copies of everything to document all that you have accom-plished.

- Keep track of everything you do. Figure out a system that works best for you and stick to it. You will be happy you did in the long run.

Chapter 8

PROMOTION AND TENURE

So far this book has addressed what we call the Basic Fundamentals (Choosing the Right Institution, What to Do Prior to Arriving at Your New Institution, and Learning About Your New Institution), the Nuts and Bolts of Success (Teaching, Research, and Service), and we are now in the third section titled The Final Steps. We have already discussed how you can document your progress and now we will specifically focus on promotion and tenure. We know how busy you will be and that ultimately you would like to earn and receive promotion and tenure. Various definitions exist for the term "tenure" in relation to university employment. One such definition is:

> Under the **tenure systems** adopted as internal policy by many universities and colleges, especially in the United States and Canada, tenure is associated with more senior job titles such as Professor and Associate Professor. A junior professor will not be promoted to such a tenured position without demonstrating a strong record of published research, teaching, and administrative service. Typical systems (such as the Recommended Institutional Regulations on Academic Freedom and Tenure[1]) allow only a limited period to establish such a record, by limiting the number of years that any employee can hold a junior title such as Assistant Professor. (An institution may also offer other academic titles that are not time-limited, such as Lecturer, Adjunct Professor, or Research Professor, but these positions do not carry the possibility of tenure and are said to be "off the tenure track.")

Academic tenure is primarily intended to guarantee the right to academic freedom: it protects teachers and researchers when they dissent from prevailing opinion, openly disagree with authorities of any sort, or spend time on unfashionable topics. Thus academic tenure is similar to the lifetime tenure that protects some judges from external pressure. Without job security, the scholarly community as a whole might favor "safe" lines of inquiry. The intent of tenure is to allow original ideas to be more likely to arise, by giving scholars the intellectual autonomy to investigate the problems and solutions about which they are most passionate, and to report their honest conclusions. In economies where higher education is provided by the private sector, tenure also has the effect of helping to ensure the integrity of the grading system. Absent tenure, professors could be pressured by administrators to issue higher grades for attracting and keeping a greater number of students. (http://en.wikipedia.org /wiki/Tenure)

For the purpose of this book, tenure is referred to as:

That condition attained by a faculty member through highly competent scholarly activities which assures the faculty member security of employment and immunity from reprisals or threats due to an intellectual position or belief which may be unpopular and which guarantees annual reappointment for the faculty member until voluntary resignation, retirement, or removal for adequate cause. (Office of Institutional Planning and Research–UF Factbook: Glossary. (n.d.). Office of Institutional Planning and Research. Retrieved August 20, 2010, from: http://ir.ufl.edu/factbook/glossary.htm#N-W)

In higher education, tenure is an honor one receives with much hard work and dedication in a field of study. Not only does the receipt of tenure offer academic freedom, but job security is often associated with this element. This chapter will focus on promotion and tenure and what is involved in the process. Whether you accept a position at a university that has focus on research, teaching, or research and teaching, tenure will be an important accomplishment to achieve in furthering your career. When does tenure occur? How do you prepare? What do you submit? What is the process? The answers to these questions and many more about documenting the work that you do can be found in this chapter. However, keep in mind that this chapter provides general answers to many frequently asked questions, but it is always best to refer to your universities specific policies and procedures regarding tenure and promotion.

When Does Promotion and Tenure Occur?

When does promotion and tenure occur? At some institutions tenure and promotion are not necessarily received together. However, it is a common thread to see new faculty members applying for tenure and promotion simultaneously. In fact, at some institutions faculty members must apply for tenure and promotion simultaneously. Promotion and tenure are typically awarded at the end of your sixth year as a faculty member, but the process is actually communicated as a seven-year process. It is common for your promotion and tenure portfolio to be submitted for review approximately five and a half years after you begin your faculty position. It then takes time to be reviewed at multitude of levels and the decision on whether to award or not award promotion and tenure happens at the end of your sixth year. We must also note that it is not a guarantee that you will remain in your current position when it is time to submit your materials for promotion and tenure. Yearly evaluations may necessitate your leaving the university if you do not satisfactorily perform in the areas of teaching, research, and service.

The time prior to being promoted and tenured is often termed a probationary period. Faculty members in this stage in their career are often referred to as junior faculty members. At most institutions, during this time your contracts for employment will be completed annually and each year there will be a reappointment decision made on your progress. Reappointment decisions can either be positive (reappointment) or negative (nonreappointment). If a faculty member is not making sufficient progress toward promotion and tenure, a reappointment decision can be denied, which means you will not be reappointed for the upcoming year and will have to find other employment. Typically, contracts at universities have a clause which allows you to continue to work at your institution for one year after a denial of tenure and promotion. This one-year period provides the faculty member time to look for other employment. Although this is an option, many faculty members choose to leave at the end of the semester to avoid feeling alienated or placing oneself in a difficult work environment. The fact that faculty members are denied tenure and promotion only reinforces the need to begin to focus on research, teaching, and service as soon you arrive at your institution. It also validates the need to continuously document your progress. Five or six years is often perceived to be a long time away, but as you know, "time flies" and promotion and tenure will be upon you quite rapidly. We have previously discussed, and would like to reiterate, the importance of being current with your activities so you will be prepared when it is time to submit your materials for promotion and tenure.

It is very important that you know exactly when you will be going up for promotion and tenure. There is an exact date you will submit your materials for promotion and tenure and more than likely this cannot be changed or modified unless there is a special circumstance like a medical leave or an extreme circumstance that would warrant "stopping the clock" in the process. For example, a faculty member may have to leave the country for a family situation and the clock (five and a half year process) may be stopped and restarted again upon their return with proper authorization from the institution. In some cases, a faculty member may go up for promotion and tenure early, but this happens less frequently. An example of when this might occur is if a faculty member brings in years of experience from another institution and negotiates an early promotion and tenure date during the offer letter process. Another reason for a faculty member to seek early tenure and promotion is if their specific record of scholarly activity exceeds the minimum requirements for tenure and promotion and is deemed exceptional in nature. However, early tenure and promotion is not the norm and faculty members should prepare to follow the published timelines for tenure and promotion.

Preparation for Promotion and Tenure

Obviously, promotion and tenure are significant aspects of employment as a faculty member in higher education. From the section above, you should already understand that every year a decision will be made on whether to renew your contract or not leading up to your promotion and tenure date. This reiterates the importance of making progress every year in the areas of teaching, research, and service. If you are not reappointed, challenges may be encountered as you seek employment at other institutions. Your future employer will want references and may question why you are leaving your current faculty position. Having to leave an institution for failure to appropriately achieve and make progress is not something that is lightly dismissed by future employers. Faculty do leave prior to promotion and tenure for many reasons (i.e., family reasons, not a good fit, and personal issues), but leaving because you were not reappointed could lay the foundation to some negative consequences in the job search process.

What all this means is, from day one, it is important to get off on the right foot in the areas of teaching, research, and service so that each year you will receive positive reviews towards promotion and tenure. This does not mean that you have to be outstanding in each area right away, but you should be making progress in all three areas. We recommend you speak with your faculty mentor, other colleagues, and your department chair often to help you prepare your career and supporting materials. Do not be afraid to ask questions, get clarifications, or get guidance if you are unaware or unsure of something. You are not expected to know every detail about the policies and procedures nor are you expected to advance through the promotion and tenure process without guidance and support, but you do need to be proactive. Again, remember that you were initially hired because the department chair, search committee, and other faculty felt you could be successful.

In Chapter 7 we highlighted how you can document your progress and in Chapters 4, 5, and 6 we highlighted the critical areas in which you will be evaluated. It is now up to you to get involved in all three areas according to the specific requirements that meet your institutions expectations. You should also be progressively improving in all areas as you move toward promotion and tenure. It seems like a long time (five and a half years), but the time goes quickly and if you wait too long to begin your work, you may find it difficult to be successful. The process itself is to give you the opportunity to show those individuals involved in the evaluation process that you are worthy of being promoted and tenured and that you are an asset to your institution in the areas of teaching, research, and service.

What Do You submit for Promotion and Tenure?

Preparing for promotion and tenure takes years of hard work and when it is time to apply for this honor/accomplishment, you need to be aware of what needs to be submitted to support your work. Depending on your institution, what you submit may vary somewhat, but in most cases, you will be required to submit some type of tenure and promotion portfolio. The portfolio could contain the following items: (a) an application packet; (b) copies of previous performance letters; (c) your most current vitae; (d) personal statements addressing teaching, research and service; (e) a value statement; and (f) supporting documentation. See Table 8.1 for a list of common materials and their descriptions.

It is very important that you are aware of what materials need to be submitted for promotion and tenure. We suggest you work with your faculty mentor very closely on this and request that he/she has his/her portfolio during your meeting so that you can view it. Included in his/her portfolio will be the same documents that you will need to submit. For instance, you might be able to see the format and structure of the teaching, research, and service statements. Table 8.2 provides a Sample Teaching Statement for Promotion and Tenure that might be similar to the one that you view in your mentor's portfolio.

Some departments may also have examples you can view and your department evaluation committee might also provide you with feedback on your portfolio prior to its submission. Preparing a high quality portfolio takes an enormous amount of time so do not procrastinate and attempt to pull it together at the last minute. Check your campus offerings when you begin to develop your portfolio. Many times universities offer workshops or supports available on your campus (possibly during the summer) to help faculty prepare for promotion and tenure. These activities will help you develop and organize your portfolio and accompanying materials. If these types of workshops or support are not available, we urge you to start putting your materials together in the summer months when your workload might be less time consuming. This will give you plenty of time to develop and revise your materials and elicit feedback from your faculty mentor, other colleagues, or your department chair. These materials need to be organized carefully and professionally as they will be a reflection of the quality of work you produce.

Table 8.1
COMMON PROMOTION AND TENURE PORTFOLIO MATERIALS

Materials	*Description*
Application Packet	There are usually university forms that need to be filled out to accompany your materials. Make sure you have the most current version of these forms.
Copies of previous Performance Letters	Copies of previous performance appraisals (your yearly evaluations) should be included. If you have misplaced them, you can usually get copies from you department chair.
Vitae	Your most current vitae documenting all that you have done in the areas of teaching, research, and service should be included.
Teaching Personal Statement	A personal statement from you about your teaching will probably be required. This should focus on your philosophy of teaching, what you have done in the area of teaching over the five and a half years while at your institution, and why your work in teaching warrants you being promoted and tenured.
Research Personal Statement	A personal statement from you about your research will probably be required. This should focus on your research record, what you have done in the area of research over the five and a half years while at your institution, and why your work in research warrants you being promoted and tenured.
Service Personal Statement	A personal statement from you about your service will probably be required. This should focus on your service record, what you have done in the area of service over the five and a half years while at your institution, and why your work in service warrants you being promoted and tenured.
Value Statement	Typically at the end, a summary statement tying teaching, research, and service should be included that addresses your total worth and value to your institution.
Documentation	Also to be included are any materials to support the work you have done in the areas of teaching, research, and service.

Table 8.2
SAMPLE TEACHING STATEMENT FOR PROMOTION AND TENURE

A. TEACHING ACTIVITIES: Write a narrative either at the beginning or end of your listing that states why you think these activities are worthy of tenure and promotion.

I believe that my performance in the classroom as an instructor, my work with students on dissertation and thesis committees, and my contributions to program and curriculum development merit my approval for tenure and promotion. In addition to supporting materials, I have included a summary statement which supports my contributions which align with the Department's long-range goals.

Instruction

I feel fortunate to have had the opportunity to teach students at the undergraduate, master, and doctoral level. I have taught 11 courses since joining the faculty of _____ University: SED 101–The Exceptional Learner; SED 202–Effective Collaboration and Teaching Exceptional and Diverse Learners II; SED 380–Transition from School to Adult Life; SED 383–Developing and Implementing Alternative Curriculum (6 credit hours); SED 440–Critical Issues in Special Education; SED 451–Facilitating Student Directed Transition Planning; SED 453–Interagency and Postsecondary Resources; SED 455–Facilitating Employment Outcomes for Individuals with Disabilities; SED 493.11–Workshop Course, Introduction to Transition Planning (1 credit hour); and SED 522–Grant Writing in Education. I had responsibility for developing and initially implementing five of those courses (451, 453, 455, 457, and 522) and I was on the course team which developed and initially implemented 383. I have continued to increase the integration of technology into my courses and am now offering hybrid courses that incorporate video lectures, online group projects, and substantive group and individual reflection activities.

In 2005, I received the University's Teaching Initiative Award in recognition of my commitment to and accomplishments in teaching. My ratings as an instructor have been consistently high. Students' ratings indicate in particular that they feel I have a thorough knowledge of the subjects I teach, have high expectations of them, provide opportunities for them to apply materials, and encourage their participation. Summary tables of students' ratings of my teaching are included in my documentation. Students' have also provided valuable written feedback for me. They frequently express appreciation for the practical nature of projects in my courses, my ability to communicate the importance of the content, my knowledge, and my enthusiasm and assistance. Comments reflecting these themes include:

I appreciate how the projects were actually useful for my students and there was direct benefit to them. _____ had a great deal of energy and passion for this topic. (SED 451, on-campus)

continued

Table 8.2–*Continued*

_____ *knows the material and does an excellent job teaching it and making known its importance. Everything in the class was relevant to our future careers. I enjoyed it a lot. (SED 383)*

Through SED 383 with _____ I was extremely challenged with both the content of the class and the projects. She had very high expectations and that made me want to try hard to achieve them. She knew so much about the content and answered all questions very detailed. She helped me when I struggled through a concept and encouraged extra practice. I really learned a lot from the class. (SED 383)

I thought the instructor did an excellent job with tasks, assignments given that can be implemented immediately in my classroom. As a result of the class, I fell that the program and students I work with will benefit from the knowledge I have gained. I would encourage the same type of assignments for future classes. (SED 453, on-campus)

Student feedback is important to me. I strive for continuous improvement of my courses so that I can more effectively assist practicing and future teachers in developing their competencies and leadership abilities. I use feedback from course evaluations and less formal procedures during the semester to make adjustments within a particular section and in future semesters.

Transition Specialist Advanced Certificate Program

One of my proudest accomplishments in teaching is the development and implementation of the graduate level Transition Specialist Learning Behavior Specialist II Advanced Certificate program. This program assists teachers in developing as leaders in supporting the transition of youth with disabilities from school to successful adult lives. The need for personnel who specialize in providing transition services is significant, as indicated by recent national studies that suggest that young adults with disabilities continue to lag behind their nondisabled peers in accessing postsecondary education, achieving quality employment outcomes, living independently, establishing financial security, and maintaining satisfactory social lives. While there has been a call nationally for training for transition specialists, the program at the University is the only active program in the state of _____. I have sole responsibility for recruitment and delivery of this program.

In 2005, I recruited the first group of campus students to take the four-course sequence. In January 2006, I recruited a second group from _____, to complete the coursework. In May 2007, 17 students completed the program. Several of those teachers went on to become the first individuals to receive advanced teaching certification as Transition Specialists from the State Board of Education. In Spring 2007, I recruited a new cohort. With limited recruitment effort, we received 35 high quality applications to the program. The current cohort includes 18 teachers from across the state of _____. I continue to answer telephone calls and emails from other teachers interested in enrolling in the program. There is clearly a need and a desire for this program.

Table 8.2–*Continued*

I am the sole faculty member responsible for implementing these courses. As such, I developed reading schedules, learning activities, and eight portfolio pieces for these four courses. I have used a widely respected model of transition services delivery to translate the individual courses into a comprehensive and cohesive program of study. I travelled to Lake County monthly from January 2006 to June 2007 to deliver instruction to that cohort, and I steadily increased my use of technology to provide off-campus students greater opportunities to network and learn from each other. I expanded my use of WebCT each semester and am now developing online modules that integrate video lectures, cooperative learning through discussions and application activities, and individual reflections on practice. I believe my efforts to integrate technology have resulted in increased program accessibility throughout the state without sacrificing critical opportunities for practicing teachers to learn from each other. I am also assuming responsibility for collecting data and preparing reports on this program for our upcoming NCATE review.

I approach graduate coursework as an opportunity to assist practicing teachers to develop into change agents in their schools. I respect the skill and knowledge they have and strive to find new ways to help them further develop. I was proud to have three of the recent program graduates present at a national conference in October to discuss how they have influenced change since enrolling in the courses and how the program structure facilitated their development as change agents.

Undergraduate Cohort

I am also proud of innovative work I have conducted in our undergraduate program. In the 2004–2005 academic year, I collaborated with two other faculty members to integrate 13 credit hours of coursework and clinical experiences for students in the semester before their Field-Based semester. We integrated the curriculum for SED 245.12, the students' first clinical experience in which they spend two full days in schools as well as time in a seminar; SED 204, an instructional strategies course; and SED 383, a curriculum development course. The content of the courses was woven together to assist students in making clearer connections among the various components of teaching practice. We co-taught these courses to one cohort of students each semester. The scholarship activities we completed through this project resulted in data-based decision-making on course delivery in our Learning and Behavior Specialist students' practicum semester. The resulting new program structure involves blocking SED 245.12 and SED 383, and delivering those courses through various models of co-teaching.

Thesis/Dissertation Committees

I am currently co-adviser with Dr. _____ for Special Education doctoral candidate _____ dissertation entitled, *An investigation of the outcomes of students receiving services in an inner city school.* I am currently advisor for two Master's students completing their thesis research. _____ is conducting a study entitled, *College*

continued

Table 8.2–*Continued*

---

freshmen's perceptions on the transition from high school to college, and _____ is conducting a study entitled, *Teachers' perceptions of transition services: An examination of the impact of two capacity-building strategies.* All three of these projects have anticipated completion dates of May 2008. I am also currently co-chairing the dissertation committee for _____, a doctoral candidate in Special Education. She is currently developing her dissertation proposal for research on teachers' perceptions of assistive technology integration for students with disabilities in general education settings. I look forward to advising additional dissertations and theses in the future.

In addition to advisement, I have had the opportunity to work on dissertation and thesis committees in both SED and Educational and Administration Foundations. Listed below are students who have completed or are in the process of completing their projects.

_____, Ed.D., Special Education, *The reliability and validity of the Supports Intensity Scale,* May 2003

_____, Ed.D., Special Education, *Secondary special education teachers' perspectives and self-reported practices related to the self-determination skills of high school students with disabilities,* August, 2007

_____, M.S., Special Education, *Student attendance: Causes, effects, and interventions,* May 2007

Independent Studies, Honors Projects, Student Research

I have advised five students on in-course honors projects and co-advised four students on an honors independent study. In-course honors projects have included examinations and comparisons of the values and services of differing vocational agencies for adults with developmental disabilities (_____, SED 380, Fall 2002); an examination and analysis of the implementation of best practices at five IEP meetings for high school youth with disabilities (_____, SED 380, Spring 2003); implementation of person-centered planning activities and development of transition planning recommendations for a high school student with multiple disabilities (_____, SED 380, Spring 2003); implementation of a comprehensive assistive technology evaluation with a reflection on the implications for curriculum adaptation and development (_____, SED 383, Fall 2004); and an analysis of interviews of low-income parents of students with disabilities, development of recommendations for improving services to these parents, and a reflection on the influence of culture in on the transition needs of families (_____, SED 383, Fall 2005). I have also been pleased to present with four graduate students at national conferences, including presenting with _____ at the 2005 Council for Exceptional Children conference and presenting with _____, _____, and _____ at the 2007 Division of Career Development and Transition conference.

Table 8.2–*Continued*

Other Teaching Activities and Accomplishments

I have been actively involved with CTLT since joining the ISU faculty. I have attended numerous training sessions and symposia sponsored by CTLT. I have been pleased to be able to contribute to those sessions as well. In October of this year, I was one of four faculty members chosen for the initial implementation of Making Teaching Visible, CTLT's new program focused on providing faculty members with opportunities to observe their colleagues' teaching and to have reflective discussions after teaching sessions. I opened my classroom twice for visitors to observe my teaching and will now work with CTLT staff to discuss how this program may be improved and expanded in future semesters. I also have presented at two CTLT events. I co-presented *Integrating coursework and early clinical experiences in a teacher education program: Lessons learned from a one-year pilot* at the January 2006 symposium, and I was on the panel presenting *Developing a teaching portfolio* at the May 2006 University Teaching Workshop.

Summary of Teaching

In summary, I believe I have excelled in this area and that I have earned the approval of tenure and promotion in regard to teaching. I have been a successful instructor in multiple courses and received university recognition of my teaching accomplishments. I have made significant contributions to curriculum development and successfully developed and implemented a graduate-level advanced certificate program that is the only one of its kind operating in Illinois. I have mentored students on graduate research and included students in national presentations. I believe that my teaching accomplishments are important contributions to the long-range goals of the Department.

Note: Permission obtained from faculty member to reprint.

This may appear to be a simplistic statement, but make sure you edit and proofread all of your materials prior to submitting them for review. It is evident to the evaluation committee that you dedicated little time to preparing your materials when the promotion and tenure packet you submitted consists of multiple errors. See Appendix G for a Sample Promotion and Tenure Packet.

What are the Procedures and Timelines for Promotion and Tenure?

You have already learned that you will be submitting your materials to be considered for promotion and tenure about five and a half years after you begin your faculty appointment. Your materials will go through many different levels of review and these will be explained in the following text. The first group of individuals to see your promotion and tenure materials will be your department evaluation committee (often referred to as Departmental Promotion and Tenure Committee (DPTAC)). This is often the same committee that evaluates the yearly annual performance portfolios. These portfolios are typically submitted to the department committee in late October to early November. Pending a positive review at the department level, which usually occurs in December, the portfolio will then go to a college evaluation committee where again, it will be evaluated. The college evaluation committee will then evaluate the materials and their decision is typically made by January. If the review is positive, the next step is to forward the materials to the Provost. At the Provost's level, two different actions can be taken. The Provost can review the materials and make a decision, or he/she may send the portfolio out for an external review.

At some institutions, promotion and tenure materials are sent out for an external review in addition to the internal review conducted by your institution. Someone in your field or a number of people in your field with expertise in an area related to your area of study are asked to review your materials to see if they feel you have earned the right to be promoted and tenured. This step is critical if there are limited individuals in your field who know the distribution and acceptance rates of journals or the value of a specific award or recognition you may have received in your field. This external review process can also be implemented at or around the college level before the materials go to the Provost.

It depends on the institution, but if external reviewers are elicited, their feedback may be incorporated with internal feedback to help make an overall decision. After materials are reviewed by the Provost, they advance to the President who communicates the decision with the Board of Trustees. If the Board of Trustees approves the recommendation, then the President will send you confirmation of promotion and tenure around mid-May (dependent upon the meeting date of the Board of Trustees). At some institutions, a letter is sent to the submitting faculty member at every stage of the process. Meaning, you may receive a letter from the provost stating he or she recommended you to the president or from the president stating he or she recommended you to the Board of Trustees. If you have received positive yearly performance evaluations, have increased your productivity in the areas of teaching, research, and service, and have properly documented all that you have done with support, you should be very successful in the promotion and tenure process.

Although not previously discussed in this book, at some institutions, collegiality is considered an element in tenure and promotion. Often this element receives a lesser weighting, but it is clear that many faculty members were denied promotion and tenure based on collegiality issues. When this occurs, it is often at the departmental level where the recommendation stems and the faculty member is typically aware and has been notified on various occasions that an issue in the area of collegiately exists. When speaking of collegiality, we are referring to professional collegiality. This term should not be confused with faculty members not "liking" a specific person. An area often addressed in collegially includes failure to communicate, collaborate, or participate in events with other faculty members. In some cases, this issue occurs when you are not on campus and the members of DPTAC do not know who you are. Just a word of caution, don't get to wrapped up in your efforts to be successful that you fail to support others, accept feedback from tenured faculty members, or disregard your role as a team member in your department.

What Happens if You Are Denied Promotion and Tenure?

In the unfortunate event that you are denied promotion and tenure, there are a couple options to consider. One option is to immediately leave your institution and look for employment elsewhere. The problem with this choice is that often the decision on tenure and promotion is made in early May, leaving you less than ample time to secure another job as a faculty member at a different institution. Typically, faculty searches are conducted in late fall and early spring so the opportunities at this time of the year are limited. However, it is not impossible to secure a job at this time. We only warn that positions may be limited. You could, however, possibly find employment somewhere as an adjunct professor, instructor, or clinical professor.

Your second option is to continue working at your current institution for one more year while you search for a new faculty position (if this is in your university's guidelines). Though it may be uncomfortable for you to continue working at your institution knowing you did not get promoted or tenured, this option allows you to continuing earning an income while seeking another faculty position. In many cases, it also guarantees that you continue with health and dental benefits while searching for another position.

Your third option is to appeal the promotion and tenure decision. There should be a committee on your campus and a procedure you can follow to appeal the decision made regarding your case. For example, the committee may be called the Faculty Review Committee, which would be responsible for considering appeals on promotion and tenure decisions. It is very uncommon for decisions to be overturned, but this committee will hear appeals, reevaluate the promotion and tenure portfolio and materials, and evaluate if the decision made was fairly and was justified. Obviously, no one wants to be put into this position, which is why we urge you to work hard, develop a plan, follow that plan, communicate effectively with others, get involved when opportunities arise, follow through on your commitments, and document all the work that you do so you are successfully promoted and tenured. If you do choose to appeal the decision, have your documentation organized and be prepared to submit a formal appeal which specifically addresses why you feel the decision should be overturned.

> *I was devastated. I knew that my reviews indicated that I was struggling with meeting the expectations for tenure and promotion, but at the last minute, I felt like I had pulled it together and was confident that I would get tenure. When I did not, I felt betrayed. Once the initial feelings of disappointment and anger (yes, I was angry) passed, I started to evaluate why I didn't do what was so clearly laid out for me to accomplish. What I finally realized was that I didn't like to write. I didn't really enjoy writing in college and why I took a job at a university that required a high level of publications is beyond me. What I found out after soul searching was that I loved the teaching part. I wanted to be a teacher and now, a few years later, here I am teaching at a junior college and loving it. This decision to leave a four-year university (Okay, I was forced to leave by my actions) was the best event that could have occurred!*

Conclusion

The information in this chapter highlighted the promotion and tenure process you will go through as a faculty member at your institution. We believe it is very important that you are aware of all the details and procedures involved with promotion and tenure so that you have the best possible opportunity to be successful. This chapter began by discussing when promotion and tenure typically occurs at most institutions of higher education. Next, the preparation for promotion and tenure was described. The materials that need to be submitted as part of the promotion and tenure process were then explained and the procedures and timelines for this process were highlighted. Lastly, possible options for you to consider and contemplate if you should not be awarded promotion and tenure were addressed.

We have no intent of trying to present the tenure and promotion process as a negative one, but we want you to be aware that this process is serious and failure to follow the proper procedure can impact the decision of the committee. Promotion and tenure are important for you to earn and your institution will only award this highly prestigious advancement to those who are deserving of such an honor. You need to be involved and show growth and maturity in the areas of teaching, research, and service and your materials need to reflect your work. You cannot be passive in this process. To be successful with promotion and tenure you need to be actively involved in all aspects of this process because your career will be greatly impacted by the outcome.

Faculty Tips about Promotion and Tenure

• The main thing for me was juggling teaching load and writing. You really have to discipline yourself not just to focus on teaching. It is exciting to be a scholar, make sure you take advantage of the opportunity.

• Promotion and tenure credentials cannot be developed in a year. Make a long-term plan for success and stick to it.

• Work with tenured faculty to find out expectations and how they prepared themselves for promotion and tenure.

Chapter 9

CREATING A HARMONY
FOR BEING SUCCESSFUL

As you have probably already figured out, being a faculty member can be a very time consuming process. There is no doubt that there are always projects that need to be developed, maintained, or completed. Knowing that you need to focus on teaching, research, and service each year, as well as over time, can be overwhelming. We have both been in your situation and have experienced all that you will experience. It is important to grow and develop in these three areas. Recognizing this is the first step to becoming successful. However, we also know that work can easily consume every aspect of your life. The ultimate goal of earning promotion and tenure can become your only focus. How do you find time to do everything? How will everything get done? Will you be successful enough for promotion and tenure? What can you do to make sure that work is not your only focus? This chapter will discuss and highlight ways that you can create a harmony for being successful so that you are still able to enjoy life (i.e., outside activities, sporting events, hobbies, quiet time, and family and friends) and still accomplish all that you need to do in the areas of teaching, research, and service toward a successful promotion and tenure.

Find Your Niche

Every faculty member has a place and role within his/her department and you will, too. It will be important for you to find out what your specific role will become. What role will you play in your department? What can you do to best serve your department? What should your focus be? How can you best serve the department in the areas of teaching, research, and service and at the same time advance your record and productivity? This is not something that anyone will probably directly tell you nor will it be something you can just look up, but it is something that you will eventually need to figure

Table 9.1
POSSIBLE AREAS TO CONSIDER AS A FOCUS

Teaching
> Curriculum Design and Revision
> Universal Design for Learning (UDL)
> Response to Intervention (RTI)
> Instructional Technology

Research
> Research Design
> Research Methodology
> Single Subject Research
> Statistical Analyses

Service
> Outreach in the Community
> State or National Legislation
> Professional Development Schools
> University/School Partnerships

out. You may elicit some feedback from your faculty mentor, colleagues on your course instructional team, the department chair, or others to help guide you, but ultimately, it is up to you to find your niche. See Table 9.1 for some possible areas that you might consider exploring in the future.

Table 9.1 is not a cumulative list but rather a starting point. If you have an area of interest that you are also knowledgeable in, consider how you may use this skill or knowledge to help others. Using your skills to help others is a great way to establish new relationships with other faculty that may lead to future projects that could benefit both you and them. If other faculty members see that you are passionate about a specific area or topic, that you are a hard worker, are diligent, and follow through with tasks, they will be more likely to consider including you in their own projects or activities. Remember, you can earn credit by producing products individually as well as collaboratively, but typically more work can get accomplished if it is spread out among others while everyone receives credit.

We also suggest you really consider incorporating teaching, research, and service in your thought processes, if at all possible. What we mean by this is that all of these components could fit together if planned properly, leading to productivity in all three areas at once. For example, a research project of yours may focus on how teachers use technology in their teaching. This information could easily be implemented in the courses you are teaching. In addition, this information may help you plan some workshops or in-services for local schools to help their teachers build their technology skills for their own teaching. You have now completed one project that impacts all three areas. You can attack each area individually, but working smarter is always beneficial and less time consuming. Believe us, you will be busy as it is, so anyway you can streamline the process will benefit yourself and your career.

Focus on your Strengths

Another way to help you find harmony is to focus on your strengths. This does not mean that you should not strive to learn new things or become involved in new areas of research, but we suggest at the beginning of your career, when you are a new faculty member, that you stay within your comfort zone. What are your existing strengths? What do you already know? What skills do you possess? We urge you to think about the knowledge, skills, and experiences that you possess and focus your time and energies in developing those areas and directions. For example, given your area of expertise, you should be requesting courses to teach that will match that knowledge and skill sets. You should be hesitant to teach courses outside your knowledge base or experience level your first year. Starting a new faculty position will pose enough challenges without adding courses to teach that contain unfamiliar content. Maybe after a year or two, you might want a new challenge and begin to teach courses that offer content outside your comfort zone, but at the beginning of your career, you should focus on performing acceptably in courses in which you are familiar.

This concept holds true for research as well. Try to publish your dissertation if you have not already, build upon the research you have already conducted, focus on what you know and your experiences. It is important that you begin to establish your research record and focus on your strengths and what you know is the most effective and efficient way to proceed in this area. There is time to try new things, address new topics, and conduct research on areas outside your main focus, but at the beginning of your career, you should try to focus on establishing a line of research and developing your area of expertise.

Lastly is the area of service and the same items we have previously mentioned apply to this area as well. You should know that you need to get involved in service activities inside and outside your institution, but do so only in areas that will benefit you and will expand your knowledge and skill sets. New service opportunities will often become available to you so you need to be sure to effectively balance your time and energy. Before you become involved or say "yes" to an opportunity, try to remember that with every opportunity there is an expected level of commitment that involves a specific amount of dedicated time. If the work involved matches what you know and the skills you possess, it will take less effort and possibly a lower level of time commitment. If the work involved does not match your knowledge and skills, however, more time and effort will be needed to accomplish this work. Make careful decisions about what you participate in as this will ultimately lead to either a positive or possibly a negative experience for you. Also, feel free to seek advice or feedback from your faculty mentor, other colleagues, or the department chair on these matters as they can offer you some great insights into these matters as well as most things related to workload.

Be Realistic

You will probably have many different opportunities that will arise for you in the areas of teaching, research, and service so one thing we suggest you do is to try and be realistic. You will not be successful if you say "yes" to every opportunity that comes your way. We have seen faculty members do this and soon they find themselves overwhelmed with responsibilities. Opportunities will arise in all research, teaching, and service activities so do not feel you have to do everything at once and say "yes" to every opportunity that arises.

> *My first semester I felt like everyone kept asking me to help them with projects and to serve on committees. I didn't want anyone to think I wasn't a team player and said yes to every opportunity presented to me. At the end of the semester I was snowed under. I couldn't keep up with my teaching or writing because I was so busy trying to finish up the things I had committed to. Luckily for me, my program coordinator recognized what was happening and helped me to prioritize and to get myself out from under all the additional projects I had agreed to participate in.*

One of the biggest challenges you will face is the ability to say "no." You need to know that this is an acceptable response and others will accept this answer; just make sure you elaborate on your response. For example, "I would really like to participate on this research project with you; however, right now I am too busy to do the type of quality work I know you would want, but if you have other opportunities in the future, please keep me in mind and I would love to collaborate with you." You will probably feel there is enough pressure on you to perform highly in the areas of teaching, research, and service without you putting more pressure on yourself. We have seen faculty take on more than they could handle and the pressure to get everything done is their undoing. They have taken on so much that they have overwhelmed themselves and actually do not get anything completed because of lack of time.

You need to make sure that you are realistic and that you set reasonable expectations for yourself. Communication is the key; if you find yourself getting stuck or having problems in a research project, you need to communicate with those you are collaborating with. If done early enough, usually the difficulties you are experiencing can be resolved. One thing that might help you is to develop an agenda or plan of where you are and where you would like to be in the future. You can also try to detail how you expect to get there. We discuss this in more detail in Chapter 5 in regard to research. You might expand and develop that plan to incorporate teaching and service. In addition to this plan, you might also have a listing of all the things you are currently working on as well as future projects. See Table 9.2 for a listing of projects and how they relate to one another.

Table 9.2
ORGANIZATION OF PROJECTS AND ACTIVITIES
IN TEACHING, RESEARCH, AND SERVICE

Teaching	Research	Service
Technology Course (in process)	PowerPoint Study (analyzing data)	PowerPoint Workshops (in process)
	iTouch Study (in process)	iTouch Workshop (in development)
	Technology Survey (in development)	
	Technology and Students With Autism (an idea)	
Research Course (in process)	Dissertation Committee Member	Action Research Workshop (in process)
	Master's Committee Member	
	Statistician for Colleague (in process)	

If you look at Table 9.2, you will see that this person is already pretty busy. To take on another project might jeopardize the projects he is already involved with. He may not, however, really be aware of all he is doing and where in the process he is with everything if he did not have a plan or chart to document his commitments. A documentation chart is fairly easy to develop, yet it is a worthwhile in helping faculty, new or old, monitor their levels of involvement in various activities and projects. Obviously, when you agree to be involved in a project, there is an expectation that you will be performing a specified amount of the work.

Following through on your word is very important for a faculty member, especially a new one. You might have heard the phrase "first impressions last a lifetime." Well, in academia, this can be true. If you are involved in a project and do everything you were asked to do and met all of the timelines, you will probably be asked to participate again in the future. On the other hand, if you are involved in a project and do not complete your assigned work or it is not completed in a timely fashion, you may not be asked again in the future to participate. What you do and how you perform is very important and this is another reason for you to be aware of all that you are involved in so that you can make very educated decisions about your involvement in future projects. The ability to follow through with projects and produce high quality work can and will impact your future and your growth and development towards promotion and tenure.

Having a good work ethic is very important whether it is individual or collaborative. If working on an individual project, you want to make sure you get the project completed in a timely fashion. We spoke previously about this in Chapter 3 in regard to setting up a timeline for how the different parts of a research project would get completed from idea development to possible publication. Adhering to these timelines and completing your work in a timely fashion is essential as you progress towards promotion and tenure, especially if you are collecting data in schools or with people. You may have a limited time to collect your data so if you have not accomplished what you need to by the time it needs to be completed, you could lose your opportunity to collect your data. Having a good individual work ethic is essential for success. It will also make your life less hectic when things are accomplished in a timely fashion and you are not always rushing at the last minute. This also applies to collaborative projects. What you do or are doing may impact the work of others. There is nothing worse than having to wait on someone who is holding up the timeline. When you do not finish your individual work, it typically only impacts you, but when you do not finish a piece of a collaborative work, it can affect many people. Having a good overall work ethic, no matter what the project or activity, will not only help you become more successful, but it will probably reduce stress in your life as well.

The last thing we want to mention is that you should feel good about your accomplishments. The work that you will be doing is not easy and you will need to juggle a multitude of projects in trying to mature in all three areas of teaching, research, and service. When you accomplish something, no matter how small, we urge you to feel good about your success and accomplishment. Every semester you should sit back and reflect on all that you have accomplished and done. It could be a student comment from class about your teaching, a presentation at a national conference, or feedback from teachers in a school where you conducted a workshop. It could be many different things, but do not get caught up in doing everything and not realizing all the good things you have done. One way to do this is to go back into your yearly file and just look at everything once in a while. Make sure you enjoy the moment and realize that the hard work you are doing is worthwhile and helping you successfully move toward promotion and tenure.

Often universities have in place a recognition program where departmental accomplishments are announced. For example, your college may produce a newsletter or your alumni association may recognize faculty accomplishments. Most of the time the items they recognize are on a larger scale and it is easy for a faculty member to not feel valued for the less visible accomplishments which support the university. As faculty members, we have seen new faculty deal with frustration about this issue. We encourage you to seriously review this recommendation and make the time to review all the large and small successes you have achieved. Remember that a small success to you may have had a very strong impact on a student, community member, or even another faculty member.

Find a Balance

The last thing to discuss is the ability to find a balance in your life. We suggest you try to find a balance between you as an individual, for work, and for family. It is important for you to find harmony in your life and concentrate on your outside interests. The goal of promotion and tenure can easily consume you as an individual. Wanting to always be better, improve, publish, do service, and so on can be very stressful. At what price, however, is it worth? Obviously we feel this is important or it would not be in this book. We have discussed this from the start of searching for a faculty position to applying for promotion and tenure. Along this path or journey you are on, or are about to take, we emphasize that there are other parts of your life that need the time, energy, and focus that you are putting forth to obtain promotion and tenure.

One area we believe is important is you as an individual. What do you like to do outside of work? What do you enjoy doing? What makes you happy? What is fun to you? What excites you? On an individual basis, you need to do some things for yourself. Build this in to your plan. Whenever you accomplish something, reward yourself. It could be going shopping or going to a movie. It could be taking a trip you always wanted to take. It could be relaxing in a hammock reading a book (nonacademic) that you have been wanting to read, or cooking a nice meal and enjoying the smells and tastes of the food. What you choose to do will be different for every person, but whatever it is, make sure that these things are built into your life plan. We have seen many faculty members come and go and those that are the most successful and well-rounded are those that have a balanced life.

We have spent much time and many different chapters focusing on work and the faculty member progressing towards promotion and tenure. Balance is important here too. You need to find balance between teaching, research, and service. What do you enjoy doing? Where is your passion? What benefits you the most? There will be some things you have a choice about doing and other things that you will have to do. How do you find a balance between all of these things? We have previously spoken about finding your niche and focusing on your strengths. This is important in your world of work so that you can be successful. It is also important to find out how to balance and juggle these three areas. As you begin your new role as a faculty member, it might be a little difficult and overwhelming. Over time, as you personally reflect and with guidance and support from others, we hope you will be able to find what works best for you and what does not.

The last area we want to address, and maybe the most important, is family. Family is often the most important area that we need balance, but also the most overlooked. Often, we see faculty focus on themselves and work, but forget about family. Family is very important and is an area that should not be overlooked. You may have extended family, a wife or husband, and possibly children. Remember that all of these people have needs as well. Make sure that you communicate effectively with them to find out what their needs are. Make sure you give them some of your time because we are sure that they will want it. For example, maybe one of your children is in basketball and all their games are on Tuesday evenings. You might try to get a teaching schedule where you do not teach on Tuesday evenings. You might dedicate your time when you get home until your children go to bed as family time to sit and help with homework, talk about the day's events, and plan for what will happen during the rest of the week. Maybe every Saturday you will vow to not do any work and just do things for your spouse or children or both. What we are trying to say is that your family is important and that to create a harmony in your life, you will need to dedicate some time to them as well. They need to know that they are important to you and that you value them as much as you value yourself and work. You need to be there for them and support them as you have people there for you who support you in your faculty position. Remember, your family is your foundation and that is who you will go home to every evening so make sure they feel happy, important, and valued. Finding a balance is important and we urge you to consider reflecting on this topic each semester. You will find you will be a more well-rounded and productive person in all aspects of your life if you have balance between yourself, work, and family.

Conclusion

The information in this chapter focused on how you could create some type of harmony for being successful as a faculty member as you move towards promotion and tenure. We believe it is very important that you are aware of all the work that you must do to prepare yourself for that day when you submit a portfolio to be evaluated for promotion and tenure. We also feel it is important that you know that having balance in your life is important as well. In addition to work, you must also play and enjoy life. In fact, having fun and experiencing life outside of work can many times rejuvenate or motivate a faculty member to be more productive. This chapter began by discussing how you should find your niche and focus on your strengths (knowledge and skill sets). Next, we addressed being realistic in what you participate in and what you get involved in. Work habits of a successful faculty member were then explained. Lastly, finding a balance between you as an individual, work, and family was addressed. We know you want to be successful in your new position and you want to successfully earn promotion and tenure, but at what cost? We have seen faculty earn these honors and yet find dissatisfaction with the rest of their life. We know that finding a balance to achieve success in both your work environment and home environment takes time and work to accomplish. Just remember, we all need support and guidance and as much as you get as a faculty member you need as an individual and as a member of a family. Do not forget about the various components of your life. If you are able to find a balance in what you do you will have better experiences all around and will be more productive at all levels, including promotion and tenure.

Faculty Tips on Being Successful

- Make sure you are realistic with your aspirations.

- Don't forget to do things for fun outside of work.

- Don't forget about family and friends. Enjoy them and spend time with them. The work will always be there—family and friends might not be.

APPENDICES

APPENDIX A

University Research Grant Application

University Research Grant Program
College of Arts and Sciences
Guidelines and Application Materials
2010–2011
(for awards beginning July 1, 2010)
Instructions for web-based submission can be found at:
http://lilt.ilstu.edu/urg/Default.aspx

This packet contains the following:

1. University Research Grant (URG) Guidelines

2. Explanation of the four URG programs:
   - The **New Faculty Initiative Grant (NFIG)**;
   - The **Pre-tenure Faculty Initiative Grant (PFIG)**;
   - The **Summer Faculty Fellowship (SFF)**; and
   - The **Faculty Research Award (FRA)**

3. Application Cover Sheets
   (Note: There are different cover sheets for each URG program.)

4. Budget Form

5. Professional Outcome Form

Please read all materials before completing your proposal. If you have any questions, please contact the College of Arts and Sciences (438-5669).

RELEVANT DATES:

October 5	In order to ensure that departments have adequate time to review proposals, it is suggested that PFIG, SFF, and FRA applications be due to departments on this date. Departments may choose, however, to set their own due date.
November 2	In order to ensure that departments have adequate time to review proposals, it is suggested that NFIG applications be due to departments on this date. Departments may choose, however, to set their own due date.
November 2	Hard copies of proposals, department rankings and ranking justifications for PFIG, SFF, and FRA applications, with all appropriate signatures, are due to College by 4:00 p.m. All

proposals and departmental rankings and justifications **must** also be uploaded at http://lilt.ilstu.edu/urg/Default.aspx by 4:00 p.m.

November 30   Hard copies of proposals, department rankings and ranking justifications for NFIG applications, with all appropriate signatures, are due to College by 4:00 p.m. All proposals and departmental rankings and justifications **must** also be uploaded at http://lilt.ilstu.edu/urg/Default.aspx by 4:00 p.m.

January 18   College submits its list of faculty awards to the Research and Sponsored Programs Office. Anticipated Professional Outcome Forms and Budget forms for funded URG projects are due to the Research and Sponsored Programs Office.

February 1   Dean announces recipients of FY11 URG awards

July 1   URG award funds available for expenditure, pending release of funds

October 12   Professional Outcome reports for awards in previous fiscal year (2009-2010) due to College

Note: University Research Grant Program Professional Outcome Form–Follow-Up Report. (n.d.). Retrieved October 9, 2010, from: www.cas.ilstu.edu/faculty/committees/docs/POFFormFollowUp.doc

University Research Grant Program College of Arts and Sciences Guidelines and Application Materials 2011–2012. (n.d.). Retrieved October 9, 2010, from: www.cas.ilstu.edu/originals/docs/URGGuidelines.doc

COLLEGE OF ARTS AND SCIENCES
UNIVERSITY RESEARCH GRANT PROGRAM GUIDELINES
2010–2011

Program Description

The College of Arts and Sciences University Research Grant (URG) program exists to:
- Foster research and creative efforts across the College;
- Stimulate development and submission of external grant proposals; and
- Support development of the research and creative programs of new faculty members.

Illinois State University defines as research, "A formal procedure which contributes to the expansion of basic knowledge or applies such knowledge to the solutions of problems in society or exemplifies creative expression in a specific field of study. The results of the research are communicated to professionals outside the university through a peer review process in a manner appropriate to the discipline."

Full-time pre-tenure and tenured CAS faculty members, except for those currently serving on the CAS Research Proposal Review Committee (RPRC), are eligible to apply for University Research Grants.

The URG program includes four grant programs (**NFIG, PFIG, SFF,** and **FRA**) that are designed to work in an incremental and complementary way to support diverse research and creative program development resource needs at different stages of faculty careers.

New Faculty Initiative Grant (NFIG)

New Faculty Initiative Grants (maximum award, $3,500) are designed to support the first stages of research and creative career development at Illinois State University. Offered to faculty members in the first or second year of their appointment at ISU, the NFIG program encourages departmental mentoring to assist applicants in strengthening their proposals. Proposals must be considered meritorious by the Research Proposal Review Committee to receive funding.

Pre-tenure Faculty Initiative Grant (PFIG)

Pre-tenure Faculty Initiative Grants (maximum award, $3,500) support faculty members once in years two through five of their appointment at ISU. Faculty members are encouraged to use PFIG funding to further their research or creative program in their progress toward tenure. The PFIG program encourages departmental mentoring to facilitate production of strong proposals. In addition to the merit of the proposal, however, the College Research Proposal Review Committee will consider the Principal Investigator's (PI) productivity since appointment at ISU in making funding decisions.

Pre-tenure faculty members are eligible to receive one NFIG and one PFIG. After receiving both grants, they must submit a grant/funding proposal to an external fund-

ing organization to become eligible to apply for Summer Faculty Fellowships (SFF) and Faculty Research Awards (FRA).

Summer Faculty Fellowship (SFF)

The Summer Faculty Fellowship (maximum award, $5,000) offers faculty salary support. All tenured faculty members are eligible for this award. Also eligible are pre-tenure faculty members who have received both the NFIG and the PFIG and who have submitted an external grant/funding proposal. These grants are very competitive. Funding decisions are based on proposal quality and the PI's record of published scholarship and grant awards. After receiving an SFF, the PI is ineligible to apply for this grant for one fiscal year following the award. That is, a PI may not apply for another SFF in a fiscal year in which he or she is receiving SFF funding. Furthermore, when applying for SFFs in subsequent years, the PI must provide documentation with each additional SFF proposal that he or she has submitted a new or revised external grant/funding proposal.

Faculty Research Award (FRA)

The Faculty Research Award (maximum award, $3,000) supports research expenses excluding salary for tenured faculty members or pre-tenure faculty members who have received both the NFIG and the PFIG awards and submitted an external grant/funding proposal. Funding decisions are based on proposal quality and the PI's record of published scholarship and grant awards. After receiving one FRA, the PI is ineligible to apply for this grant for one fiscal year following the award. That is, a PI may not apply for another FRA in a fiscal year in which he or she is receiving FRA funding. Furthermore, when applying for FRAs in subsequent years, the PI must provide documentation with each additional FRA proposal that he or she has submitted a new or revised external grant/funding proposal.

College of Arts and Sciences University Research Grant Programs

New Faculty Initiative Grant (NFIG)	Pre-tenure Faculty Initiative Grant (PFIG)
Eligibility: First- or second-year tenure-track faculty members. Faculty members who are awarded an NFIG must hold the terminal degree in their discipline by the time the money is to be awarded. **A faculty member may receive this grant only once.**	***Eligibility:*** Pre-tenure faculty members holding the terminal degree in their discipline who are in years 2–5 of ISU service. **A faculty member may receive this grant only once.**
Costs supported: Salary and/or project expenses.	***Costs supported:*** Salary and/or project expenses.
Maximum award amount: $3,500.	***Maximum award amount:*** $3,500.
Criteria for funding: All meritorious proposals will be supported, subject to availability of funds.	***Criteria for funding:*** All meritorious proposals will be supported, subject to availability of funds.

Accountability: Professional Outcome Form required. *Submission deadline to College:* November 30	*Accountability:* Professional Outcome Form required. *Submission deadline to College:* November 2.
Summer Faculty Fellowship (SFF)	**Faculty Research Award (FRA)**
Eligibility: • Pre-tenure faculty members who have received both NFIG and PFIG awards and submitted an external grant/funding proposal and • Tenured faculty members.	*Eligibility:* • Pre-tenure faculty membes who have received both NFIG and PFIG awards *and* submitted an external grant/funding proposal; and • Tenured faculty members
Sit-out: Faculty members who have received an SFF are ineligible to apply for another SFF for one fiscal year following that award.	*Sit-out:* Faculty members who have received an FRA are ineligible to apply for another FRA for one fiscal year following that award.
External grant requirement: After receiving one SFF, a faculty member must submit a different external grant/funding proposal for each additional SFF for which he or she applies in subsequent years.	*External grant requirement:* After receiving one FRA, a faculty member must submit a different external grant/funding proposal for each additional FRA for which he or she applies in subsequent years.
Costs supported: Faculty salary only.	*Costs supported:* Project expenses *excluding* faculty salary.
Maximum award amount: $5,000. Co-PIs may apply for a joint SFF totaling $10,000.	*Maximum award amount:* $3,000. Co-PIs may apply for a joint FRA totalling $6,000.
Criteria for funding: Highest quality proposals will be funded, subject to availability of funds.	*Criteria for funding:* Highest quality proposals will be funded, subject to availability of funds.
Accountability: Professional Outcome Form required.	*Accountability:* Profesional Outcome Form required.
Submission deadline to College: November 2.	*Submission deadline to College:* November 2.
Note: Applicants may apply concurrently for an FRA for the same or different project if they meet the eligibility requirements for that program.	*Note:* Applicants may apply concurrently for an SFF for the same or different project if they meet the eligibility requirements for that program.

Additional Program Guidelines:

• Co-PIs may apply for URG grants for collaborative projects. Any project in which funds are requested for salary for two or more ISU faculty members is considered a collaborative project. Co-PIs need only submit one proposal for a collaborative SFF project and only one proposal for a collaborative FRA project. In an SFF proposal, the role of each PI must be clearly delineated and justified. In an FRA proposal, the need for additional funds beyond the funds allocated to a single PI must clearly be justified. If a collaborative project is funded, sit out and external grant/funding requirements will apply equally to all PIs. Total award amounts will be determined by the tenure and program eligibility status of each co-PI.

- PIs from the College of Arts and Sciences are encouraged to collaborate with colleagues from other ISU colleges. Each PI must submit a proposal to his/her college's URG program, indicating each PI's contribution to project activities. Funding decisions will be made by each college's dean.

- The URG program will not consider proposals for support of costs associated with faculty development, student research/thesis projects, or travel unrelated to the conduct of original research or creative efforts (e.g., travel to conferences to present results). Equipment requests will be funded only if the equipment is directly and specifically related to the proposal. Ordinarily, requests for computers or technology available from College or departmental resources will not be funded.

- If a faculty member who has been awarded a URG leaves Illinois State University employment prior to the beginning of the award period, s/he will forfeit the award. If a URG recipient leaves Illinois State University employment during the fiscal year of the award, s/he will resign the award and return to the College any money that has already been allocated to him/her.

- Ordinarily, projects supported by external grants will not receive simultaneous support from the URG program. If URG support is needed to *enhance* the scope of an externally funded project, the proposal should clearly describe and justify project components for which URG support is requested.

- PIs may choose the division [Science/Mathematics (A), Social Sciences (B), or Humanities (C)] in which their URG proposal will be evaluated. Methodological considerations should guide this decision.

- For projects involving human or animal subjects, appropriate approval (from IRB or IACUC) must be obtained before research begins.

Professional Outcome Forms

All applicants to the URG program must submit a Professional Outcome Form indicating the anticipated results of the proposed research or creative effort. Results may include (but are not limited to) presentations, publications, manuscript submissions, external grant proposal submissions, or other scholarly outcomes recognized by the applicable academic disciplines. In projecting outcomes, URG applicants should include results likely to occur within one year from the date of the award (July 1).

Outcomes of URG-funded activities are indicated on Professional Outcome Forms submitted in the fiscal year following the award. For an award beginning on July 1, 2010, URG recipients will be required to submit a Professional Outcome Form to the College by October 11, 2011, which identifies all scholarly results of work funded by the grant. Failure to submit the Professional Outcome Form will result in all investigators involved in the URG-funded project being ineligible for further URG competition for a period of five years. Furthermore, URG recipients will be required to submit a second Professional Outcome Form to the College one year after submission of the first Professional Outcome Form to document URG project outcomes not previously completed and reported. This Professional Outcome Form is due to the College on October 10, 2012.

Requests to Review Successful Proposals

Any faculty member may ask to examine successful URG proposals. Requests should be made in writing (hard copy or e-mail) to the Associate Dean for Research Support of the College with a brief explanation of the reason for the request.

Evaluation Criteria

University Research Grant proposals are mentored and receive their initial review at the department level. They are then forwarded for consideration and recommendation to the CAS's RPRC. **Because URG proposals are reviewed by both departmental and College committees, proposals must both demonstrate disciplinary expertise and communicate clearly to the non-specialist reader.** Proposals will be evaluated on the basis of the following criteria:

1. *Clarity of purpose and focus*
   The proposal must clearly articulate a statement of the research or creative effort the applicant intends to undertake.
2. *Significance of research or creative effort*
   With reference to scholarship, the proposal must indicate the need for the proposed work, its significance for the discipline, and the gap in scholarship it will fill.
3. *Objectives of research or creative effort*
   In a manner appropriate to the discipline, the proposal must clearly describe the research or creative objectives. These objectives may be stated as research questions, hypotheses, thesis statements, anticipated conclusions, or projected creative goals, and must be linked to the project's purpose and focus.
4. *Clarity and adequacy of research/creative plan*
   In a manner appropriate to the discipline and–where appropriate–supported by citation of prior literature, the proposal must describe the research or creative plan, methodology, or approach by which project objectives will be achieved. In cases where more than one person will work on a project, the proposal must discuss each person's contribution.
5. *Link between project goals and budget request*
   The budget request, whether for research costs or salary, should be clearly linked to proposed project activities and goals. Successful proposals, especially for the SFF, will clearly describe in the narrative section as well as the budget justification how the requested support will benefit the project.
6. *Adherence to URG guidelines and format*
   All required elements are included and length restrictions are followed. Deviations from guidelines and format requirements may result in disqualification of the proposal.
7. *(For NFIG proposals) Preparation to do proposed work*
   Faculty members applying for NFIG awards must include a one-page Vitae indicating year of terminal degree and publications related to their area of expertise.

8. *(For PFIG proposals) Research and/or creative activity at Illinois State University*
Faculty members applying for PFIG awards must demonstrate scholarly activity since their appointment at ISU.

9. *(For SFF and FRA proposals) Research and/or creative record*
The scholarly record of the applicant will be a significant element in the RPRC's evaluation of the applicant's capacity to complete the research proposed and to disseminate it to an academic audience. In the case of equivalent proposals, the College committee will give preference to applicants with superior records of published scholarship and/or grant awards.

10. *(For FRA proposals for pre-tenure faculty members who have received both an NFIG and a PFIG award, and for tenured faculty members who have received one FRA or one SFF) Proof of submission of a grant/funding proposal to an external funding organization.*
After receipt of a previous URG award, the applicant must include with the URG proposal a copy of the "Blue Sheet" (Proposal Submission Form) accompanying an external grant proposal submitted through the Research and Sponsored Programs Office or a copy of a submission and /or award letter from an external funding agency that did not require RSP processing.

Applicants should also note that all parts of the proposal may be considered by the committee in its evaluation and ranking. This includes the budget and justification, the list of publications and grants, and the Professional Outcome Form.

Format

All of the following items must be submitted, in the order listed, in order for a proposal to be complete.

1. COVER SHEET (form provided): Applicants may ask for review in Group A (Sciences and Mathematics), Group B (Social Sciences), or Group C (Humanities).

2. NARRATIVE: no more than *three pages, single-spaced (1,800 word maximum) for NFIG, PFIG, and SFF programs and two pages, single-spaced (1,200 word maximum) for the FRA program* that shall include:
   A. Abstract: Name, department, and statement (not to exceed 150 words) summarizing the project;
   B. Statement of Need/Significance of Research or Creative Effort: Indicate the problem to be addressed or the need for research/creative effort, together with the significance of the proposed work for the discipline;
   C. Objectives of Research or Creative Effort: In a manner appropriate to the discipline, these should be stated as research questions, hypotheses, or projected outcomes (e.g., for a creative project);
   D. Research or Creative Plan: In a manner appropriate to the discipline, the proposal should make clear how project objectives will be achieved. Approaches to information collection and analyses should be specifically described and linked to project objectives.

The narrative should be written clearly and should be accessible to the general scholarly community. Terms specific to the discipline (jargon) should be avoided where possible or, at a minimum, defined parenthetically.

3. BIBLIOGRAPHY: an optional one-page bibliography of works cited in or supporting the narrative.
4. APPENDIX: an optional one-page appendix providing material (e.g., maps, graphs, other) supporting the narrative.
5. BUDGET PAGE (form provided).
6. BUDGET JUSTIFICATION: One-page explanation of budget items, linking project costs to project activities and goals. If more than one person will be working on the project, the role of each contributor (PIs, graduate assistants, student workers, etc.) must be briefly discussed.
7. PROFESSIONAL OUTCOME FORM (form provided): Indicates anticipated outcomes of project work in terms of research or creative productivity.
8. (**For SFF and FRA proposals**) LIST OF PEER REVIEWED PUBLICATIONS AND EXTERNAL GRANT/FUNDING AWARDS: Each PI should list all peer reviewed publications from the past 10 years (providing full citations in a manner appropriate to the discipline) and all external grant/funding awards (including the funding organization, dates, and award amount). These should be listed by category (e.g., publications, awards).
9. (*For NFIG proposals*) ONE-PAGE VITAE INDICATING YEAR OF TERMINAL DEGREE AND PUBLICATIONS RELATED TO AREA OF EXPERTISE
10. (*For PFIG proposals*) DESCRIPTION OF RESEARCH OR CREATIVE ACTIVITIES SINCE APPOINTMENT AT ISU
11. (*For pretenure faculty who have received both an NFIG and PFIG and who are applying for either an SFF or an FRA or for tenured faculty who have received one FRA and are applying for subsequent FRAs*) EXTERNAL FUNDING SOURCE IDENTIFICATION FORM.

Submission

The suggested date that completed applications should be delivered to the department for departmental review is October 5, 2009 (for PFIG, SFF, and FRA programs) or November 2, 2009 (for the NFIG program). Please ask your department chair about the number of copies you should submit and if you need to upload your proposal at http://lilt.ilstu.edu/urg/Default.aspx. This site will be available to upload URGs for departmental review; Departments can choose whether or not they will utilize the on-line option for departmental review. **At least one hard copy submitted to the department office should have the original signature of the applicant(s).**

Departmental committees will review all proposals from department faculty and provide written feedback to applicants. However, their responsibilities will vary for each program.
- Departmental committees will review and mentor NFIG and PFIG proposals to make certain that those submitted to the RPRC are meritorious.
- Departmental committees will provide substantive written evaluations of each NFIG proposal to the RPRC. Evaluation forms to be used for departmental review are available on the College website. They are listed as evaluation forms under URGs on the CAS A-Z. Departmental reviews will be returned to the PI.

- Departmental committees will rank proposals from department faculty for PFIG, SFF, and FRA funding, and will provide substantive written justification of the ranking of each proposal to the RPRC. Co-PIs from the same department will be co-ranked. Evaluation forms to be used for departmental review are available on the College website. They are listed as evaluation forms under URGs on the CAS A-Z. Departmental reviews will be returned to the PI.

Proposals and departmental reviews **must** be uploaded at http://lilt.ilstu.edu/urg /Default.aspx **and** one hard copy of the proposal with the departmental review attached and with the original signatures of the applicant(s) and the department chairperson must be delivered to the College Office no later than 4:00 p.m. November 2, 2009 (PFIG, SFF and FRA applications) and no later than 4:00 p.m. November 30, 2009 (NFIG applications).

Evaluation of proposals at the College level will be conducted by the RPRC. In the event that RPRC ranking differs from departmental ranking of its proposals, the chair of the RPRC will notify the chairperson of the department. The department will have five (5) working days from the date of notification to respond to the committee. Responses may be in writing or take the form of a request for a meeting with the RPRC. Departments may provide information to support the RPRC's decisions, but the RPRC is responsible for the funding recommendations made to the Dean, who makes the final funding decisions. Applicants will receive notification of their funding status no later than February 1, 2010. Specific feedback in the form of the departmental review submitted with a proposal will be provided to the applicant when his or her proposal is not funded.

SUBMISSION CHECKLISTS FOR UNIVERSITY RESEARCH GRANT PROGRAM PROPOSALS:

NEW FACULTY INITIATVE GRANT (NFIG) CHECKLIST
ELIGIBILITY: PRE-TENURE FACULTY IN FIRST OR SECOND YEAR WHO WILL HOLD THE TERMINAL DEGREE BY THE TIME MONEY IS AWARDED

- Signed Cover Sheet for New Faculty Initiative Grant proposals
- Narrative of no more than three pages and optional bibliography and appendix
- Budget Form and budget justification
- Professional Outcome Form
- One-page Vitae indicating year of terminal degree and publications related to area of expertise

PRE-TENURE FACULTY INITIATIVE GRANT (PFIG) CHECKLIST

ELIGIBILITY: PRE-TENURE FACULTY IN YEARS TWO-FIVE OF ISU SERVICE WHO HOLD THE TERMINAL DEGREE

- Signed Cover Sheet for Pre-tenure Faculty Initiative Grant proposals
- Narrative of no more than three pages and optional bibliography and appendix
- Budget Form and budget justification

- Professional Outcome Form
- Description of research or creative activity since appointment at ISU

SUMMER FACULTY FELLOWSHIP (SFF) CHECKLIST

ELIGIBILITY: TENURED FACULTY MEMBERS. ALSO, PRE-TENURE FAC-ULTY WHO HAVE RECEIVED BOTH NFIG AND PFIG AWARDS AND SUB-MITTED AN EXTERNAL GRANT/FUNDING PROPOSAL

- Signed Cover Sheet for Summer Faculty Fellowship proposals
- Narrative of no more than three pages and optional bibliography and appendix
- Budget Form and budget justification (Faculty salary support only)
- Professional Outcome Form
- List of Peer Reviewed Publications and External Grant/Funding Awards (past 10 years)
- (For pre-tenure faculty who have received both NFIG and PFIG awards) Copy of the Proposal Review Form or the Individual Submission and Award Reporting Form accompanying an external grant proposal submitted through the Research and Sponsored Programs Office to an external funding organization or a copy of a submission and /or award letter from an external funding agency that did not require RSP processing.

FACULTY RESEARCH AWARDS (FRA) CHECKLIST

ELIGIBILITY: TENURED FACULTY MEMBERS. ALSO, PRE-TENURE FAC-ULTY WHO HAVE RECEIVED BOTH NFIG AND PFIG AWARDS AND SUB-MITTED AN EXTERNAL GRANT/FUNDING PROPOSAL

- Signed Cover Sheet for Faculty Research Award proposals
- Narrative of no more than two pages and optional bibliography and appendix
- Budget Form and budget justification (Project expenses excluding faculty salary)
- Professional Outcome Form
- List of Peer Reviewed Publications and External Grant/Funding Awards (past 10 years)
- (For pre-tenure faculty who have received both NFIG and PFIG awards and tenured faculty members who have received one FRA) External Funding Source Identification Form and verification from Research and Sponsored Programs Office that the faculty member has submitted a proposal through them to an external funding organization or a copy of a submission and /or award letter from an external funding agency that did not require RSP processing.

UNIVERSITY RESEARCH GRANT PROGRAM
COLLEGE OF ARTS AND SCIENCES
NEW FACULTY INITIATIVE GRANT

Evaluation Group: _____A (Sciences & Mathematics)

_____B (Social Sciences)

_____C (Humanities)

Principal Investigator	Department	Year of Appointment at ISU

Project Title: _____

_____

Does this research involve the use of human subjects?   Yes_____   No_____

Does this research involve the use of animal subjects?   Yes_____   No_____

TOTAL AMOUNT requested for projects (from budget page) _____

Investigator Signature: _____ Date _____

. . . .

DEPARTMENT ACTION

Proposal is eligible for submission to the College.   Yes_____   No_____

Chair Signature: _____ Date: _____

. . . .

Please submit the original proposal, plus as many copies as specified by your department chair, to your department chair by November 2, 2009 or deadline stated by your Chair. Departments must forward original proposal with signatures and you must submit your on-line proposal to the College Office by 4:00 P.M. on November 30, 2009.

UNIVERSITY RESEARCH GRANT PROGRAM
COLLEGE OF ARTS AND SCIENCES
PRE-TENURE FACULTY INITIATIVE GRANT

Evaluation Group: _____A (Sciences & Mathematics)

_____B (Social Sciences)

_____C (Humanities)

Principal Investigator	Department	Year of Appointment at ISU

Project Title:_____

_____

Does this research involve the use of human subjects?   Yes_____   No_____

Does this research involve the use of animal subjects?   Yes_____   No_____

TOTAL AMOUNT requested for projects (from budget page) _____

Investigator Signature:_____ Date_____

. . . .

DEPARTMENT ACTION

Proposal Rank: _____ out of _____ proposals submitted by the department in the
Pre-tenure Faculty Initiative Grant category.

Chair Signature: _____ Date: _____

. . . .

Please submit the original proposal, plus as many copies as specified by your department
chair, to your department chair by October 5, 2009 or deadline stated by your Chair.
Departments must forward original proposal with signatures and you must submit your on-
line proposal to the College Office by 4:00 P.M. on November 2, 2009.

UNIVERSITY RESEARCH GRANT PROGRAM
COLLEGE OF ARTS AND SCIENCES
SUMMER FACULTY FELLOWSHIP

Evaluation Group: _____A (Sciences & Mathematics)

_____B (Social Sciences)

_____C (Humanities)

Principal Investigator	Department	Tenure Status	Year of Appointment at ISU

Project Title:_____

_____

An External Funding Source Identification Form and verification from Research and Sponsored Programs Office that the faculty member has submitted a proposal through them to an external funding organization or a copy of a submission and /or award letter from an external funding agency that did not require RSP processing must accompany a Summer Faculty Fellowship proposal for pre-tenure faculty who have received both NFIG and PFIG awards and tenured faculty members who have received one SFF.

Does this research involve the use of human subjects?   Yes_____ No_____

Does this research involve the use of animal subjects?   Yes_____ No_____

TOTAL AMOUNT requested for salary (from budget page) _____

Investigator Signature: _____ Date _____

. . . .

DEPARTMENT ACTION

Proposal Rank: _____ out of _____ proposals submitted by the department in the Summer Faculty Fellowship category.

Chair Signature: _____ Date: _____

. . . .

Please submit the original proposal, plus as many copies as specified by your department chair, to your department chair by October 5, 2009 or deadline stated by your Chair. Departments must forward original proposal with signatures and you must submit your on-line proposal to the College Office by 4:00 P.M. on November 2, 2009.

UNIVERSITY RESEARCH GRANT PROGRAM
COLLEGE OF ARTS AND SCIENCES
FACULTY RESEARCH AWARD

Evaluation Group: _____A (Sciences & Mathematics)

                            _____B (Social Sciences)

                            _____C (Humanities)

Principal Investigator	Department	Tenure Status	Year of Appointment at ISU
Co-Prinicipal Investigator (Both PIs must submit proposals	Department	Tenure Status	Year of Appointment at ISU

Project Title:_____

_____

An External Funding Source Identification Form and verification from Research and Sponsored Programs Office that the faculty member has submitted a proposal through them to an external funding organization or a copy of a submission and /or award letter from an external funding agency that did not require RSP processing must accompany a Faculty Research Award proposal for pre-tenure faculty who have received both NFIG and PFIG awards and tenured faculty members who have received one FRA.

Does this research involve the use of human subjects?   Yes_____   No_____

Does this research involve the use of animal subjects?   Yes_____   No_____

TOTAL AMOUNT requested for projects (from budget page) _____

Investigator Signature: _____ Date _____

. . . .

DEPARTMENT ACTION

Proposal Rank: _____ out of _____ proposals submitted by the department in the Faculty Research Award category.

Chair Signature: _____ Date: _____

. . . .

Please submit the original proposal, plus as many copies as specified by your department chair, to your department chair by October 5, 2009 or deadline stated by your Chair. Departments must forward original proposal with signatures and you must submit your on-line proposal to the College Office by 4:00 P.M. on November 2, 2009.

UNIVERSITY RESEARCH GRANT PROGRAM
COLLEGE OF ARTS AND SCIENCES BUDGET

Investigator: _____

Project Title: _____

A.   PERSONNEL   AMOUNT
                          Faculty Salary*
          Name: _____   _____
          month to be paid beginning July 1, 2010:_____

          Name: _____   _____
          month to be paid beginning July 1, 2010:_____

     Civil Service . . . .   _____

     Graduate Assistants . . . .   _____

     Student Help . . . .   _____

B.   OPERATIONS

     Contractual . . . .   _____

     Postage . . . .   _____

     Travel . . . .   _____
     Destination, purpose and dates of travel from
          July 1, 2010 through June 30, 2011 only

     _____

     Commodities . . . .   _____

     Printing . . . .   _____

     Equipment . . . .   _____

     Computer Services . . . .   _____

     Telephone Tolls . . . .   _____

TOTAL REQUEST . . . .   _____

* Salary may only be requested for New Faculty Initiative Grant (NFIG), Pre-tenure Faculty Initiative Grant (PFIG) and Summer Faculty Fellowship (SFF).

Please attach a narrative of no more than one page explaining budget expenses. <u>REQUIRED</u>.

University Research Grant Program
Professional Outcome Form

Check appropriate boxes:

Type of outcome: Faculty Status:
  ❏ Intended Professional Outcome   ❏ Tenured   ❏ Pre-Tenured
  (Submit with URG proposal)   URG Category
  ❏ Accomplished Professional Outcome   ❏ New Faculty Initiative Grant
  (Due October 11, 2011)   (NFIG)
    ❏ Pre-Tenure Faculty Initiative
    Grant (PTFIG)
    ❏ Summer Faculty Fellowship
    (SFF)
    ❏ Faculty Research Award
    (FRA)

Principal Investigator(s)–Please print.   College/Department(s)

_____   _____

_____   _____

_____   _____

_____   _____

Title of Proposal:

_____

Briefly describe the URG project (3–5 lines)

List the intended outcome(s) (i.e. the product/work/result) of this URG briefly and clearly. Be specific regarding the number of items in each category listed. **Outcomes must be completed by October 11, 2011.**

Signatures:

P.I._____ Date: _____

P.I._____ Date: _____

Chair_____ Date: _____

Dean_____ Date: _____

University Research Grant Program
College of Arts and Sciences

Faculty Research Award
External Funding Source Identification Form

MUST BE COMPLETED BY PRE-TENURE FACULTY WHO HAVE RE-CEIVED NFIG AND PFIG AWARDS, FOR EACH SUBSEQUENT FRA APPLIED FOR BY ANY TENURED FACULTY MEMBER WHO HAS RECEIVED ONE FACULTY RESEARCH AWARD, AND FOR EACH SUB-SEQUENT SFF APPLIED FOR BY ANY TENURED FACULTY MEMBER WHO HAS RECEIVED ONE SUMMER FACULTY FELLOWSHIP AWARD.

A. Identifying Information

Principal Investigator(s): _____

_____

Title of Proposal: _____

_____

B. Funding Source Information

Name of Agency: _____

Address: _____

_____

_____

C. Date External Proposal Was Submitted: _____

D. Dates of URG Awards:

FRA Awards (years) _____

SFF Award (years) _____

Note: Please attach a copy of the "Blue Sheet" associated with submission of the external grant proposal indicated above or a copy of a submission and /or award letter from an external funding agency that did not require RSP processing.

University Research Grant Program Professional Outcome Form–Follow-Up Report. (n.d.). Retrieved October 9, 2010, from www.cas.ilstu.edu/faculty/committees/docs/POFFormFollowUp.doc

University Research Grant Program College of Arts and Sciences Guidelines and Application Materials 2011–2012. (n.d.). Retrieved October 9, 2010, from www.cas.ilstu.edu/originals/docs/URGGuidelines.doc

APPENDIX B

Sample Undergraduate Syllabus

Department of Special Education–591
SED 203: Measuring and Affecting Student Academic and Social Behavior I
3 Hr.
Gladly We Learn and Teach

Instructor:	Dr._____, Professor of Special Education
Office:	_____
Office Hours:	Wednesdays 1:00-1:30, Thursdays 4:00-4:45 and by appointment
Office Phone:	(____) _____-_____
E-Mail:	_____ (Please use email within Blackboard for all class contacts).
Section, day & time:	03 M., W., 2:00–3:15 p.m.
Room:	02–DeG 305
Semester:	Spring 2009

I. Catalog Course Description

203 MEASURING AND AFFECTING STUDENT ACADEMIC AND SOCIAL BEHAVIOR I 3 F, *S. SED 201 and Adm to Teacher Ed req. Conc reg in SED 202. Includes Clin Exp: Approx. 10–12 hours.* Teaching as a reflective process. Fundamentals of data-based instructional design; evaluation of instruction; formal, alternative, and curriculum-based assessment.

Expanded Course Description

SED 203 is the first course in a series of two (with SED 204) that introduces teaching and learning as a continual process of assessment, planning, direct intervention, and evaluation of student learning, learning environments, and teacher effectiveness. The primary topics covered are the fundamentals of assessment. Addresses legal, family, and diversity issues related to them. May be taken concurrently with SED 202.

II. Purpose of the Course: Professional Standards and Student Outcomes

The Department of Special Education at _____ University is committed to preparing special educators who promote a high level of competence and integrity in practicing their profession. Graduates will contribute to *"Realizing the Democratic Ideal"* by providing excellence in teaching, thus enhancing the quality of life potential for all learners, including those with disabilities. Courses offered through the department develop and assess the knowledge, performance, and disposition standards required of the professional special educator. Standards adopted by the department include those of the Council for Exceptional Children (CEC), the Interstate New Teachers Assessment and Support Consortium (INTASC), and the content area standards and Illinois

Professional Teaching Standards (IPTS) required by the Illinois State Board of Education (ISBE).

A. Common Core Content Standards for Special Educators

Principles of Assessment
CC5D. The effects of teacher attitudes and behaviors on all students.
CC3G. Influences of disabilities, culture, and language on the assessment process.
CC3A. Assessment as an educational model.
CC3B. Terminology used in assessments.
CC9C. Central concepts and methods of inquiry for reflecting on practice and problem solving.
CC3J. Matching appropriate assessment procedures to purposes of assessment.
CC3F. Strengths and limitations of various assessment tools.

Legal Aspects of Assessment
CC3C. Legal provisions, regulations, and guidelines regarding assessment of individuals with disabilities.
CC1H. Conducting the professional activities of assessment, diagnosis, and instruction consistent with the requirements of law, rules, and regulations, and local district policies and procedures.
CC3I. Accommodations and modification of national, state, and local assessments and the Illinois Alternate Assessment.

Ethical Practices
CC7C. Ethical practices for confidential communication to others about individuals with disabilities.
CC8L. Maintaining confidentiality of medical and academic records and respect for privacy of individuals with disabilities.

Roles and Responsibilities of Assessment Team Members
CC7G. Roles and responsibilities of school-based medical and related services personnel, professional groups, and community organizations in identifying, assessing, and providing services to individuals with disabilities.
CC3L. Collaborating with families and other professionals in conducting individual assessment and reporting of assessment results.
CC7K. Collaborating with a team, including families, to develop and implement individual student programs (Individualized Education Programs [IEPs], Individualized Family Service Plans [IFSPs], transition plans, etc.).
CC3O. Using performance data and information from teachers, other professionals, individuals with disabilities, and parents collaboratively to make or suggest appropriate modifications in learning environments, curriculum, and/or instructional strategies.

Gathering and Interpreting Data About Learners
CC3K. Gathering background information regarding academic history.
CC7H. Information generally available from family, school officials, legal system, and community service agencies.
CC4M. The process for inventorying instructional environments to meet a student's individual needs.
CC3P. Evaluating learning environments and matching necessary supports to individual learners' needs.
CC3N. Developing individualized assessment strategies for instruction and using appropriate procedures for evaluating results of that instruction.
CC3H. A variety of procedures for identifying students' learning characteristics and needs, monitoring student progress, and evaluating learning strategies and instructional approaches.
CC3Q. Creating and maintaining accurate records.
CC3E. Strategies for modifying and adapting formal tests.
CC3M. Interpreting information from formal and informal assessment instruments and procedures.
CC3D. Interpreting information obtained from standardized tests including age/grade scores, standard scores, percentile ranks, stanines, measures of central tendency, standard deviations, and standard error of measurement.

Planning Instructional Programs
CC4L. Short- and long-range plans consistent with curriculum goals, learner diversity, and learning history.
CC5L. Identifying realistic expectations for student behavior in various settings.
CC4Q. Developing and/or selecting relevant instructional content, materials, resources, and strategies that respond to cultural, linguistic, gender, and learning style differences.
CC5W. Designing, implementing, and evaluating instructional programs that enhance an individual's social participation in family, school, and community activities.
CC1I. Considering the continuum of placement and services within the context of least restrictive environment when making educational recommendations for students.

III. Required Text(s)/Materials

Alberto, P. A., & Troutman, A. C. (2006). *Applied behavior analysis for teachers* (7th ed.). Columbus, OH: Merrill-Prentice Hall. (Keep this text for SED 204!). We will use only a few chapters.
Cohen, L. G., & Spenciner, L. J. (2007). *Assessment of children and youth with special needs* (3rd ed.). Boston, MA: Allyn and Bacon. (Keep this text for 204!). This is our primary text.
English Grammar & Punctuation by Quick Study Academic ($4.95), a guide for effective writing (ISBN 157222531-9) (Recommended).
Fifteen 3 by 5 inch note-cards for class activities.

Readings and Study Guides in Blackboard:

Cummings, K., Atkins, T., Allison, R., & Cole, C. (2008). Response to inter-
    vention: Investigating the new role of special educators. *Teaching Exceptional
    Children, 40*(4), 24–31.
Rinaldi, C. & Samson, J. (2008). English language learners and response to
    intervention. *Teaching Exceptional Children, 40*(5), 6–14.
Tomlinson, C.A. (2008). Learning to love assessment. *Educational Leadership,
    65*(4). 8–13.

IV. Course Requirements/Learning Activities

*This syllabus lists assignments and point values for all assignments. I will also provide
detailed descriptions and explanation of evaluation guidelines for all projects. Please
record your scores (and your attendance) in your class folder to monitor your own progress
and grade in the course.*

Exams
These two learning activities (i.e., midterm & final) will be closed-book exer-
cises with objective (e.g., multiple choice) questions. The purpose of these exer-
cises is to monitor your reading and to help you prepare for your content area
tests required for state licensure. The final exam (comprehensive) will be given
during finals week with review of important mid-term content as well as new
material covered after the midterm. Study guides will be posted in Blackboard
approximately one week before the test dates to help you prepare.

Readings
It is essential that you to keep up with the daily readings! Read carefully, take
notes, highlight, do whatever works best for you to come prepared to class and
fully participate in all class activities.

In-Class Learning Activities
Students will participate in topic-related activities as pertinent to assessment
tools and planning for instruction. These activities may include small group
projects, role-playing, completion of individual case studies, etc. Points may be
given for these activities; you cannot earn these points if you are absent.

Professional Behavior/Dispositions
It is important that future special education teachers exhibit appropriate attitudes and professional behaviors on-campus, in classes, as well as during
school visits and clinical experiences. These dispositions include behaviors
related to respect, honesty, reverence for learning, emotional maturity, flexibility, collaboration skills, and responsibility. You may earn up to 20 disposition points throughout the semester from a compilation of my rating of your
professional attitudes and behaviors and one from your cooperating teacher.
Red-flag behaviors (e.g., multiple absences, texting during class) will be discussed with you, if needed and SED's guidelines (see LiveText)will be followed.

Score Record

1. PPVT paper   40 points _____
2. In-class activities/participation   up to 30 points_____
3. CEAR worksheets   64 points _____
4. Comprehensive educational assessment report (CEAR)   90 points _____
5. Powerpoint of Curriculum-based Measure   10 points _____
6. Mid-term Exam   50 points _____
7. Final Exam   75 points _____
8. Professional Behavior/Dispositions   20 points _____
9. Case studies? (up to 3 at 5 points each)   15 points _____
10. Reading study guides   38 points _____

V. Additional Description of Some Course Requirements:

1. Peabody Picture Vocabulary Test (PPVT) Paper

I will assign you to a partner to prepare and then administer the PPVT. You will be given 2 class periods for these activities. Next, you will score the test protocol and complete a paper about this experience. The grading criteria for this project appear. . . . If you miss class on either of the scheduled dates, you must schedule an appointment and administer the test to me or earn a zero on this project.

2. School Activity Worksheets 1–7

These worksheets will guide you through planning and gathering data for your Comprehensive Educational Assessment Report, (CEAR) which is **the major** project for this course and an SED portfolio item. The worksheets also provide several opportunities for reflection about your case and the assessment process. Save these templates, then add your information to help write your CEAR report. Turn them as in as scheduled for full credit.

3. CBM PowerPoint

You will prepare a power-point presentation of 4-6 slides explaining your CBM, the task and exact objective it measures, directions for teacher and student and any changes you'd make before continuing to use this CBM. We will design the grading rubric for this 10-point presentation together in class. You will also present this (weeks 14 -15) and be graded with the class rubric by both the instructor and peers.

4. Comprehensive Educational Assessment Report (CEAR)
  (This project is divided into 5 sections as described below).

The Comprehensive Educational Assessment is designed to provide you with about 10 hours of clinical experience. You will gather various types of assessment data about one student (preschool to grade 12) with a documented disability. We will provide a placement for you with a 203 partner. However, if you **commute** and would find it more convenient to find your own school placement, you may do so. Note that you will need **5–6 school visits scheduled outside of class time** to gather this assessment data.

The CEAR report is divided into five sections. Each section will require particular assessment steps guided by the activity worksheets mentioned in #2 above. These will be discussed in detail during class meetings. The final CEAR project and rubric will be posted in Blackboard. We will offer your teacher a copy of your graded CEAR which may require you to make additional editorial changes. The final CEAR step is for you to get your cooperating teacher's signature and evaluation of your professional behaviors.

Six Steps to Gathering Data for the CEAR
1. Review the student's IEP for demographic and background data. Use worksheets 1 and 2.
2. Observe instruction and discuss relevant variables. Use worksheet 3.
3. Design your assessment plan with KWHL (You need not be at the school to do this (wrksht 4).
4. Conduct a brief interview of your student's special education teacher and of your student before giving the CBM) (worksheets 5a and b)). **The interviews (only) should be done with your 203 partner. However, all your reports are to be written independently.**
5. Collect systematic observational data (**203 partners must record different behaviors**, observe and collect data during two sessions) worksheet 6.
6. Create a Curriculum Based Measure (CBM) for one of your student's IEP goals. After your student interview as an ice-breaker, administer the measure twice to your student (worksheet 7).

VI. Standards for Written Work (spelling, grammar, etc.)
The assignments in this class require critical thinking and writing. Sentence structure, appropriate grammar use, and correct spelling are required, since these are required of special education teachers. You are expected to carefully proofread and have another person proofread your assignments before you submit them. If sentence structure, organization, grammar use, and spelling need serious attention, the paper will be returned to you before grading and a **10% deduction will be taken from the possible points on that assignment**. I may suggest that you use the services of the University Center for Learning Assistance at Stevenson Hall 103 for individual assistance.

VII. Late Project Procedures & Grade Scale
Projects are due on my desk before the class start time on the listed due dates. Projects turned in late without my prior permission will earn only 50% of the possible points.

Letter grades for the course will be based on the following scale:

A =	92% or more of the total
B =	84–91% of the total
C =	76–83% of the total
D =	65–75% of the total
F =	64% or less of total

General guidelines for **all written assignments** are listed below:
1. Use person first language (e.g., person with a disability, child with a learning disability, etc.).
2. Use double spacing throughout all assignments.
3. Write about facts rather than opinions. Tell what you saw or heard.
4. Use the active rather than the passive voice (e.g., Mrs. Jones saw, rather than John was seen by Mrs. Jones).
5. All assignments must be typed, using a word processing program of your choice. Always save your work! Make a hard copy and back-up your work at each stage to save yourself from catastrophe!
6. Use spell check. Points will be deducted for spelling errors.
7. Organize your work to maximize a reader's understanding. Use headings to match both the order and required elements from each assignment checklist.
8. All assignments must be professional-looking, stapled or neatly clipped, or in a paper folder with your name and a title page.

VIII. Other Course Standards (i.e., participation)

Your participation is important to your success in the course as it will be to your success as a professional educator. I expect you to arrive on time and to attend class faithfully. Please let me know **ASAP by email** if you will be absent from class due to illness or other emergency. Individual participation folders available before class begins will allow you to record your attendance. If a course member misses a class meeting, that course member is responsible for what has been presented and discussed during the missed class. This includes obtaining notes and/or copies of handouts from **classmates**. There will be no make-up dates or arrangements for activities. Permission to make up exams will be granted only for serious and documented circumstances. Make-up exams may not be the same format as those administered in class.

I consider two absences as serious and three class absences as unacceptable. **After a third absence, you must see make an appointment with me to discuss your attendance and performance.**

What You May Expect of Me:

A sincere effort to facilitate your study and learning of the material in this course. I will be on time and prepared for class. I will work to make the material as interesting and understandable as possible.

I will be accessible to you should you ask for assistance (either during office hours or with a timely appointment).

I will return scores and papers in a timely manner.

When you are speaking, I will be respectful and attentive.

I will tell you when I don't know an answer to a question and help you find the answer. I admit I don't have all the answers!

I will give prior notice if I find it necessary to change the syllabus.

I will provide specific information about how assignments will be evaluated prior to deadlines.

I do NOT change final grades, unless I made a computation or clerical error. In that case, I will correct errors cheerfully.

What I Expect of You:
A sincere effort to learn the material in this course.
Prompt arrival for class; that you stay for entire class period.
That you prepare for class thoughtfully and get engaged with the course content.
That you turn **off** cell phones: no calls or text messaging during class!
When I am speaking, I ask you to be respectful and attentive. When other class members are speaking, I again ask you to listen respectfully and attentively.
That you communicate with all stakeholders in this endeavor appropriately including me as instructor, your 203 CEAR partner, and your 203 cooperating teacher.
Ask questions as they occur to you. I can help more before an assignment is due!
Give me prior notice of important events/conditions that may affect your performance in this class. Prior notice is needed if I might be able to assist you in any way.

IX. Academic Integrity

Academic integrity is expected in all class-related endeavors. Students are expected to be honest in all academic work. Offenses involving academic dishonesty include, but are not limited to, the following: cheating on quizzes or examinations, computer dishonesty, plagiarism, grade falsification or collusion (see Student Handbook for definitions and University regulations regarding academic dishonesty). Acts involving academic dishonesty will be reported to the Department Chairperson and the Student Judicial Office. The penalties for academic dishonesty may be severe, ranging from failure on the particular class requirement, to failure in the course, to expulsion from the major or the University (see catalog and Student Handbook for a description of adjudication procedures).

Plagiarism will result in a **failing grade** for any assignment. Note that plagiarism consists of not only writing another's work verbatim, but also paraphrasing without giving credit to the original source. You will be assigned to work with a 203 classmate on the same student case for the CEAR. However, **all of your written work is to be done individually** rather than collaboratively. The interviews should be conducted with your 203 partner. However, your written report about the interviews is to be done independently. All work on the CEAR is to be done **by you during this semester for this class only.**

X. Special Needs

Students who need accommodations based on a disability may contact the Office of Disability Concerns and are encouraged to discuss the specific nature of the accommodations needed with the course instructor.

Revised Course Schedule (May be adjusted by the instructor if needed!)

Week Day & Date	Topics *In-class activities*	Readings listed are to be completed before each class. Text chapters note: Cohen & Spenciner (C& S) Alberto & Troutman (A & T) Materials in Blackboard 203.03**
Week 1 M 1/12	**Course overview** *Finding two 203 buddies (home group)* *What is assessment and the buzz?* *Brainstorm in home groups of 3*	Turn in 3 x 5 card information Folders
Week 1 W 1/14	**Foundations & the law** Key court cases Assign cases Syllabus quiz	C & S chapter 1 Bring more info about assigned court case by home group *Be prepared for a syllabus quiz*
Week 2 M 1/19	MLK, Jr., Day	No class
Week 2 W 1/21	Family rights–Asking questions *Letters for teachers*** Dispositions Good Communication	C & S, 2, pp. 21–28 C & S, 17, pp. 355–359 **Email your teacher ASAP, send me a copy. Call the school as a back-up.**
Week 3 M 1/26	Response to Intervention (RTI)	Cummings et a., 2008** Study guide for Cummings due
Week 3 W 1/28	Reliability & Validity	C & S, chapter 3 **Make follow-up contact to your teacher as needed.**
Week 4 M 2/02	Technical skills *The Bell Curve-converting scores*	(Bring text to class)
Week 4 W 2/04	Technical skills *The Bell Curve-converting scores*	(Bring text to class)
Week 5 M 2/09	*Intro to the PPVT, scoring, and the paper*	C & S, chapter 8, pp. 156–168 & 181–182
Week 5 W 2/11	*Meet at Milner* *Prepare to give PPVT (assign pairs)* *Administration questions*	*Meet at Milner* C & S, 2, pp. 32–33 & pp. 65–67 Answer PPVT prep questions
Week 6 M 2/16	*Meet at Milner* *Give PPVT-mark score protocol*	*Meet at Milner* Copy needed tables for paper
Week 6 W 2/18	Writing reports & Scientific writing Discuss CEAR worksheets 1–3	C & S chapter 7

Week 7 M 2/23	So what else is assessment? The RIOT matrix Review of records activity	Read Tomlinson 2008** Study guide questions School visit 1 (record review; use worksheets 1 & 2)
Week 7 W 2/25	KWHL with Dan (practice worksheet 4 & 5)	**PPVT paper is due** C & S chapter 5 After record review, create your assessment plan (**worksheet 4**)
Week 8 M 3/02	Interviewing Open-ended vs. closed	**Bring worksheet 4 and interview questions on worksheet #5a, to class** **Turn in for preapproval.**
Week 8 W 3/04	More about interviews Classroom observations *Class check-up*	Worksheets 1–2 are due A & T, pp. 59–62 C & S, Chapter 5, pp. 70–83 **School visit #2 for teacher interview**
Week of 3/09	Spring Break	**Note: Your school's break may be different from ISU's!**
Week 9 M 3/16	*Systematic Observations Event recording Let's count this . . .*	**School visit #3 to observe instruction** **Worksheet 3**
Week 9 W 03/18	*CBMs Samples*	**Worksheet 4 is due** C & S, pp. 172–175, 195–196, 215–216, 261, 263
Week 10 M 3/23	More about CBMs *Small group work on CBM*	C & S, pp. 175–183 & 200–207 **Worksheet 3 is due** *School visit #4 , do event recording (worksheet 6)*
Week 10 W 3/25	Other assessment approaches *Catching up . . . Clinical exp. Forms Teacher evals and envelopes*	**Bring your CBM to class** (Worksheet 7 through materials, completed) **Worksheet 5a is due**
Week 11 M 3/30	Goals & Objectives *Writing goals and objectives*	A & T 2 *School visit #5 for student interview & to give your CBM Thank your teacher for his/her help Take forms with you*
Week 11 W 4/01	*No class today–extra CEAR time!*	
Week 12 M 4/06	More about goals/objectives	**Worksheets 5b & 6 are due** C & S, Chapter 9

Week 12 W 4/08	Reading	***Professional Draft of CEAR 1–2 is due with rubric***
Week 13 M 4/13	Math *CEARs 1–2 back to you*	C & S, chapter 12, pp. 251–258; 266–269 **Worksheet 7 is due**
Week 13 W 4/15	*Clapping institute* *Designing rubrics*	C & S, chapter 11, pp, 106–122 ***Professional Draft of CEAR 3–5 is due with rubric***
Week 14 M 4/20	Diversity Issues/ELL *CEARS 3–5 back: make changes now!* *Teacher letters & envelopes out* *Finalize the CBM powerpoint rubric*	**Read Rinaldi (2008) paper** **Rinaldi study guide is due** ***Send or take your teacher a thank you***
Week 14 W 4/22	IAA *CBM powerpoints*	**Final CEAR is due with rubric** ***Grade CBMs with rubric***
Week 15 M 4/27	*CBM powerpoints*	C & S, 15, pp. 313–331 ***Grade CBMs with rubric***
Week 15 W 4/29	*CBM powerpoints* *CEARs back to you*	C & S, 299–302 ***Grade CBMs with rubric***
W 5/06	1:00 p.m.	***Final exam*** ***Signed teacher evals are due!***

Peabody Picture Vocabulary Test (PPVT) Paper Outline

Write a paper title. Begin with an introduction paragraph telling the purpose of this paper. Why are you writing it and what are the major sections? (Use no heading for this section.)

Basal and Ceiling

Explain the importance of a basal and ceiling. Tell how you applied the basal and ceiling rules with your student. What did you learn about basal and ceiling from this test administration? Highlight the rules on the test protocol (i.e., test form) or manual to support your work.

Chronological Age

Calculate your student's chronological age (CA) on the date of your test administration using the test's rules. Show your work following C & S and place in a word table or chart. Label your columns.

Test Protocol

Attach completed protocol with basal and ceiling marked and all scores calculated correctly. Attach copies of all charts and tables (highlight the rows) you used to find your scores.

Test Results

Recreate a word table listing all test results (e.g., raw scores, standard scores, percentile scores, etc.) Label your columns.

Summary of Test Results

Interpret your student's test results comparing your student's scores to mean scores on that test, for your student's age, and with the 90% confidence interval.

Reflect on your administration skills on this test. Talk about your strengths and areas to improve.

Conclusion Section

What were the major sections of this paper? What did you learn about giving and scoring a standardized test from this experience? How might this experience be useful to you in your future teaching?

Note: I will evaluate, not only the content of your paper, but also the writing as related to clarity of writing, use of section headings (i.e., to match this outline), grammar, and spelling (10 points).

APPENDIX C

Sample Graduate Syllabus

_____ University
Department of Special Education
Spring 2008

Course Number & Title:	SED 422: Teaching Diverse Learners
Course Credit:	3 semester hours
Room & Time:	DeG 305
	5:30–8:20 p.m. Thursdays
Instructor:	_____, Professor of Special Education
	(___) ____-_____ (office phone)
	FAX: (___) ____-_____
	_____ (Office)
E-mail:	_____ (this is the best way to reach me!)
Office Hours:	Wednesdays 10:00–11:00, Thursdays 3:45–4:45, and by appointment

Catalog Description

SED 422 TEACHING DIVERSE LEARNERS 3 Hr. FORMERLY SED 422 TEACHING STUDENTS WITH LEARNING DISABILITIES *Preq. SED 101, 145 or 411 or equivalent.* **Topics: Curriculum, instructional objectives, methods, learning strategies, and materials for education of students who require adaptations for learning.**

Expanded Course Description

This course provides in-depth study of recent research related to effective curriculum, instructional objectives, methods, and materials for educating children/youth who require adaptations for learning. Additional emphasis is on learning theory and application of learning theory to strategies for students. Topics include: reading decoding, fluency and comprehension, written composition and spelling, mathematics instruction, teaching in the content areas, grouping and social skill instruction, learning theory and strategies, interactive teaching, as well as multicultural considerations. The content is applicable to teaching all students requiring support in learning.

Purpose of the Course

The Department of Special Education at _____ University is committed to developing special educators who seek to *"Realize the Democratic Ideal"* by developing the highest education and quality of life potential for all learners, including those with disabilities. Courses offered through the department seek to develop the knowledge, performance, and disposition standards required of the professional special educator. These standards have been defined by National Board for Professional Teaching

Standards (NBPTS), the Council for Exceptional Children (CEC), the Interstate New Teachers Assessment and Support Consortium (INTASC), and the Illinois State Board of Education (ISBE) for advanced certification as Learning Behavior Specialist 2: Curriculum Adaptation. This course is focused on developing the professional standards that follow.

This action research project in this course serves as a portfolio entry and **Aligns with NBPTS Entry 2: Fostering Communications Development**, National Board for Professional Teaching Standards for All Teachers

A7.   Incorporate the prevailing theories of cognition and intelligence in their practice.
B3.   Develop the critical and analytical capacities of their students.
B4.   Command specialized knowledge of how to convey and reveal subject matter to students.
B5.   Know the preconceptions and background knowledge that students typically bring to each subject and strategies and instructional materials that can be of assistance.
B6.   Know where difficulties are likely to arise and modify their practice accordingly.
B7.   Create multiple paths to the subjects they teach.
B8.   Teach students how to pose and solve their own problems.

National Board for Professional Teaching Standards: Exceptional Needs Specialist

3A.   Know the connection between communication and learning.
3B.   Use communication skills to help students acquire, access, comprehend, and apply information knowledge.
4B.   Ensure access to quality learning opportunities for all students.
10C. Use strategies to assist students in assuming responsibility for learning.
10D. Foster intellectual risk taking among students.
10E. Teach students to work independently and collaboratively.

Learning Behavior Specialist II Curriculum Adaptation Standards

2A.   Learning research and implications for students with disabilities.
2B.   Impact of various disabilities, levels of disabilities, and combination of disabilities on learning and skill development.
2C.   Impact of listening skills on the development of critical thinking, reading comprehension, and oral and written language.
2D.   Impact of language development on the academic and social skills of individuals with disabilities.
3E.   Varied test-taking strategies.
3I.   Systematically measures and evaluates the effectiveness of curricular adaptations and/or modifications in instructional strategies on student learning.
3J.   Conducts student error analyses to identify needed instructional modifications.
3L.   Assesses reliable methods of response of individuals who lack communication and performance abilities.

4D. Strategies for modifying materials, changing teaching procedures, altering task requirements, or selecting an alternative task based on students' learning styles and needs.

4E. Modifies general curricula by analyzing what is taught, how it is taught, how the student will demonstrate proficiency, and the instructional setting needed by the student for successful learning.

4F. Tries the least intrusive intervention or adaptation first.

4G. Matches individual learning style with appropriate curricular adaptations.

4I. Selects instructional materials which engage students in meaningful learning.

5A. Reinforcement theory and its application to learning.

5B. The impact of the environment on student learning.

5C. Modifies the learning environment based on a student's learning strengths, curricular needs, and appropriate instructional strategies.

6A. Various methods for adapting content, instructional strategies, instructional settings, and materials to maximize learning.

6B. Various student learning strategies that increase capacity for learning.

6C. Study strategies to assist students in the completion of various tasks.

6D. Various methods for grouping students to maximize learning.

6E. How technology may be used to maximize learning.

6G. Adapts content, materials, and instructional strategies in reading to meet individualized needs.

6H. Adapts content, materials, and instructional strategies in mathematics to meet individualized needs.

6I. Adapts content, materials, and instructional strategies in language arts to meet individualized needs.

6J. Adapts content, materials, and instructional strategies in academic content areas (e.g., science and social studies) to meet individualized needs.

6K. Adapts content, materials, and instructional strategies related to social skills, life skills, vocational skills, and study skills to meet individualized needs.

6L. Uses research-supported instructional strategies and practices.

6M. Uses adaptations and strategies for facilitating maintenance and generalization of skills across environments.

6N. Uses assistive technology devices to meet individualized needs and maximize learning.

6O. Teaches students cognitive strategies which maximize learning.

Director of Special Education Certification Standards

1A. Knows and understands differing population needs in a pluralistic society.

1B. Knows and understands theories and methodologies of teaching and learning including the adaptation and modification of curriculum to meet the needs of all learners.

1K. Facilitates and engages in activities that promote the success of all students in the least restrictive environment by understanding responding to an influencing the larger political, social, economic, legal, and cultural context.

2A. Knows and understands the principles of human growth and development ranges of individual variation in their application to the school environment and instructional program.

2E. Knows and understands cognition, learning theories, and interventions and their relationship to instruction.

2I. Understands affects of the cultural and environmental milieu of the child and the family, including cultural and linguistic diversity, socioeconomic level, abuse/neglect, and substance abuse on behavior and learning.

2J. Has knowledge of techniques for modifying instructional methods, curricular materials, technology, and the learning environment and students' needs including technologies that are developmentally appropriate.

2N. Facilitates and engages in activities that use best practices and sound educational research to promote improved instructional techniques, intervention strategies, and specialized curricular materials.

2U. Facilitates and engages in activities that systematically conduct, act upon, and report assessment of individual student educational performance and evaluation of the instructional program.

2V. Facilitates and engages in activities that connect educational standards to specialized instructional services.

4B. Knows and understands effective intervention strategies and processes that are prerequisite to a referral case study evaluation.

4D. Knows and understands the continuum of programs and array of services available to students with disabilities.

4L. Facilitates and engages in activities that promote a free appropriate public education in the least restrictive environment.

4M. Facilitates and engages in activities that promote programs and related services for children based upon a thorough understanding of individual differences.

4P. Facilitates and engages in activities that evaluate a student success in participation in the general educational curriculum.

Required Text(s)/Materials

Readings have been compiled for you and are available in WebCT. A WebCT demonstration will be provided in class on the first night for new users.

Course Requirements

Assigned readings are to be completed before the class meeting time to facilitate discussion and activities related to the concepts. A part of membership in a learning community is the preparation for group work prior to meetings. As professionals within this learning community you will be expected to demonstrate this behavior at all times during the semester. I encourage you to participate during class discussions in both small groups and the larger group. Your comments, insights and questions will facilitate the learning of your classmates.

Attendance is expected at all class meetings. If you must be absent, please let me know as soon as possible. I do consider 2 absences from a 3-hour class to be excessive. Some in-class activities may be graded and if you are absent from class you will not have the opportunity to make these activities up.

Completion of all assigned activities on the scheduled due date is required as a component of professional behavior. If you cannot complete the assignment within the given timeframe, you **must** discuss this with the professor **prior** to the due date. Assignments that are turned in late without prior arrangement will have points deducted.

Assignments Listing

1. Case studies (in groups)	3 at 5 points each
2. Preparation/Participation	2 points per reading
3. Problem scenario or material sharing	5 points
4. Quizzes (2 at 25 pts. each)	50 points
5. In-Service	49 points
6. Action Research Project	155 points
7. Presentation of Final Project	20 points

Assignments Description:

1. Case Studies
Students will read and analyze three case studies which will cover several different disability areas. These will be in-class group activities with no make-up option for absences.

2. Participation/Preparation
Students will prepare for class by reading each article and keyboarding either a response to the paper or a thoughtful discussion question for each reading. Please be prepared to discuss the readings in class including the highlights of the reading, response and discussion questions about the readings. We would be particularly interested in hearing about your experiences using any of the strategies with your own clients and students and any other suggestions for our future instructional practice.

3. Problem Scenario or Material Sharing
Each student will prepare one brief problem-solving activity to facilitate class discussion (by sign-up). This can employ the following (e.g., I have a student who . . . or I am in need instructional method or materials that . . .). In either case the purpose of this is to engage classmates in problem-solving.

4. Tests or Quizzes
Two quizzes, consisting of short answer and application questions, will be administered during the course. These quizzes are designed to give you feedback on their knowledge of the course content. Study guides will be provided one week before each quiz to facilitate your preparation. These will be closed-book, closed-note activities.

5. In-Service Presentation
This assignment involves small groups of approximately five students (assigned) who will present about ways effectively employ current research-based educational interventions appropriate for students with disabilities. You may select any teaching approach or strategy for which you find a minimum of 8 peer-reviewed supportive journal articles. The topic(s) you select may or may not be included in course read-

ings. Course readings may be used in addition to but not toward the minimum requirement of 8 articles. Sample topics are provided in a list at the end of this description. Some class time will be devoted to preparation of the in-services which should be approximately 35 minutes long.

6. Action Research Project (Portfolio piece)

The purpose of this project is to design and deliver instruction for communication development and/or literacy learning with a student or students with special learning needs with communication and/or literacy learning challenges using a broad definition of communication/literacy. Student progress monitoring and critical reflection are essential elements of this project. The project will consist of both a written commentary as well as video-recordings of instruction (DVDs or mini-DVDs, standard-sized or mini-videotapes). You will exchange video-recordings with different 422 classmates for feedback and integrate their feedback with your own in your reflection commentary. An outline and rubric for this project are included in this document.

7. Brief Presentation of Action Research Project.

The purpose of this activity is to allow 422 participants to share their completed action research project with classmates at the last regular class meeting. The presentation (approximately 5 minutes in length) should include the following: a clear definition of the target student's characteristics, the purpose of the intervention, description of the strategy or intervention steps, presentation of data and results, and a reflection of ways to improve or recognize the teaching strategy.

Grading System:

The final grade for the course will be based on performance on the written quizzes and all graded assignments.

Letter grades for the course will be based on the following scale:

A=93-100%, B=85-92%, C=78-84%, D=72-77%, F= <72%

Standards for Written Work (spelling, grammar, etc.)

All course papers and abstracts are expected to be typed and submitted without typographical errors. The following criteria will be included in the appraisal of course papers:
1. Grammatical accuracy
2. Freedom from typographical errors
3. Use of the format of the American Psychological Association (APA 5th ed.) for references and headings
4. Please carefully proofread your work before handing it in.

Class Attendance

Class attendance is required. It is strongly encouraged that you attend each class session. Should something significant occur and you are unable to attend the scheduled class session, it will be your responsibility to contact the instructor to acquire the information from him/her, other students, and/or handouts presented in the class session. Again, it is your responsibility to make the decision as to whether or not an event or circumstances require that you miss a class. Your professional future will require similar decisions. Repeated unexcused absences will be discussed and penalized.

Academic Integrity
Academic integrity is expected in all class-related endeavors; students are expected to be honest in all academic work. Offenses involving academic dishonesty include, but are not limited to, the following: cheating on quizzes or examinations, computer dishonesty, plagiarism, grade falsification or collusion (see *Student Handbook* for definitions and University regulations regarding academic dishonesty). Acts involving academic dishonesty will be reported to the Department Chairperson and the Student Judicial Office. The penalties for academic dishonesty may be severe, ranging from failure on the particular class requirement, to failure in the course, to expulsion from the major or the University (see catalog and *Student Handbook* for a description of adjudication procedures).

Special Needs
Students who need accommodations based on a disability may contact the Office of Disability Concerns and are encouraged to discuss the specific nature of the accommodations needed with the course instructor.

COURSE SCHEDULE

Date	Topic
January 17	Introduction of class and materials
January 24	Week 2–Effective instruction/interventions *Designing lesson plans and interventions* *Case study 1–Jack* *Group time*
January 31	Week 3–Response to interventions & evidence *Monitoring progress* *Writing behavioral objectives* *Group time*
February 7	Week 4–Reading *Group time*
February 14	Week 5–Testing Video-recording 1 and lesson plan due to instructor. Also describe your participants or sample and why chosen. *Group time*

February 21	Week 6–Instructional Grouping *Group time?*
February 28	**Mid-term quiz** **Video exchange 1**
March 6	Week 7–Peer tutoring In-service 1
March 13	No Class–Spring Break
March 20	Week 8–Cooperative Learning **Video exchange 2** In-service 2
March 27	Week 9–Math In-service 3
April 3	Project Night (no class)
April 10	Week 10–Self-strategies **Video exchange 3** In-service 4
April 17	Week–11 Social skills In-service 5
April 24	Week 12–Writing In-service 6
May 1	Action research presentations; **Action Research Project Due**
May 8	**Final Quiz**

Ideas for In-Service and Action Research Intervention Topics

1. cooperative learning
2. peer tutoring, classwide or cross-age
3. direct or explicit instruction
4. stimulus and response prompting
5. self-instruction for various content area tasks
6. self-monitoring of on-task behavior or attention
7. cognitive mediation strategies (social or academic problem-solving)
8. keyword mnemonics
9. learning strategies (e.g., RAP from the University of Kansas)
10. study & test-taking strategies
11. coached elaborations or elaborative interrogations

12. social stories or other social skills instruction
13. text structure strategies
14. main idea or self-questioning instruction for reading comprehension
15. reciprocal teaching
16. Math word problem strategies (e.g., SOLVE, POSSE)
17. Others?

Outline for In-service

1. Present the goals/objectives of this presentation.

2. Describe the intervention. What characterizes this intervention? Based on the available knowledge, what unique aspects of this intervention contribute to its effectiveness with students with n disabilities?

3. Research Support What research support did you find for this intervention?

4. Describe the characteristics of the students who might benefit from this intervention. Provide examples of the manifestations of their learning or behavioral difficulties. Describe participants in the studies you reviewed as well as other populations for which this intervention might be useful and any needed adaptations for other age or disability groups (e.g., adaptations for students at the elementary level; the secondary level? Other adaptations which might be used for students with other types of disabilities?)

5. Describe specific procedures for implementation considering the phases of student learning as appropriate acquisition, fluency and implications for generalization, as appropriate. How would a teacher implement this intervention? What are the steps for success?

6. Describe a data-collection tool or plan you could use to measure student learning outcomes to measure as a direct result of this intervention.

7. Additional materials and references. What other materials might be used while using this intervention? Provide an APA reference list with appropriate citations within the presentation with a minimum of six peer-reviewed references.

Outline for Action Research Project

The purpose of this project is to design and deliver instruction for communication development and/or literacy learning with a student or students with special learning needs who present communication and/or literacy learning challenges using a broad definition of communication/literacy. Student progress monitoring and critical reflection are essential elements of this project.

Use this outline and the rubric to guide you through your written project and supporting artifacts for sections 1–7 as appropriate.

1. Introduction–Who you are, your background, why you took this course? What had you hoped to learn? Other thoughts as you begin this project?

2. Review of research. Provide a summary of research support from peer-reviewed journals or edited book chapters for the intervention(s) you selected. Explain how this intervention package fit the particular needs of your sample.

3. Design of Instruction. Tell more about your sample. Who, why, and how chosen? Tell how instruction was planned and implemented with 9–10 lesson plan (6 formal lesson plans, the remaining lessons provide notes/logs for support. Materials and other artifacts are clearly described and/or included.

4. Implementation of instruction. This section includes video-recordings of 9-10 lessons, with teacher/client logs and some general daily reflections. The implementer is the focus of this section.

5. Evidence of student learning. Tell how you made instructional decisions and revised your implementation plan based on evidence of student learning. Make a case for the connection between the instruction provided and this data. Include professional-looking, data-based instruction/graphs, charts, etc. as well as student work samples.

6. Collaboration and reflection with relevant supervisors, colleagues, 422 peer reviewers and yourself is the focus of this section. With whom did you collaborate and why? How thoroughly did you consider/ reflect on peer feedback throughout project development and incorporate it into your decision-making and reflections?

7. Concluding remarks and final reflection. This section is an overall summary of the project and what was learned. Describe, analyze, and evaluate instructional decisions, implementation, as well as reflect on student learning, teacher learning. Also compare your results to the literature and describe the effect of this project on your future professional practice.

APPENDIX D

Sample Human Subjects Proposal Form

Illinois State University Institutional Review Board

Research with Human Subjects

IRB Number _____

Protocol Submission Form

Federal regulations and Illinois State University policy require that all research involving humans as subjects be reviewed and approved by the University Institutional Review Board (IRB). Any person (ISU faculty member, staff member, student, or other person) wanting to engage in human subject research at or through Illinois State University must receive written approval from the IRB before conducting research. For more information, templates, and forms please go to www.rsp.ilstu.edu

> **Please complete and forward this form and all supporting documents to your Department/Unit IRB representative.** Handwritten applications will not be accepted. If you have any questions, please contact your Departmental/Unit IRB representative or the Research Ethics & Compliance Office, (REC) 438-2520, Campus Box 3330.

I. General Information

A. Protocol Information

Protocol Title:

Purpose of Project (Please check only one box) ☐ Dissertation ☐ Thesis

☐ Class project (Please give course number) _____ ☐ Other

☐ Externally funded faculty/staff research (Complete Appendix B) ☐ Non-externally funded faculty/staff research

B. Principal Investigator Information (PI must be an ISU faculty or staff member)

Principal Investigator		☐ Faculty ☐ Staff	
Dept	Mail Code	Telephone Number	Email Address

Co-Principal Investigator Information							
Co-Principal Investigator			☐ Faculty	☐ Staff	☐ Grad. Student		☐ Undergrad. Student
Dept	Mail Code	Telephone Number		Email Address			
Co-Principal Investigator Information							
Co-Principal Investigator			☐ Faculty	☐ Staff	☐ Grad. Student		☐ Undergrad. Student
Dept	Mail Code	Telephone Number		Email Address			

II. Principal Investigator Assurance

As Principal Investigator, I certify that to the best of my knowledge:
1. The information provided for this project is correct
2. No other procedures will be used in this protocol
3. I agree to conduct this research as described in the attached supporting documents
4. I will request and receive approval from the IRB for changes prior to implementing changes (including but not limited to changes in cooperating investigators or any changes in procedures).
5. I will comply with IRB and ISU policies for conducting ethical research.
6. I will be responsible for ensuring that the work of my co-investigator(s)/student researcher(s) complies with this protocol.
7. Any unexpected or otherwise significant events in the course of this study will be promptly reported to the REC.
8. In the case of student research, I assume responsibility for ensuring that any student will comply with University and Federal regulations regarding the use of human subjects in research.
9. In the case of externally funded research, I will request a modification to my approved protocol if any relative changes to the project's scope of work are requested by the agency.
_____   _____
Principal Investigator Signature   Date

III. Protocol Description

A. Provide a **brief** description, in **layperson's terms,** of the proposed research. State the goals and/or hypotheses of this study and how these goals relate to previous research in this area.

B. Methodology

a. Identify all participant groups in the study and indicate criteria for including or excluding individuals from participation.

b. How many participants will be included in the study?

    Number: Male _____ Female _____ Total _____

    (N/A _____ if not targeting males/females specifically)

    Age range:_____ to _____

c. Justify use of any protected populations (e.g., children, mentally disabled individuals, prisoners, pregnant women). Complete whichever is appropriate, Appendix C-F, for that population.

d. How will you identify potential participants and get access to contact information? Please include documentation of permission to use any proprietary sources, i.e., listserv, organization roster, etc.

e. How will participants be recruited? Attach all recruitment documentation, (i.e., e-mail letters, flyers, telephone scripts, etc.) and indicate how they will be contacted and by whom.

f. Who will obtain informed consent/assent and what procedures will be used (and in what order) to secure informed consent/assent?

g. How will the risk of coercion be minimized?

h. Where will the research take place? Please be as specific as possible. If research is confidential in nature, please explain how location will help preserve confidentiality.

If consent, permission, and assent forms are being used, attach copies. If presented verbally, a copy of any presentation script must be submitted. **Examples of informed consent and parent permission can be found at http://www.rsp.il stu.edu/research/human_subjects/index.shtml**

C. Procedure

a. Who will collect data?

b. What are you asking the participants to do? In what order?

c. Will you involve them in a psychological intervention, biomedical procedure, or deception? If so, complete relevant Appendix G, H, or J.

d. If participants are receiving compensation for participation (e.g., payment, gifts, extra credit, etc.) indicate type and amount of compensation, how it will be disbursed, and identify the funding source.

e. Will you record audio _____ , video _____, or still images_____ of participants whether by film, tape, digital or other media? Please check and complete Appendix K.

D. Instruments/Apparatus

What forms, surveys, equipment, etc. will you use? (**Attach copies** of all forms, surveys and instruments to be used.) If online surveys will be used, please identify the system to be used and describe the system's confidentiality protections.

E. Data

a. How/where will the data be stored and kept secure? Please specify building and room number.

b. Who will have access?

c. How will the data be used (during and after the research)? Will it be disseminated through publication, presentation, or other means?

d. How and when will the data be disposed of?

F. Risks

a. What are the physical, psychological, or social (loss of reputation, privacy, or employability) risks?

b. How will the risks be minimized?

c. Will the data be anonymous _____ or confidential_____? (Please check one.)

G. Benefits

a. What do you hope to learn?

b. Who might find these results useful?

c. How will the participants directly benefit? If they will not, please state that. Compensation is not a benefit.

d. Explain how the benefits justify the associated risks.

IV. Checklist

This checklist must be completed and attached to all protocols or Department Representatives will return them to the PI. Please note that for any items checked "yes" you must attach the designated, completed appendices and relevant forms and instruments.

_____ Yes _____ No   Informed consent procedures/ documentation have been clearly explained. (**All** protocols must have a completed **Appendix A**.)

_____ Yes _____ No   Is your research being funded? (If yes, complete **Appendix B**.)

_____ Yes _____ No   Are you recruiting and enrolling subjects 0–7 years old? (If yes, complete and attach **Appendix C**.)

_____ Yes _____ No   Are you recruiting and enrolling subjects 8–17 years old? (If yes, complete and attach **Appendix C**.)

_____ Yes _____ No   Are you recruiting and enrolling prisoners as subjects? (If yes, complete and attach **Appendix D**.)

_____ Yes _____ No   Are you recruiting and enrolling pregnant women as subjects? (If yes, complete and attach **Appendix E**.)

_____ Yes _____ No   Are you recruiting and enrolling mentally incapacitated individuals as subjects? (If yes, complete and attach **Appendix F**.)

_____ Yes _____ No   Will the subjects of this study be exposed to the possibility of harm, including physiological, psychological, or social (e.g., loss of reputation, privacy, or employability). (If yes, complete and attach **Appendix G**.)

_____ Yes _____ No   Will the subjects of this study be exposed to any psychological interventions such as contrived social situations, manipulation of the subject's attitudes, opinions or self-esteem, psychotherapeutic procedures, or other psychological influences. (If yes, complete and attach **Appendix H.**)

_____ Yes _____ No   Will this study involve any elements of deception? (If yes, complete and attach **Appendix I.**)

_____ Yes _____ No   Will the proposed research involve any biomedical procedures (e.g., the taking or withholding of medication, ingestion of any food or other substances, injections, blood drawing, or any other procedure which would normally be done under medical supervision). (If yes, complete and attach **Appendix J.**)

_____ Yes _____ No   Will all or some of the subject(s) of the proposed research be audio or videotaped or recorded in any other manner? (If yes, complete and attach **Appendix K.**)

_____ Yes _____ No   Will this proposed research involve any elements of technology? (i.e., web-based subject recruitment, email recruitment, web survey, etc.)

Appendix A: Elements of Informed Consent

Please ensure that all of these elements are included in the protocol and consent documents before checking "Yes". The informed consent procedures and documents outlined in this protocol must contain all of the following:

_____ Yes   1. A statement that the study involves research

_____ Yes   2. An explanation of the purposes of the research

_____ Yes   3. The duration of the participant's participation

_____ Yes   4. A description of procedures to be followed

_____ Yes   5. A description of foreseeable risks or discomforts to the participant

_____ Yes   6. A description of any benefits to the participants or any others that may be expected from the research

_____ Yes   7. A statement describing the extent, if any, that confidentiality will be maintained

_____ Yes   8. An explanation as to whom to contact concerning questions about the research, research participants' rights, and/or a research related injury or adverse effect. This should include the Principal Investigator's name and contact information as well as the Research Ethics & Compliance Office name and number: (309) 438-2520.

_____ Yes   9. A statement that participation is voluntary

_____ Yes   10. A statement that refusal to participate involves no penalty or loss of benefits

_____ Yes   11. A statement that the subject may discontinue participation at any time without penalty or loss of benefits

Do the consent procedures and documents outlined in the protocol contain the following?

____ Yes ____ N/A   1. Identification of any experimental procedures

____ Yes ____ N/A   2. A disclosure of appropriate alternative procedures or courses of treatment, if any that might be advantageous to the subject

____ Yes ____ N/A   3. An explanation about any compensation or medical treatments that may be available if injury occurs, what they may be, and where to get further information

Appendix B: Funded Projects

If your research will be funded please answer the following questions.

1. Project:_____ Has been _____ Will be   submitted to the following agency:

Name of Sponsor:	
Address:	
Contact Person:	

2. Funding decision: _____ is pending   _____ has been awarded
   Agency assigned grant number:

3. How is the research funded:
   _____ Internal departmental funds
   _____ External grant/ contract
   _____ Corporate sponsor
   _____ Foundation
   _____ Federal Grant–A copy of the grant must be submitted with the
   IRB protocol

If you would like certification of approval sent to your funding agency, please provide the name and address of your contact person at the agency:

Name:	
Address:	
Fax Number:	

REC Number _____ (To be completed by the REC)

Appendix C: Research Involving Minors as Subjects

If some or all of the subjects of the proposed research will be minors (under the age of 18), provide the following information.

1. Provide a justification for the inclusion of minors that documents the benefits that are likely to accrue to a child participating in the project.

2. Specify how parental permission will be obtained and documented. Attach copies of all letters and permission forms.

3. Specify how you will obtain **assent** of minor subjects. Attach copies of assent forms for children who can read (8 to 17 years) or script (for children under 8 years) for verbal assent.

4. If subjects are school children and class time is used to collect data, describe in detail the activity planned for nonparticipants. Who will supervise those children? This information must be included in the consent form.

5. For projects involving children under 8 years of age, what nonverbal cues will you watch for to indicate the child is ready to end or pause participation?

6. Specify provisions for minimizing **coercion** on minors to participate.

Appendix D: Prisoners

If some or all of the proposed research subjects are prisoners, specify provisions for minimizing coercion on prisoners to participate.

Appendix E: Pregnant Women

If some or all of the proposed research involves pregnant women, you must **justify** the inclusion of pregnant women and specify how risks to mother and fetus will be minimized.

Appendix F: Mentally Incapacitated Individuals

If all or some of the study subjects are mentally incapacitated, provide the following information:

1. Describe the procedures to be used to explain the study in ways that will be understandable to the mentally incapacitated subjects.

2. Explain the role of legal guardians, if any, in the informed consent process.

Appendix G: Special Risk to Human Subjects

If the subjects of this study be exposed to the possibility of harm, including physiological, psychological, or social (e.g., loss of reputation, privacy, or employability).

1. Identify and describe possible risks to subjects.

2. **Justify** those risks by explaining how they are outweighed by the sum of the benefits to the individual subject and to the importance of the knowledge to be gained (discuss the alternative ways of conducting this research and why the one chosen is superior).

3. Explain fully how the **rights** and **welfare** of such subjects at risk will be protected (e.g., equipment closely monitored, psychological screening of prospective subjects, medical exam given prior to procedure).

Appendix H: Research Involving Psychological Intervention

Will the subjects of this study be exposed to any psychological interventions such as contrived social situations, manipulation of the subject's attitudes, opinions or self-esteem, psychotherapeutic procedures, or other psychological influences?

1. Identify and describe the **psychological intervention and behavior** expected of subject(s) and the context of the behavior during the psychological intervention.

2. Describe how data resulting from this procedure will be gathered and recorded.

3. Identify anticipated and possible psychological, physiological, or social **consequences** of this procedure for the subjects.

4. Indicate the investigator's competence and identify his/her **qualifications** by training and experience, to conduct this procedure.

Appendix I: Deception

A study is deceptive if false information is given to subjects, false impressions created, or information relating to the subjects' participation is withheld from the subjects.

1. Describe in detail the **deception** involved, including any instructions to subjects or false impressions created.

2. Explain in detail why deception is necessary to accomplish the goals of the research (care should be taken to distinguish cases in which disclosure would invalidate the research from cases in which disclosure would simply inconvenience the investigator).

3. Describe, in detail, the plan for **debriefing** subjects (attach a copy of any debriefing statement).

Appendix J: Biomedical Procedures

If the proposed research involves biomedical procedures (e.g., the taking or withholding of medication, ingestion of any food or other substances, injections, blood drawing, or any other procedure which would normally be done under medical supervision), please provide the following information:

1. Describe, in detail, the biomedical **procedures** involved in this project.

2. Identify anticipated and possible physiological **consequences** of this procedure for the subject(s) and steps to be taken to screen out subjects who may be at exceptional risk.

3. Identify the **site** where the procedure will occur.

4. Indicate the investigator's competence and identify his/her **qualification**, by training and experience, to conduct this procedure.

Appendix K: Video/Audio Taping

1. If all or some of the subject(s) of the proposed research will be audio or video-taped, **justify** why the use of audio or videotaping is necessary to the study.

2. Who will have access to the tapes and for what purposes?

3. Where will the tapes be stored and what security measures will be taken to prevent unauthorized persons from accessing the tapes?

4. What are your plans for the ultimate use and disposal of the tapes?

Note: Laws. (n.d.). Forms: Research & Sponsored Programs. *Research & Sponsored Programs: Illinois State University.* Retrieved October 9, 2010, from: http://www.rsp.ilstu.edu/forms/human_irb.shtml

APPENDIX E

Sample Human Subjects Reviewer Form

Illinois State University
Institutional Review Board (IRB)

IRB Number _____

Department/Unit Representative Protocol Review Form

After completing this review form, please attach a copy of the entire protocol to this form and forward to the Research Ethics & Compliance–Campus Box 3330. For more information, templates, and forms go to **www.rsp.ilstu.edu**.

I. Project Description

Project Title	
PI Name	

Co PI Last Names				

(Write one or two sentences briefly describing the proposed research)	

II. Methodology

A. Participants:	
1. How many of each type will be recruited?	_____ Total Adults (over 18) = _____ Males _____ Females
	_____ Total Adults (over 18) = _____ Males _____ Females
2. Of the above numbers, how many participants will be specifically recruited from the following populations?	_____ Prisoners _____ Mentally Handicapped _____ Mentall Ill _____ Physically Disabled _____ Pregnant Women _____ Physically Ill _____ Other: (please specify)
3. How will they be recruited?	
4. Informed Consent for Participants over 18	Does the study include an informed consent process that includes all of the elements? ___ Yes ___ No Is the informal consent form included? ___ Yes ___ No

5. Consent for Minors or those requiring a guardian	Does the study include a parent/guardian permission process that includes all of the elements? ___ Yes ___ No Is the parent/guardian permission form attached? ___ Yes ___ No Are appropriate assent forms or scripts attached? ___ Yes ___ No		
B. Procedure(s)			
1. Which techniques will be used to collect data	___ Questionnaire ___ Interview ___ Treatment ___ Other:	___ Files/Records ___ Physical Exercise ___ Observation	___ Task(s) ___ Specimens ___ Tests
	Recording: ___ Audio ___ Video ___ Still Image Could identification of subjects and/or their responses be damaging to standing, employability, insurability, reputation, or be stigmatizing?		
	___ Yes	___ No	
2. Will the study involve . . .	Psychological Intervention? ___ Yes ___ No Biomedical Procedures? ___ Yes ___ No Deception? ___ Yes ___ No		
3. Does the protocol adequately state a plan for . . . ?	Storing the data securely? ___ Yes ___ No Access to the data? ___ Yes ___ No Use of the data? ___ Yes ___ No Disposition of the data? ___ Yes ___ No		

III.   Risks

For each of the following potential risks below, does the protocol adequately described how risks will be minimized?			
Psychological Intervention?	___ Yes	___ No	___ N/A
Biomedical Procedures?	___ Yes	___ No	___ N/A
Deception?	___ Yes	___ No	___ N/A
Coercion of Minors	___ Yes	___ No	___ N/A
Coercion of Prisoners	___ Yes	___ No	___ N/A
Risks to Mother and Fetus	___ Yes	___ No	___ N/A
Risks to Social Standing and Reputation	___ Yes	___ No	___ N/A
Other:			

IV.   Benefits

Does the protocol state anticipated benefits? ___ Yes ___ No

V.   Department Representative Recommendation

Please review your responses above carefully! All shaded areas indicate an expedited or full level of review.

Name (please print):	Date:
Recommended Level of Review: ___ **Exempt** ___ **Expedited** ___ **Full**	

Comments:

Note: Laws. (n.d.). Forms: Research & Sponsored Programs. *Research & Sponsored Programs: Illinois State University.* Retrieved October 9, 2010, from: http://www.rsp.ilstu.edu/forms/human_irb.shtml

APPENDIX F

Completed Human Subjects Proposal

Illinois State University Institutional Review Board

Research with Human Subjects

IRB Number _____

Protocol Submission Form

Federal regulations and Illinois State University policy require that all research involving humans as subjects be reviewed and approved by the University Institutional Review Board (IRB). Any person (ISU faculty member, staff member, student, or other person) wanting to engage in human subject research at or through Illinois State University must receive written approval from the IRB before conducting research. For more information, templates, and forms please go to www.rsp.ilstu.edu

> **Please complete and forward this form and all supporting documents to your Department/Unit IRB representative.** If you have any questions, please contact your Departmental/Unit IRB representative or the Research Ethics & Compliance Office, (REC) 438-8451, Campus Box 3330.

I. General Information

A. Protocol Information
Protocol Title:
Educators' Attitudes and Perceptions Regarding the Flex Process
Is this research part of a thesis or dissertation proposal? ☐ No ☐ Yes
If yes, has the thesis or dissertation proposal been approved? ☐ No ☐ Yes

B. Principal Investigator Information (PI must be an ISU faculty or staff member)	
Principal Investigator	Department
Telephone Number	Email Address
Fax Number	Mailing Address
Co-Principal Investigator Information	
Co-Principal Investigator	Department
Telephone Number	Email Address
☐ Faculty ☐ Staff ☐ Grad. Student ☐ Undergrad. Student	Mailing Address

Co-Principal Investigator Information	
Co-Principal Investigator	Department
Telephone Number	Email Address
☐ Faculty ☐ Staff ☐ Grad. Student ☐ Undergrad. Student	Mailing Address

II. Principal Investigator Assurance

As Principal Investigator, I certify that to the best of my knowledge:

1. The information provided for this project is correct
2. No other procedures will be used in this protocol
3. I agree to conduct this research as described in the attached supporting documents
4. I will request and receive approval from the IRB for changes prior to implementing changes (including but not limited to changes in cooperating investigators or any changes in procedures).
5. I will comply with IRB and ISU policies for conducting ethical research.
6. I will be responsible for ensuring that the work of my co-investigator(s)/student researcher(s) complies with this protocol.
7. Any unexpected or otherwise significant events in the course of this study will be promptly reported to the REC.
8. In the case of student research, I assume responsibility for ensuring that any student will comply with University and Federal regulations regarding the use of human subjects in research.
9. In the case of externally funded research, I will request a modification to my approved protocol if any relative changes to the project's scope of work are requested by the agency.

_____   _____
Principal Investigator Signature   Date

III. Protocol Description

A. Provide a **brief** description, in **layman's terms**, of the proposed research.

The field of education seems to always be changing in order to address the varied needs of students. Historically, if a child has struggled in the regular education setting, he or she may be referred for special education services, assessed, and educated through a pull-out program if found eligible. During the 1980s, some research indicated that pull-out programs were ineffective. At this time, the Regular Education Initiative (REI) was introduced and was aimed at merging regular and special education in order to better address the needs of all children. REI served as an early foundation for the flexible service delivery system in Illinois. Flex involves a collaborative, problem-solving team which focuses on making adaptations and modifications to address a student's difficulties in the general education environment. The purpose of the present study will be to examine educators' perceptions regarding the flexible service delivery system in one central Illinois elementary school district. Educators' perceptions regarding flex procedures, academic and behavioral interventions, the benefits of the process, and educator satisfaction will be studied.

The targeted school district's superintendent and other administrators have been contacted, and the proposed study has been explained to them. All administrators will allow the survey to be conducted at building faculty meetings in the fall.

The survey will be administered at four different faculty meetings. Prior to administering the survey at the faculty meeting, the cover letter will be read which describes the topic of the survey, the purpose behind it, that participation is voluntary, that no benefits will be lost as a result of not participating, and that responses will remain confidential. After the cover letter has been read and questions have been addressed, the survey will be distributed to the teachers. Administrators will also be given the opportunity to complete a survey at their faculty meetings. After the surveys have been completed, the school secretary will collect all surveys and will return them to the researcher via interschool mail. Related services personnel will receive a copy of the cover letter and survey in their mailboxes at their assigned schools. The same procedure will be followed for teachers not in attendance at the meeting. Surveys may be placed in a designated envelope following the meeting, or they can be returned directly to the researcher via interschool mail.

B. Methodology

1. Participants (**ALL** protocols must have a completed Appendix A)

   a. How many participants will be included in the study?

      Number: Male 11 __ Female 101 __ Total 122 __
      (N/A _____ if not targeting males/females specifically)

      Age range: __ 22_ to __60_

   b. Where will participants be recruited?

      Participants will include special educators, general educators, related services personnel, and administrators. They will be recruited at their school faculty meetings.

   c. How will they be recruited? (Attach all recruitment documentation, i.e., letters, flyers, etc.)

      The researcher will contact the district's superintendent and administrators for permission to administer the survey at building faculty meetings. The cover letter will be read and distributed to those attending the faculty meeting.

   d. What procedures will be used (and in what order) to secure informed consent/assent?

      Everyone will be given a copy of the cover letter and survey at the faculty meeting. The cover letter will be read to them. They give their consent by completing the survey.

If consent (and assent) forms are being used, attach copies. If presented verbally, a copy of any presentation text must be submitted. **Templates for informed consent,**

parent consent/permission, and minor assent can be found at www.rsp.ilstu.edu

2. Procedure

    a. What are you asking the participants to do? In what order?

    The participants are being asked to read the cover letter and then complete the attached survey.

    b. Will you involve them in a psychological intervention, deception, or biomedical procedure?

    No.

    c. Will you audio _____ , or videotape _____, or record in any other manner _____ , participant responses? Please check.

3. Instruments/Apparatus

    What forms, surveys, equipment, etc. will you use? (Attach copies of all forms, surveys, and instruments to be used.)

    A copy of the cover letter and survey are attached.

4. Data

    a. How/where will the data be stored and kept secure?

    The data will be stored in a locked file cabinet in the principal investigator's office.

    b. Who will have access?

    The researchers in this study will be the only people who will have access to the data.

    c. How will the data be used (during and after the research)?

    The data will be used to examine educators' perceptions regarding the flexible service delivery system in one central Illinois school district. Educators' perceptions regarding flex procedures, academic and behavioral interventions, the benefits of the process, and teacher satisfaction will be studied.

    d. How will the data be disposed of?

    After five years, all paper documents will be shredded.

C. Risks

1. What are the physical, psychological, or social (loss of reputation, privacy, or employability) risks?

   Breach of confidentiality is the only risk associated with this study; however, no individual names will be used, and data will be coded with numbers. In addition, data will be reported in groups and not by individuals.

2. Will the data be anonymous _____ or confidential____X____?
   (Please check one)

D. Benefits

1. What do you hope to learn?

   We hope to gain insight into educators' attitudes and perceptions regarding flex procedures, academic and behavioral interventions, the benefits of the process, and overall educator satisfaction.

2. Who might find these results useful?

   We believe that these results will be useful to the district's administrators, the individual buildings' flex teams, and the local special education cooperative which oversees the implementation of the flex program.

3. How will the participants directly benefit?

   Based upon their input, changes could be made to the flex process. These changes could result in increased satisfaction with the process and better student outcomes.

IV. Checklist

This checklist must be completed and attached to all protocols or Department Representatives will return them to the PI. Please note that for any items checked "yes" you must attach the designated, completed appendices.

__X__ Yes _____ No	Informed consent procedures/ documentation have been clearly explained. (**All** protocols must have a completed **Appendix A**.)
_____ Yes __X__ No	Is your research being funded? (If yes, complete **Appendix B**.)
_____ Yes __X__ No	Are you recruiting and enrolling subjects 0–7 years old? (If yes, complete and attach **Appendix C**.)
_____ Yes __X__ No	Are you recruiting and enrolling subjects 8–17 years old? (If yes, complete and attach **Appendix C**.)

_____ Yes __X__ No   Are you recruiting and enrolling prisoners as subjects? (If yes, complete and attach **Appendix D**.)

_____ Yes __X__ No   Are you recruiting and enrolling pregnant women as subjects? (If yes, complete and attach **Appendix E**.)

_____ Yes __X__ No   Are you recruiting and enrolling mentally incapacitated individuals as subjects? (If yes, complete and attach **Appendix F**.)

_____ Yes __X__ No   Will the subjects of this study be exposed to the possibility of harm, including physiological, psychological, or social (e.g., loss of reputation, privacy, or employability). (If yes, complete and attach **Appendix G**.)

_____ Yes __X__ No   Will the subjects of this study be exposed to any psychological interventions such as contrived social situations, manipulation of the subject's attitudes, opinions or self-esteem, psychotherapeutic procedures, or other psychological influences. (If yes, complete and attach **Appendix H**.)

_____ Yes __X__ No   Will this study involve any elements of deception? (If yes, complete and attach **Appendix I**.)

_____ Yes __X__ No   Will the proposed research involve any biomedical procedures (e.g., the taking or withholding of medication, ingestion of any food or other substances, injections, blood drawing, or any other procedure which would normally be done under medical supervision). (If yes, complete and attach **Appendix J**.)

_____ Yes __X__ No   Will all or some of the subject(s) of the proposed research be audio or videotaped or recorded in any other manner? (If yes, complete and attach **Appendix K**.)

_____ Yes __X__ No   Will this proposed research involve any elements of technology? (i.e., web-based subject recruitment, email recruitment, web survey, etc.)

Cover Letter

My name is _____, and I am currently conducting a research project in order to fulfill requirements for completing my Master's Degree in Special Education at _____ University. I have chosen to research flex by conducting a survey. This survey will be distributed to regular education teachers, special education teachers, related services personnel, and administrators working within the district.

This survey was designed to examine educators' attitudes and perceptions regarding flex. I am asking you to complete the attached survey which includes demographic information and 24 Likert survey items. It should only take you 10–15 minutes to complete.

Your participation in this survey is completely voluntary. You may withdraw from the study at any time without penalty. The names of the school district and of individuals working within the school district will not be mentioned

in the study. Every precaution will be taken to ensure your responses are confidential. The purpose of this study is to identify educators' attitudes and perceptions regarding flex. Your input is valued and appreciated.

By returning the completed survey you are consenting to participate in this research study. Please place your completed survey in the designated envelope at your faculty meeting, or send it directly to _____ at _____ School through inter-school mail.

I thank you for taking the time to share your feelings regarding the flex process. Your participation is greatly appreciated and will allow me to learn more about educators' attitudes and perceptions of the flex process. If you have any questions, please contact Dr. _____ or myself.

Name
Address
Phone
eMail

Research at _____ University that involves human participants is carried out under the oversight of the Institutional Review Board. Questions or problems regarding these activities should be addressed to IRB Chairperson, Research and Sponsored Programs Office, Campus Box _____, City, State, zip code, or phone (___) _____-_____.

Flex Survey

Part I: Please provide some information about yourself by circling below.

School at Which You Work	Central Jr. High Lincoln Washington
Role at the School	General Ed. Teacher Special Ed. Teacher
	Related Services Personnel Administrator
Grade Level Taught	Pre-K K 1 2 3 4 5 6 7 8
Years of Experience	0–4 5–9 10–14 15–19 20–24 24–28 29+
Gender	Male Female

Part II: Please respond to following survey items by circling the appropriate number (1=strongly disagree, 2=somewhat disagree, 3=somewhat agree, 4=strongly agree).

	Strongly Disagree	Somewhat Disagree	Somewhat Agree	Strongly Agree
The flex process helps to address the needs of students who are struggling academically.	1	2	3	4
Interventions developed in flex meetings are an effective way of addressing students' behavioral needs.	1	2	3	4
I am satisfied with the way in which flex is implemented in our school.	1	2	3	4
Time and energy spent on the development and implementation of interventions is worthwhile.	1	2	3	4
The academic interventions which are developed in flex result in increased academic achievement.	1	2	3	4
The flex process helps to address the needs of students with behavioral concerns.	1	2	3	4
I am supported when interventions are difficult to implement.	1	2	3	4
The flex process helps to ensure that the needs of all students are met.	1	2	3	4
Interventions developed in flex meetings are an effective way of addressing students' academic needs.	1	2	3	4
Flex can address the needs of students who exhibit off-task behavior.	1	2	3	4
All teachers have similar experiences with the flex process.	1	2	3	4
Students benefit from the flex process.	1	2	3	4

Academic concerns can be remediated through the flex process.	1	2	3	4
For students exhibiting acting out behavior, behavioral interventions developed in flex can lead to a decrease in the undesirable behavior.	1	2	3	4
The flex process is too time-consuming.	1	2	3	4
Data collection is a valuable component of flex.	1	2	3	4
I have seen students make academic gains following the implementation of an intervention.	1	2	3	4
During a flex meeting, the effectiveness of a behavioral intervention is determined by examining the data collected.	1	2	3	4
My concerns regarding students' academic or behavioral concerns are heard and addressed in flex meetings.	1	2	3	4
Flex results in fewer students being identified for special education services.	1	2	3	4
Data is used to determine the effectiveness of an academic intervention in a flex meeting.	1	2	3	4
Flex interventions can eliminate problematic behaviors.	1	2	3	4
Flex is a good way to address the academic and behavioral needs of struggling students.	1	2	3	4
Using flex allows more students to be successful in the general education classroom.	1	2	3	4

Thank you for taking the time to complete this survey. Your participation is greatly appreciated.

APPENDIX G

Sample Promotion and Tenure Packet

TENURE AND PROMOTION RECOMMENDATION
COE Supplementary Material
Revised 9/2007 with new Provost form

Start the tenure/promotion binder with the required Provost Materials (You can label the section separately as well.). http://www.provost.ilstu.edu/resources/doc uments/ApplicationForTenure_Promotion.pdf

The binder should be no wider than 3 inches. The CFSC requests that you avoid placing material in plastic sleeves. However, you can add dividers to clearly separate the Provost materials from the summaries and appendices.

Sections A, B, C will be completed by the faculty member. Sections D and E will be completed by the DFSC. One can attach appendices to supplement each of the three sections. Faculty members are encouraged to examine portfolio binders submitted in previous years. Please note that the forms and binder width requirements have changed over time, but the substance remains the same.

A. TEACHING ACTIVITIES: Write a narrative either at the beginning or end of your listing that states why you think these activities are worthy of tenure and promotion.

I believe that my performance in the classroom as an instructor, my work with students on dissertation and thesis committees, and my contributions to program and curriculum development merit my approval for tenure and promotion. In addition to supporting materials, I have included a summary statement which supports my contributions which align with the Department's long-range goals.

Instruction

I feel fortunate to have had the opportunity to teach students at the undergraduate, master, and doctoral level. I have taught 11 courses since joining the faculty of _____ University (ISU): SED 101–The Exceptional Learner; SED 202–Effective Collaboration and Teaching Exceptional and Diverse Learners II; SED 380–Transition from School to Adult Life; SED 383–Developing and Implementing Alternative Curriculum (6 credit hours); SED 440–Critical Issues in Special Education; SED 451–Facilitating Student Directed Transition Planning; SED 453–Interagency and Postsecondary Resources; SED 455–Facilitating Employment Outcomes for Individuals with Disabilities; SED 493.11–Workshop Course, Introduction to Transition Planning (1 credit hour); and SED 522–Grant Writing in Education. I had responsibility for developing and initially implementing five of those courses (451, 453, 455, 457, and 522) and I was on the course team which developed and initially implemented 383. I have continued to increase the integration of technology into my courses and am now offering hybrid courses that incorporate video lectures, online group projects, and substantive group and individual reflection activities.

In 2005, I received the University's Teaching Initiative Award in recognition of my commitment to and accomplishments in teaching. My ratings as an instructor have been consistently high. Students' ratings indicate in particular that they feel I have a thorough knowledge of the subjects I teach, have high expectations of them, provide opportunities for them to apply materials, and encourage their participation. Summary tables of students' ratings of my teaching are included in my documentation. Students' have also provided valuable written feedback for me. They frequently express appreciation for the practical nature of projects in my courses, my ability to communicate the importance of the content, my knowledge, and my enthusiasm and assistance. Comments reflecting these themes include:

> *I appreciate how the projects were actually useful for my students and there was direct benefit to them. _____ had a great deal of energy and passion for this topic. (SED 451, on-campus)*

> *_____ knows the material and does an excellent job teaching it and making known its importance. Everything in the class was relevant to our future careers. I enjoyed it a lot. (SED 383)*

> *Through SED 383 with _____ I was extremely challenged with both the content of the class and the projects. She had very high expectations and that made me want to try hard to achieve them. She knew so much about the content and answered all questions very detailed. She helped me when I struggled through a concept and encouraged extra practice. I really learned a lot from the class. (SED 383)*

> *I thought the instructor did an excellent job with tasks, assignments given that can be implemented immediately in my classroom. As a result of the class, I felt that the program and students I work with will benefit from the knowledge I have gained. I would encourage the same type of assignments for future classes. (SED 453, on-campus)*

Student feedback is important to me. I strive for continuous improvement of my courses so that I can more effectively assist practicing and future teachers in developing their competencies and leadership abilities. I use feedback from course evaluations and less formal procedures during the semester to make adjustments within a particular section and in future semesters.

Transition Specialist Advanced Certificate Program

One of my proudest accomplishments in teaching is the development and implementation of the graduate level Transition Specialist Learning Behavior Specialist II Advanced Certificate program. This program assists teachers in developing as leaders in supporting the transition of youth with disabilities from school to successful adult lives. The need for personnel who specialize in providing transition services is significant, as indicated by recent national studies that suggest that young adults with disabilities continue to lag behind their nondisabled peers in accessing postsecondary education, achieving quality employment outcomes, living independently, establishing financial security, and maintaining satisfactory social lives. While there has been a call nationally for training for transition specialists, the program at _____ is the only active program in the state of _____. I have sole responsibility for recruitment and delivery of this program.

In 2005, I recruited the first group of campus students to take the four-course sequence. In January 2006, I recruited a second group from _____, to complete the coursework. In May 2007, 17 students completed the program. Several of those teachers went on to become the first individuals to receive advanced teaching certification as Transition Specialists from the _____ State Board of Education. In Spring 2007, I recruited a new cohort. With limited recruitment effort, we received 35 high quality applications to the program. The current cohort includes 18 teachers from across the state of _____. I continue to answer telephone calls and emails from other teachers interested in enrolling in the program. There is clearly a need and a desire for this program.

I am the sole faculty member responsible for implementing these courses. As such, I developed reading schedules, learning activities, and eight portfolio pieces for these four courses. I have used a widely respected model of transition services delivery to translate the individual courses into a comprehensive and cohesive program of study. I travelled to _____ monthly from January 2006 to June 2007 to deliver instruction to that cohort, and I steadily increased my use of technology to provide off-campus students greater opportunities to network and learn from each other. I expanded my use of WebCT each semester and am now developing online modules that integrate video lectures, cooperative learning through discussions and application activities, and individual reflections on practice. I believe my efforts to integrate technology have resulted in increased program accessibility throughout the state without sacrificing critical opportunities for practicing teachers to learn from each other. I am also assuming responsibility for collecting data and preparing reports on this program for our upcoming NCATE review.

I approach graduate coursework as an opportunity to assist practicing teachers to develop into change agents in their schools. I respect the skill and knowledge they have and strive to find new ways to help them further develop. I was proud to have three of the recent program graduates present at a national conference in October to discuss how they have influenced change since enrolling in the courses and how the program structure facilitated their development as change agents.

Undergraduate Cohort

I am also proud of innovative work I have conducted in our undergraduate program. In the 2004–2005 academic year, I collaborated with two other faculty members to integrate 13 credit hours of coursework and clinical experiences for students in the semester before their Field-Based semester. We integrated the curriculum for SED 245.12, the students' first clinical experience in which they spend two full days in schools as well as time in a seminar; SED 204, an instructional strategies course; and SED 383, a curriculum development course. The content of the courses was woven together to assist students in making clearer connections among the various components of teaching practice. We co-taught these courses to one cohort of students each semester. The scholarship activities we completed through this project resulted in data-based decision-making on course delivery in our Learning and Behavior Specialist students' practicum semester. The resulting new program structure involves blocking SED 245.12 and SED 383, and delivering those courses through various models of co-teaching.

Thesis/Dissertation Committees

I am currently co-adviser with Dr. _____ for Special Education doctoral candidate _____ dissertation entitled *An investigation of the outcomes of students receiving services in an inner city school.* I am currently advisor for two Master's students completing their thesis research. _____ is conducting a study entitled *College freshmen's perceptions on the transition from high school to college,* and _____ is conducting a study entitled *Teachers' perceptions of transition services: An examination of the impact of two capacity-building strategies.* All three of these projects have anticipated completion dates of May 2008. I am also currently cochairing the dissertation committee for _____, a doctoral candidate in Special Education. She is currently developing her dissertation proposal for research on teachers' perceptions of assistive technology integration for students with disabilities in general education settings. I look forward to advising additional dissertations and theses in the future.

In addition to advisement, I have had the opportunity to work on dissertation and thesis committees in both SED and Educational and Administration Foundations. Listed below are students who have completed or are in the process of completing their projects.

_____, Ed.D., Special Education, *The reliability and validity of the Supports Intensity Scale,* May 2003.

_____, Ed.D., Special Education, *Secondary special education teachers' perspectives and self-reported practices related to the self-determination skills of high school students with disabilities,* August 2007.

_____, M.S., Special Education, *Student attendance: Causes, effects, and interventions,* May 2007.

Independent Studies, Honors Projects, Student Research

I have advised five students on in-course honors projects and co-advised four students on an honors independent study. In-course honors projects have included examinations and comparisons of the values and services of differing vocational agencies for adults with developmental disabilities (_____, SED 380, Fall 2002); an examination and analysis of the implementation of best practices at five IEP meetings for high school youth with disabilities (_____, SED 380, Spring 2003); implementation of person-centered planning activities and development of transition planning recommendations for a high school student with multiple disabilities (_____, SED 380, Spring 2003); implementation of a comprehensive assistive technology evaluation with a reflection on the implications for curriculum adaptation and development (_____, SED 383, Fall 2004); and an analysis of interviews of low-income parents of students with disabilities, development of recommendations for improving services to these parents, and a reflection on the influence of culture in on the transition needs of families (_____, SED 383, Fall 2005). I have also been pleased to present with four graduate students at national conferences, including presenting with _____ at the 2005 Council for Exceptional Children conference and presenting with _____, _____, and _____ at the 2007 Division of Career Development and Transition conference.

Other Teaching Activities and Accomplishments

I have been actively involved with CTLT since joining the _____ faculty. I have attended numerous training sessions and symposia sponsored by CTLT. I have been pleased to be able to contribute to those sessions as well. In October of this year, I was one of four faculty members chosen for the initial implementation of Making Teaching Visible, CTLT's new program focused on providing faculty members with opportunities to observe their colleagues' teaching and to have reflective discussions after teaching sessions. I opened my classroom twice for visitors to observe my teaching and will now work with CTLT staff to discuss how this program may be improved and expanded in future semesters. I also have presented at two CTLT events. I co-presented *Integrating coursework and early clinical experiences in a teacher education program: Lessons learned from a one-year pilot* at the January 2006 symposium, and I was on the panel presenting *Developing a teaching portfolio* at the May 2006 University Teaching Workshop.

Summary of Teaching

In summary, I believe I have excelled in this area and that I have earned the approval of tenure and promotion in regard to teaching. I have been a successful instructor in multiple courses and received university recognition of my teaching accomplishments. I have made significant contributions to curriculum development and successfully developed and implemented a graduate-level advanced certificate program that is the only one of its kind operating in _____. I have mentored students on graduate research and included students in national presentations. I believe that my teaching accomplishments are important contributions to the long-range goals of the Department.

B. **SCHOLARLY PRODUCTIVITY:** Write a narrative either at the beginning or end of your listing that states why you think these activities are worthy of tenure and promotion.

My scholarship has been focused on directing a federal grant related to public benefits and youth with disabilities, transition from school to adult life for youth with disabilities, family-school collaboration, and teacher education. In addition to the following narrative, I have provided documentation in the following areas of scholarly productivity to support my application for tenure and promotion: (1) documentation of work completed as part of a federal grant; (2) copies of articles published in peer reviewed journals and chapters from edited books; (3) national and state presentations; and (4) externally and internally funded research grant proposals.

Social Security Transition Project ($697,221 total; $570,887 transferred to _____ University)

Since October 2001, I have been the Principal Investigator for the Social Security Transition Project, a U.S. Department of Education model demonstration project. I transferred the grant from the University of _____ to _____ University when I joined the faculty here, changing my time commitment to the grant from 1.0 FTE to .25 to .50 FTE. My research appointment of .25 FTE was contributed as a cost share obligation for the grant for my first four years at _____. Due to receiving a no-cost extension for this project, it continued as an active project until September 30, 2007. I am currently developing the final report to submit to the Department of Education.

The focus of this project was to develop outreach and training materials and systems to support adolescents and young adults with disabilities access public benefits systems. Since 1996, many youth with severe disabilities have had difficulty accessing or maintaining Supplemental Security Income benefits through the Social Security Administration. These benefits are critical for many youth who require life-long support through adult services or who are at risk for living in poverty.

Through this federal grant, I collaborated with the _____ County Health Care Consumers to develop a volunteer advocate training program, develop advocate training materials, and implement a plan to sustain the advocate program after the grant period. I also collaborated with the _____ State Board of Education to develop training materials, which are now included in the Transition Outreach Training for Adult Life (TOTAL) technical assistance project and have been disseminated across the state. I recruited two area secondary special educators to develop additional resources for teachers. I am currently making modifications to training materials for the _____ Special Education District and the Special Education District of _____.

My work on the project has involved project management and annual performance reporting, development of teacher training materials, development of advocate training materials, supervision of the community subcontractor, and implementation of outreach and training sessions for families and school personnel. The grant funding period ended September 30, 2007. I am currently developing the final report for the grant, which will be submitted in December of this year.

Scholarly Publications

In addition to directing the Social Security Transition Project for six years, I have been actively involved in several other areas of research. My current research addresses transition services structure, family-school collaboration, and teacher education and professional development. I have co-authored 3 articles in peer-reviewed professional journals and five book chapters since joining the _____ University. I have one additional article under review and multiple active research projects related to transition services and family-school collaboration.

Funded Grant Proposals

In the past six years, I have secured $3,084,363 in grant funding. In 2001, I secured two U.S. Department of Education grants, the $697,221 model demonstration project and a $2,349,892 capacity building grant. I brought the model demonstration grant with me when I accepted the position at _____, while the capacity building grant remained at the University of _____. In addition to receiving federal grants, I have received several smaller grants to support my work. I was honored to receive a $10,000 grant from the College of Education with colleagues to support research on our innovative junior year cohort experience. This research has resulted in one journal article and a second article is currently being developed. That project was also supported by a small grant from the _____ Association of Teacher Educators Research Mini Grant program. I also received a $10,000 action research grant with four department colleagues from the _____ Low Incidence Association and _____ Public Schools to support research on the use of personal digital assistants as employment supports for teens and young adults with significant disabilities. I have also received two COE URG grants.

National and State Presentations

Since 2002 I have made 20 presentations at national and state professional conferences. I have two additional national conference presentations that have been accepted for 2008. My presentations have primarily addressed findings and activities from the Social Security Transition Project, findings from studies on family involvement with schools, and findings and philosophy related to teacher education.

Additional Scholarship Activities

I am a member of the team developing and authoring the Supports Intensity Scale-Children, which will be published by the American Association on Intellectual and Developmental Disabilities in late 2008. I am a Consulting Editor for *Career Development for Exceptional Individuals,* the leading journal in my area of specialization. I have reviewed grants for two U.S. Department of Education Office of Special Education and Rehabilitation Services (OSERS) competitions, and I attended the OSERS Project Directors' meetings in 2002, 2003, and 2004.

Summary of Scholarly Productivity

I believe that my record of scholarship in multiple areas merits approval of tenure and promotion. I wrote and have served as the Principal Investigator and Project Director of a U.S. Department of Education grant. Despite the time commitment to the federal grant, I have successfully published in respected journals and key edited books in my field. My direction of the Social Security Transition Project has brought visibility to the newly developed graduate-level Transition Specialist Advanced Certificate program at _____. I am actively involved in research related to implementation of transition services, collaborating with families, and professional development. As I gain momentum on my research agendas outside of the grant, I am successfully collaborating with graduate students on that work. I feel my scholarship has successfully complimented my teaching and service activities. Lastly, I feel my scholarship is consistent with the long-term goals and needs of the Department of Special Education.

C. **SERVICE ACTIVITIES:** Write a narrative either at the beginning or end of your listing that states why you think these activities are worthy of tenure and promotion.

I have been committed to both external and internal service. Externally, I have assisted individual families, provided training to teachers and social workers, and assisted in building a sustainable system of support to families navigating the Supplemental Security System. I have also been a partner with the _____ State Board of Education on several initiatives related to providing professional development and technical assistance related to transition. I have also been active on the national level in supporting transition-related capacity building. Finally, I have been active on numerous department and university committees. I believe my combined efforts on local, state, and national fronts, as well as my service to _____ University, are deserving of tenure and promotion.

Social Security Transition Project

My work with the Social Security Transition Project has resulted in numerous service activities to families and schools. The project has focused heavily on providing support and advocacy services to individuals and their families. Through the project, we have assisted 871 families and trained 52 volunteer advocates. The assistance to families has addressed completing applications, filing appeals, compiling necessary documentation, and generally understanding their rights and responsibilities within the system. I have also conducted training sessions and provided technical assistance for special education personnel from _____ Unit 4 District, _____ School District 116, _____ District 61, _____ County Rural Special Education Cooperative, _____ Special Education District, Special Education District of _____, _____ Special Education District, and numerous other districts through statewide trainings conducted in conjunction with the _____ Board of Education Transition Outreach Training to Adult Living Project. Training and technical assistance materials have been disseminated statewide through the TOTAL project. I have also provided outreach services to groups of parents in numerous counties.

I was also pleased to use the Social Security Transition Project to sponsor a summer institute in 2006. I recruited teams from high poverty high schools and special education cooperatives and specialized district programs that serve areas with higher than average poverty rates. Participants attended the institute in teams to discuss the unique barriers encountered in trying to implement transition services with families who live in poverty and within high poverty districts and programs. Thirty-two people in 12 teams attended the two-day institute. Content experts and facilitators assisted teams in developing action plans to implement change in their local schools and programs. I was also pleased to be able to accept some Institute participants into the current Transition Specialist cohort.

Additional External Service

In 2005 I was invited to serve on the National Secondary Transition Technical Assistance Center (NSTTAC), Capacity Building Expert Panel. The NSTTAC is a federally funded research and dissemination project with the charge of generating and synthesizing transition-related research, disseminating information on evidence-based practices, and developing strategies to assist states in improving capacity building efforts. I believe my invitation to participate on the 10-person Capacity Building Expert Panel was recognition of my accomplishments and commitment to not only the provision of capacity building activities but also the evaluation of the effectiveness of those efforts.

My work with transition services development in the state of _____ also led to my participation as a member of the _____ team at two national state leadership forums, in 2004 and 2007. These forums are opportunities for teams of state agency leaders to identify priorities and develop action plans to improve transition services in their states. I have also consulted with the _____ Interagency Coordinating Council Education Subcommittee on the need for professional development related to transition. I served on the 2002 Expert Panel for the development of the Learning and Behavior Specialist 2: Transition Specialist certification examination for the _____ Board of Education. In 2006, I represented _____ at the Symposium on Trauma, Stress, and Education for _____ Youth in Foster Care, convened by the Center for Child Welfare and Education at _____ University.

Internal Service Contributions

I also believe it is important to serve the _____ community. I have taken that service obligation seriously, serving on five College of Education committees and five Department committees. On the college level, I have served on College Council (2003–2009), Diversity (2003–2006), Curriculum (2003–2005), Research (2005–2006; 2007–2009), and the Technology Planning Committee (ad hoc; 2003). As a member of the Diversity committee, I developed and implemented with Dr. _____ a symposia series on college students with psychiatric disabilities. This four-session series included speakers from the community and university and offered faculty members opportunities to gain understanding of the nature of various psychiatric disabilities, to discuss challenges, and to share strategies. For the last year, I have also served on the College of Education task force for planning the College's Sesquicentennial activities.

On the department level, I have served on the Curriculum Committee (2003–2005), the Masters Degree Committee (2004–present), the Research Committee (2004–present), and the Resource Allocation Committee (2006–present). I believe one of my most significant contributions to the department was my leadership on the Department Retreat in 2007. I chaired the ad hoc group that not only planned the one-day retreat, but also planned and implemented a pre-retreat curriculum mapping process. The curriculum mapping process provided an opportunity for all faculty members to share information on the content of their courses, their concerns about overlaps and gaps within our curriculum, and other concerns about the nature of our undergraduate program. We used the information gained through the two-week mapping activity to develop problem-solving and action-planning groups at the retreat. Since the April retreat, this group has continued to meet to implement strategies identified at the retreat and to continue the curriculum mapping process for specific areas of concern. I believe that we have initiated an effective and sustainable continuous improvement strategy. I also served on the teams compiling program proposals for the _____ Board of Education for approval of the LBS2: Transition Specialist and LBS2: Multiple Disabilities programs. I also served on the Faculty Search Committee in the 2003–2004 academic year. (Note: Permission obtained from faculty member to reprint.)

Summary of Service

I believe my external and internal service contributions warrant tenure and promotion. I have provided assistance to families and teachers throughout the state so that young people with disabilities living in poverty can receive public benefits that sustain them and make it possible for them to access long-term support programs. At the same time, I have assisted with developing a sustainable program in _____ County that will allow this type of assistance to continue now that grant funding is expired. I have worked at both the state and national level to provide assistance and consultation on professional development and other capacity building efforts related to transition planning. I feel my service contributions have brought recognition to _____ University both nationally and statewide in the area of transition from school to adult life for youth with disabilities. Finally, I have made significant contributions on both College and Department committees.

INDEX

241

- Rumrill, Phillip D., Jr., Brian G. Cook, & Andrew L. Wiley—**RESEARCH IN SPECIAL EDUCATION: Designs, Methods, and Applications. (2nd Ed.)** '11, 288 pp. (7 x 10), 2 il., 9 tables.

- Sandeen, Arthur—**ENHANCING LEADERSHIP IN COLLEGES AND UNIVERSITIES: A Case Approach.** '11, 232 pp. (7 x 10).

- Jones, Carroll J.—**CURRICULUM DEVELOPMENT FOR STUDENTS WITH MILD DISABILITIES: Academic and Social Skills for RTI Planning and Inclusion IEPs. (2nd Ed.)** '09, 454 pp. (8 1/2 x 11), 50 tables, $63.95, (spiral).

- Nicoletti, John, Sally Spencer-Thomas & Christopher M. Bollinger—**VIOLENCE GOES TO COLLEGE: The Authoritative Guide to Prevention and Intervention. (2nd Ed.)** '10, 392 pp. (7 x 10), 9 il., 8 tables, $87.95, hard, $59.95, paper.

- Hickson, Mark III, & Julian B. Roebuck—**DEVIANCE AND CRIME IN COLLEGES AND UNIVERSITIES: What Goes on in the Halls of Ivy.** '09, 268 pp. (7 x 10), 5 tables, $57.95, hard, $37.95, paper.

- Hunt, Gilbert H., & Dennis G. Wiseman, Timothy J. Touzel—**EFFECTIVE TEACHING: Preparation and Implementation. (4th Ed.)** '09, 316 pp. (7 x 10), 58 il., 1 table, $62.95, hard, $42.95, paper.

- Lassonde, Cynthia A., Robert J. Michael, & Jerusalem Rivera-Wilson—**CURRENT ISSUES IN TEACHER EDUCATION: History, Perspectives, and Implications.** '08, 270 pp. (7 x 10), 1 il., $58.95, hard, $38.95, paper.

- Bakken, Jeffrey P. & Festus E. Obiakor—**TRANSITION PLANNING FOR STUDENTS WITH DISABILITIES: What Educators and Service Providers Can Do.** '08, 214 pp. (7 x 10), 4 il., 25 tables, $51.95, hard, $31.95, paper.

- Jones, Carroll J.—**CURRICULUM-BASED ASSESSMENT: The Easy Way to Determine Response-to-Intervention. (2nd Ed.)** '08, 210 pp. (8 1/2 x 11), 59 tables, $35.95, (spiral) paper.

- Milner, H. Richard—**DIVERSITY AND EDUCATION: Teachers, Teaching, and Teacher Education.** '08, 288 pp. (7 x 10), 4 il, 1 table, $61.95, hard, $41.95, paper.

- Wiseman, Dennis G. & Gilbert H. Hunt—**BEST PRACTICE IN MOTIVATION AND MANAGEMENT IN THE CLASSROOM. (2nd Ed.)** '08, 316 pp. (7 x 10), 10 il, $62.95, hard, $42.95, paper.

- Burns, Edward—**The Essential SPECIAL EDUCATION GUIDE for the Regular Education Teacher.** '07, 326 pp. (7 x 10), 16 tables, $76.95, hard, $49.95, paper.

- Goodman, Karen D.—**MUSIC THERAPY GROUPWORK WITH SPECIAL NEEDS CHILDREN: The Evolving Process.** '07, 318 pp. (8 x 10), 21 tables, $69.95, hard, $49.95, paper.

- Hargis, Charles H.—**ENGLISH SYNTAX: An Outline for Teachers of English Language Learners. (3rd Ed.)** '07, 308 pp. (7 x 10), 6 tables, 6 il., $69.95, hard, $44.95, paper.

- Walker, Robert—**MUSIC EDUCATION: Cultural Values, Social Change and Innovation.** '07, 340 pp. (7 x 10), 28 il., 2 tables, $69.95, hard. $49.95, paper.

- Adams, Dennis & Mary Hamm—**MEDIA AND LITERACY: Learning in the Information Age—Issues, Ideas, and Teaching Strategies. (3rd Ed.)** '06, 290 pp. (7 x 10), 38 il., $61.95, hard, $42.95, paper.

- Hargis, Charles H.—**TEACHING LOW ACHIEVING AND DISADVANTAGED STUDENTS. (3rd Ed.)** '06, 182 pp. (7 x 10), $34.95, paper.

- Burke, Peter J. & Robert D. Krey—**SUPERVISION: A Guide to Instructional Leadership. (2 nd Ed.)** '05, 462 pp. (7 x 10), 22 il., $89.95, hard, $63.95, paper.

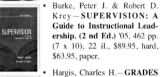

- Hargis, Charles H.—**GRADES AND GRADING PRACTICES: Obstacles to Improving Education and to Helping At-Risk Students. (2nd Ed.)** '03, 132 pp. (7 x 10), 1 il., $48.95, hard, $33.95, paper.

- Hunt, Gilbert H., Dennis G. Wiseman & Sandra Bowden — **THE MODERN MIDDLE SCHOOL: Addressing Standards and Student Needs. (2nd Ed.)** '03, 256 pp. (7 x 10), 45 il., 12 tables, $42.95, paper.